WHISPERED CALL

HIS VOICE TO HIS CHILDREN

SUE PIPER AND
SANDY PETTY

WHISPERED CALL

HIS VOICE TO HIS CHILDREN

SUE PIPER AND
SANDY PETTY

Dedicated to the God who calls us forth

and makes all things possible

PREFACE

I have not come to undo you; truly I have come to bind you up. The slings and arrows of all of man's days create bleeding, aching heart wounds, confusion, and void; I have come to fill that void; I have come to heal those wounds; I have come to banish that confusion with My light and life. To your prayer closet I come, Me … My very presence, My very person; not to find fault, I come Child to release you from your prisoner stance. Hear now these words of freedom; let them permeate your mind and spirit; they have great power to overcome your long practiced restraining voices, forever holding you back, holding you down, forever speaking lies … 'He cannot love me.' 'He does not care.' 'I am not enough.' Child, I hear your whispered pain; now you hear My Whispered Call to your heart. Let My words of love, of mercy, of affection echo against your cavernous need, bouncing and rebounding across the years of your fractured and lonely life. I've come and you never again step alone; I've come and you never again stand alone; I've come and you never again reach out to find no one reaching back; I've come to speak; hear now My Whispered Call, and know wholeness.

Your Abba Father

ACKNOWLEDGMENTS

Our appreciation to all those who have shared with us how God has impacted their lives and hearts using the words in *God Whispers* and *Still... God Whispers*. Your stories have, and continue to spur us on. It is with humble gratitude that we also thank those who faithfully answer His call to pray for us, that it would always be God who is the author of our efforts and not we ourselves.

We particularly wish to acknowledge Andre Mickel, DDS, MSD who has generously provided hundreds of these devotionals to some of His hurting children in crisis situations. May the seeds you plant bear much fruit for His Kingdom!

We thank our dear friend and sister, Karin Nethery, once again for her tireless and uncomplaining editing.

INTRODUCTION

Neither Sandy nor I ever intended to be the authors of a book, much less three books. But God, we have learned, often has different plans than the ones we anticipate for ourselves. Even so, it is with some trepidation that we once again claim that these "whisperings" voice God's heart of love for His children. We know, however, that we dare not let false humility stand in the way of messages that He would impart to His own.

We pray that the Comforter and Counselor, the promised Holy Spirit, would reveal Himself to each person through these meditations. May He increase and we decrease as you read until you only hear His heart for you in these words.

May His whispered call urge you forth, and may His healing touch lead you out of the darknesses of this world and ever deeper into the light of His love.

Additional copies of this book may be purchased directly from the authors or from www.amazon.com or www.barnesandnoble.com. (Quantity discounts are available through the authors.) Various eBook formats are available from www.smashwords.com, www.barnesandnoble.com, www.amazon.com, and iTunes.

If you would like to contact us, please feel free to email us at SandPiper1122@gmail.com.

DEAR READERS …

If, as you read the words in this devotional, your heart stirs; if you hear God's gentle whisper in your spirit; if you'd like to have a personal relationship with God, but you can't figure out how to begin or what to say, we share a short prayer of reflection, repentance, and redemption with you. It's not the words that matter; it's your heart's yearning to draw close to God and accept the grace and love that He offers through His Son Jesus Christ. What God desires most from you is a sincere heart and an unflinching honesty about where you are and what you need from Him.

Dear Heavenly Father, I acknowledge that in my lifetime I've done a lot of wrong things toward others, toward myself, and toward You. I've made a mess of much of my life, and I'm tired of being in charge. Father, I ask forgiveness for my sins and I ask you, Jesus, to come into my heart and be Lord over it all. Only You, Father, have the ability and the willingness to take all that I am, and all that I'm not, and turn it around. Thank You for saving me; thank You for loving me; thank You for reaching out for me.

We encourage you to get a copy of The Bible that you can read and understand. (The Message Bible is a great place to start if you've never read The Bible.) Also needed for your growth and emotional well-being is a good church with people that are willing to reach out to you and come along side you in this journey of life with Him.

If you've made a commitment to Christ or you have more questions, we'd love to hear from you. Please email us at: SandPiper1122@gmail.com

January 1

Give ear and come to me; hear me, that your soul may live. I will make an everlasting covenant with you, my faithful love promised to David. Isaiah 55:3

Draw near and worship Me! Draw near and glorify Me! Draw near and bow before Me! Little baby born is King of Kings and Lord and Lords, and My baby arms even today are not too short to save you. Your praises and your penitence reach My throne. Draw near; come close. Do not let anyone else worship for **you**. My sons, My daughters, I need to hear **your** voice; I need to hear **your** heart; I need to see **your** bowed spirit. Bare your soul to Me this first day of this new year. Praise Me! Glorify Me! Bow before Me! I am King and Lord. I am your Redeemer. I am child just born who will save your heart and soul, here and now and forever more. Come! I invite you today. Put aside your tiredness from the world's revelry and come. Dear heart, come; COME to Me! Let Me embrace you as you bow before Me, as you surrender all of yourself to Me this day. Make a clean start, a new start, that I might do new things in your life. Taste … and see … for I the Lord am good.

January 2

It is written: "'As surely as I live,' says the Lord, 'every knee will bow before me; every tongue will confess to God.'" Romans 14:11

Tremble at My coming. Bow in the face of My holiness. Stand amazed at My presence. You have become far too used to the ordinary landscape of your life, and you do not see Me because you do not look for Me. You too often miss My coming to you because your eyes are closed to the spiritual; too enmeshed in the things of this world, you have let your spirit harden, and you miss the things of Me. I come with love, with peace, with kindness, but remember that it is I who come, not some whimpering, useless, powerless presence. I will open your eyes, and you will see Me as I truly am and fall prostrate before Me.

January 3

The house of the wicked will be destroyed, but the tent of the upright will flourish. There is a way that seems right to a man, but in the end it leads to death. Proverbs 14:11-12

The world has built memorials to wealth and to power, but I see the hearts of men. It is not what you have but who you are that matters to Me. Do not be easily swayed by the package a life comes in, for the outer wrapping is just that and only that. What appears comfortable, what appears important, what seems easy, fun, or even meritorious is often just an outer layer that disguises the stench of death and despair. Judge not by the world's standards, for what the world constructs and what it values holds little measure of My truth. Blessed are the meek not the proud. Blessed are those who seek after My righteousness and not the riches of the world, for in My kingdom it is they who will be filled, they who will be satisfied.

January 4

He found him out in the wilderness, in an empty, windswept wasteland. He threw his arms around him, lavished attention on him, guarding him as the apple of his eye. Deuteronomy 32:10 (MSG)

I have taken hold of you, and in that relentless holding is the power that causes you to take hold of Me. The apple of My eye, sheltered under the shadow of My wings, and encompassed by My loving embrace and My Father heart, I continually search for you to draw you close. Your leaning in is not of your initiative or your strength; rather it is your spirit heart swaying in tempo to the overtures of your Creator God. Struggle not against the close abiding to which I call you. Come forth from the empty wilderness places. Leave the desert behind and step out into the oasis of My love and nurture. Abide in Me in the places I have prepared for you. Do not cower in the darkness of the past or in ignorance of the future unaware that I have already restored the wounds of the past and prepared both the high and the low places of your future. Take My hand; abide in Me!

January 5

If you, then, though you are evil, know how to give good gifts to your children, how much more will your Father in heaven give good gifts to those who ask him! Matthew 7:11

Child, the ability to color your world with different shades and hues I place in your hand. This ability you've always had, but it's been locked away, hidden; hidden behind shame and insecurity and fear and rejection. Now, Child, you have glimpsed the box of crayons that I have made available to you, and your soul stirs with excitement. Reach for new colors; see the deep, rich hues of the new tints available to you. Do not worry about staying within the lines, right now; it's about the new color; it's about taking crayon to old paper and re-coloring the areas of life that have been miss-colored in grays and beiges. Take the colors that YOU choose, and with bold hand and confident heart make these spaces of bland burst with new color. I give you this gift as I have given it to all; albeit, late in life you receive it, do not be dismayed by that fact. As others' colors begin to fade and lose their vibrancy, your colors will ignite and shine with a brilliance that will re-ignite others' colors. I am pleased, Child, that you see now the box of colors I've set aside for you; use them, revel in them, enjoy them, for this resounds glory back to Me.

January 6

Can a mother forget the baby at her breast and have no compassion on the child she has borne? Though she may forget, I will not forget you! See, I have engraved you on the palms of my hands. Isaiah 49:15-16

I do not need to be reminded of My love for you, for it is I who have called you and I who have chosen you. Your imperfections do not alarm Me; your unholy ways do not drive you from Me. You are in My sights all the time and none of your ways are hidden from Me. Why do you worry? Do you not know that I have your todays in My hand? Reach out and I am there; listen and you will hear Me already speaking; look and you will find that My gaze is already focused on you. I will never forget you; I will never leave nor forsake you. I will repair your broken down walls. I will nurse you back to health. I will speak peace when there is no peace. Trust Me in **all** this Child.

January 7

"Am I not a God near at hand" - God's Decree - "and not a God far off?" Jeremiah 23:23 (MSG)
For you who faces today with false cheer or a pasted on smile, who greets your today with tears in your eyes, and who can barely worship because of what's going on in your life, it's for **you** that I came … and it's for you that today I come. There are no easy answers for you to understand, My Child, why life is so difficult sometimes, and I know your pain and your grief and your questions and your concerns would swamp you. But, like Peter, I have given you the power to walk on water; I have given you the power to stand where there is no firm place to stand because I, Child, **I** am your firm place. I am the One who loves you best with a love that will carry you from your problems, through your problems, from your grief and through your grief, into My arms. Breathe, Child; breathe, and lift up your head, and meet **M**y eyes and **My** gaze, and feel **My** arms of love around you, for until we are reunited in My Kingdom forever, there is no other safe place; there is no other haven. I invite you to **My** haven because I love you.

January 8

You gave bread from heaven for their hunger, you sent water from the rock for their thirst…. You gave them your good Spirit to teach them to live wisely. You never stinted with your manna, gave them plenty of water to

drink. **You supported them forty years in that desert; they had everything they needed; Their clothes didn't wear out and their feet never blistered. Nehemiah 9:15.20-21 (MSG)**

Do not doubt My sufficiency. Neither doubt My close by presence, My hunkering down into your life today, and My Spirit fullness. Assume that I abide and you will find Me. Assume that My today manna is sufficient for your needs. You have gone out to the fields with Me; you have collected My heart and My words for you; now live in them securely. Find your way through this day not by means of your intellect but through the working of My spiritual nourishment within you. You are not alone, My Child, for I abide in you and with you and fill you for all your needs. I love you so much that the manna I have given you is exactly what you need for the day that I will bring you. Rejoice in that!

January 9

The tongue has the power of life and death, and those who love it will eat its fruit. Proverbs 18:21

With your words you speak life, or with your words you speak death. What you utter toward another brings My grace and My healing, or it brings destruction and pain. Your mouth is a force in My world. Though small, it is mighty. Words thoughtlessly spoken hold no less power; carelessness does not keep the seed from growing. It is good for you to remember the impact what you say can have on another's heart and life. Pause and think: *'Is this life giving? Or is this death breathing?'* In that pause, hope can spring. Be no less conscious of the words you speak to yourself. The subconscious mutterings of a heart about itself are more powerful than you know. You can destroy your very soul from the inside, damaging your own tender tissue with the thoughts you think and the words you speak about you. Remember whose you are; remember who you are. Be careful what you say to My loved ones, yourself included.

January 10

This is how God showed his love for us: God sent his only Son into the world so we might live through him. This is the kind of love we are talking about - not that we once upon a time loved God, but that he loved us and sent his Son as a sacrifice to clear away our sins and the damage they've done to our relationship with God. 1 John 4:9-10 (MSG)

Bow at My feet. Prostrate yourself. Do not take the offering of Myself to you lightly, for My blood was shed and My life was given that you might see My love clearly. Abiding in Me is not some heavenly game of hide and seek in reverse. Rather it is Holy God coming down, giving up rights to rescue you, to find you, to redeem you, to restore you. I call not for recognition (although I deserve that) but for surrender, not for intellectual consent (although that must be there too) but for your will to bow. Your rightful place in the universe is in submission and surrender to Me, the Holy God who loves you.

January 11

[B]ecause the Lord disciplines those he loves, as a father the son he delights in. Proverbs 3:12

You cry and hide your face from Me, stung by My discipline. Child, you have brought this calliope of circumstances upon yourself. In your haste, in your anger, in your rebellion, you chose your path. Now Satan serves you up a double portion of misery for your trouble. Are you yet done with your own way? Have you yet reached the end of your own wisdom? Can you yet bend your knee and once again hear My voice of direction? None of this is pleasurable for Me, Child; My heart aches for your pain; My arms burn for you to return to their embrace. My love for you changes not, not in your obedience nor your rebellion; My ear is ever open to your cry. My discipline is meted out because the cruelest thing parents can do is to allow their beloved child to continue down a path destined to be that child's undoing and not cry out loud and long ... **'STOP!'** while creating the painful encouragement for them to do so. I love you thusly Child; My hand of correction is the same hand that has your name engraved upon its palm.

January 12

Then Joseph said to his brothers, "Come close to me." Genesis 45:4
Like Joseph's unfaithful, fearful brothers, you stand afar from Me. What you have done, who you have been, banishes you from My sight in your own eyes. Your past makes a present with Me impossible, just as Joseph's brothers felt about their repugnant treatment of him. Expecting retribution and justice, they feared the worst for themselves. And so it is with you. You cannot begin to imagine My mercy stretched toward you, nor My love poured out. You know who you are, what you have done, and, even despite your best intentions, what you have failed to do. In your heart, you know that you do not deserve either My forgiveness or My love, and so when I implore you to come close, you envision punishment rather than mercy at the end of that command. It is your faithlessness that needs Me so desperately, and in no way will I turn you away when you come. No punishment awaits you, for I have already taken your just retribution upon Myself. Only My joy at our reunion awaits; only the washing away of the past with My great love fills the present. Fear not; come close to Me!

January 13

O Lord, the king rejoices in your strength. How great is his joy in the victories you give! You have granted him the desire of his heart and have not withheld the request of his lips. Psalm 21:1-2
As I have promised you, My Child, your praises have indeed called Me close to you this morning. So hear My word to your heart. Remember: I **will** be victorious. When you are chained by circumstances, remember, I will be victorious.

When you are chained in defeat and by disease and health issues, remember, I will be victorious. When you are chained by loss and grief and despair, remember, I will indeed be victorious. You are My Mordecai. You may not know the end of the story, but I know it. So be faithful. The gallows that Haman has set out before your eyes to taunt you with the noose, and the chain that you feel around your neck created by the enemy of your heart, I will reverse those, My Child. Haman will die on His own gallows. The enemy will be defeated. Your praise calls My presence forth. It reminds you, My Child, **I WILL BE VICTORIOUS**!

January 14

"Comfort, yes, comfort My people!" Says your God. "Speak comfort to Jerusalem, and cry out to her, That her warfare is ended, That her iniquity is pardoned; For she has received from the Lord's hand Double for all her sins." Isaiah 40:1-2 (NKJV)
You walk this world with a taut chain around your neck, a choke collar designed and held by the Great Pretender. The world and its master would convince you to go this way and that, guided by your lusts and by your cravings, enthralled by its enticements. You feel powerless, held by its sway, held captive by a will and a force other than your own. Do you not yet realize, Child; have you not yet heard? The power of My Son crucified fills you. The authority that brought Him forth from the grave has been given to you. Look at yourself! You have the power to break the choke collar that you wear, that the world and its master use to lead you to and fro. You have the authority to put a chain around **his** neck, around the world's neck, subduing in My name the lust of your eyes, your cravings for this world, the defeat and the despair of circumstances, for My power is your power. Cower no longer like a dog mistreated by its cruel master. I am your Master, and I have given you authority in My name to defeat the grasp of this world and all its horrors. You are free; you are released; you are pardoned; you are loved. Walk in that truth.

January 15

Remember: A stingy planter gets a stingy crop; a lavish planter gets a lavish crop…. As one psalmist puts it, He throws caution to the winds, giving to the needy in reckless abandon. His right-living, right-giving ways never run out, never wear out. This most generous God who gives seed to the farmer that becomes bread for your meals is more than extravagant with you. He gives you something you can then give away, which grows into full-formed lives, robust in God, wealthy in every way, so that you can be generous in every way, producing with us great praise to God.
2 Corinthians 9:6,9-11 (MSG)

I speak truth to you. I give you My Word, My seed, My love. In times of abundance and in times of lack, there is always some seed that I leave you with. My truth is clear: what you sow, you will reap. If you sow nothing, you will reap nothing. This is the law of the harvest. Your greatest sacrifice in times of desperate need and relentless grief is to look to the future, not just the present. Do not hold so tightly what you fear is too little for the present that you cannot sow it into the future. The hard places of your life produce the tears that will soften the hard ground around you; what causes you to cry is exactly what will enable a future healthy harvest. Give heed to your tears; loose the cries that you have suppressed in your captivity. Take the seed that I have given you; relinquish your tight grasp of fear that there will be no more, and sow it; plant it. My Holy Spirit imbues your heart with constancy and expectation, for there will never come a time when I won't provide spiritual seed enough to sustain you, nor will there ever be a time when I don't call you to plant while thinking of the future and not just the present. When tears stream down your face, when circumstances feel overwhelming, that is when I call you to plant. The planting of My seed is not always done with the sun shining and the sky blue. Often I call you to plant when the seed has almost run out, when you have to choose between eating in the present and sowing for the future, when you have to trust that what I give you today is also intended to be a harvest for tomorrow.

January 16

The Lord Almighty has sworn, "Surely, as I have planned, so it will be, and as I have purposed, so it will stand." Isaiah 14:24

My plans will not be thwarted; My intentions will not be denied. You have heard it said that you can run but not hide; that is true of your relationship with Me as well. You may turn a deaf ear. You may avert your gaze. You may even deny both Me and My ways. Yet nothing will change Me, and nothing can make Me deny My love for you. I have purposed long before time began; long before you knew Me, I knit together not just you but all time and people and places. From your vantage point, it seems the world spins out of control. It is not so, Child, for its spinning is held safely in My hands. I use even the straying of My most wayward child. I reverse plans meant for evil, repurposing all things for good that will live eternally. You do not need to understand My ways in order to trust them. I am not some helpless, subdued, defeated god of cardboard or wax. I am the Holy One, the great I AM, the Alpha and the Omega. I am the Omniscient and Righteous One. What I intend will come to pass. What I purpose I will bring forth. Despite all the evil intentions that live and reign on this fallen earth, My good plans will prevail.

January 17

[B]y abolishing in his flesh the law with its commandments and regulation. His purpose was to create in himself one new man out of the two, thus making peace. Ephesians 2:15

I embrace the whole of you. I do not look upon you as a buffet, picking and choosing pieces and parts of you to make up a plate of the best, the choicest pieces of you, then to offer you up to the world. Why would a plastic world need a plastic version of "you" as an offering? No Child, I take you as a plate set before Me, **as is**, the good, the not so good, and the downright unappealing of you, and I season it with My salt, and I blow My Spirit breath on you to make you the right temperature. This is what will affect the world: the real of you, the struggling you, the hopeful you, the faithless you, the trusting you, the joyful you, and the heartbroken you. The world has had its fill of plastic Christians, quoting overused and under-lived scriptures; now is the time I have set for My people to shed the skin of religion and to stand vulnerable and naked and REAL before the plastic gods of this world. You, all of you, every piece of you is written down in My book, created for My glory, and called for such a time as this.

January 18

God was wonderful to us; we are one happy people. And now, God, do it again - bring rains to our drought-stricken lives So those who planted their crops in despair will shout hurrahs at the harvest, So those who went off with heavy hearts will come home laughing, with armloads of blessing. Psalm 126:3-6 (MSG)

Can you find your way toward My harvest, the one that calls you to trust in the unseen, the unknown, the future? You have learned to trust Me in the present. Can you trust that what I call you to do in the present will lead to a future that you can't yet see, a harvest that will bring joy that you can't imagine? Be greedy for Me, hungry for Me. See yourself standing in the midst of the chain of your days, surrounded by choices that affect your future, your harvest, your spiritual prosperity. I will teach you what is for you to eat today and what is to sow for your tomorrows. I will instruct you to fast sometimes, to relinquish what feels like overwhelming hunger, so that you might instead sow into an eternal harvest. Do not think that your tears are without purpose. They are, in fact, what will nourish that which you surrender to Me. If I capture them in a bottle, don't you think they are precious to Me? Don't you think they matter? Don't you think I use them?

January 19

The remnant of the saved in Mount Zion will go into the mountains of Esau And rule justly and fairly, a rule that honors God's kingdom. Obadiah 1:21 (MSG)
Don't play by the rules of the world's old game, for I have turned the table and changed the rules. I usher forth a new way: a way of compassion rather than cruelty, of generosity rather than recompense. Fair takes on new meaning, for the forgiveness side of justice reigns. Harbor vengeance no longer; instead look for ways to bring healing and health to broken situations. My people must be My new Kingdom's vanguard. Establish peace, even in the midst of the little wars that rage about you. Be the righter of wrongs; be willing to make new friends out of old enemies. I know this way seems topsy-turvy, insufficient somehow when your heart cries for justice. But My justice is of a different kind since My Son has come. I call you to bring a new kind of Light to the nations, a redemption having its roots in forgiveness that turns its cheek and harbors no ill will. This is the new kind of rule and reign that I have chosen for My loved ones.

January 20

I tell you the truth, whatever you did for one of the least of these brothers of mine, you did for me.... I tell you the truth, whatever you did not do for one of the least of these, you did not do for me. Matthew 25:40,45
I, the Creator, took on the form of creature because of My great love for you. I call you to do similarly. Take on the needs and the concerns of the least of them. Sacrifice your ease and your entitlements in order that refuge and safety might come to those who have none. Your blessings are not yours to hold tightly in your grasp; rather, hold them loosely in your outstretched hand, offering them to Me and to those whose lives I call you to impact. Mine is the way of surrender, of giving up, of offering that which you hold most dear.

January 21

Blessed are those who mourn, for they will be comforted. Matthew 5:4

Because you dwell in darkness, think not that My presence has left you; I dwell with you. Because you cannot lift your heart to Me in praise because of your own pain, do not think I turn away offended; I dwell with you. Because this day dawns bright and clear, but your heart prefers the shadow lands because of your grief, do not think I criticize you; I dwell with you. As mourners of old sat with the grief-stricken, so My spirit sits with you. I, like them, at times can only offer My presence. Lean against My bosom; let your tear-swollen eyes rest, your grief encased heart find safety; I dwell with you. Brighter days **will** come; joy will again spring forth, and laughter will someday find its way to your heart. But, until that time comes, I join with you; I will not leave you … I dwell.

January 22

He shall say: "Hear, Israel: Today you are going into battle against your enemies. Do not be fainthearted or afraid; do not panic or be terrified by them. For the Lord your God is the one who goes with you to fight for you against your enemies to give you victory."
Deuteronomy 20:3-4

There is a time to rest, a time to quiet yourself before Me in peaceful repose. But, Child, there is also a time to war, a time to pick up sword and shield, and run to the battle. A time to rout the enemy, shouting your warrior shout and brandishing your warrior steel, a time to leave the comfort and rest of hearth and home for the discipline and lack of the battlefield. Have no mercy on the enemy of your life, for if you do anything less than remove the head of the demon-hoard, they will regenerate and return to your home to pillage and rape and kill. So rouse yourself Warrior-Child; shake off the lethargy that comes from too much food and too much leisure. Your family looks to you for protection; will you watch them tortured and ravaged and dragged away by your foe? Bang the rust from your sword; take up shield and breastplate; take your place at the wall. Be vigilant; be watchful; be ready; I call you to battle.

January 23

All these blessings will come down on you and spread out beyond you because you have responded to the Voice of God, your God: God's blessing inside the city, God's blessing in the country; God's blessing on your children, the crops of your land, the young of your livestock, the calves of your herds, the lambs of your flocks. God's blessing on your basket and bread bowl; God's blessing in your coming in, God's blessing in your going out. Deuteronomy 28:2-5 (MSG)

Choose **Me**.   Choose to hear **My** voice. Choose to be obedient to **My** call. Do not silence the cry, the murmur of My still, small voice that speaks within the hidden recesses of your heart. You are Mine; allow Me to draw you deeper into My heart. Turn your will toward Mine, and I will give you My power and My strength to walk in My ways. Surrender your heart, moment by moment, day by day, as My Counselor Spirit prods and nudges you to see and hear the truth, and I will reorder your steps, lead you to the high places, take you deep into situations and hearts where you can be the transformative vessel of My love. You make choices all day long, choices that are either obedience or disobedience at the core, choices that call you toward either surrender or independence. Choose Me. You know My voice; choose **Me**.

January 24

Israel's watchmen are blind, they all lack knowledge; they are all mute dogs, they cannot bark; they lie around and dream, they love to sleep. They are dogs with mighty appetites; they never have enough. They are shepherds who lack understanding; they all turn to their

own way, each seeks his own gain. Isaiah 56:10-11

Be careful My Child, for I have told you that many are called but few are chosen. You **are** My chosen one, part and parcel of My plan for My creation's redemption. My watchman on the heights keeping guard; My shepherd in the pastures watchful and caring. If you make this your calling about yourself rather than Me, it will be to My people's peril and not just your own. Blow My horn; sing My praises; fellowship with My people, and bless them with your love, your caring affection. Do not be a guard for My house who slumbers and only revels in his own pleasure and satisfaction. The time is short; My Day is not far below the horizon. My sheep need protection and leading. My house needs cared for and guarded. It is you I have called to these tasks. You who I have picked out from the masses to be one of My faithful ones. It is you who I have given the order to walk in My footsteps, dwell in My presence, and be My image bearer. Speak My truth. Guard My people. Share My bounty. Be My holy one.

January 25

Let me give you a new command: Love one another. In the same way I loved you, you love one another.
John 13:34 (MSG)

Love My children. Be an empty vessel, and I will fill you up and pour you out. Be willing to step into the dark places of the world where I put you, and be My light. Be My grace; be My love in due season. I gave Myself to you to redeem you, but your redemption is not just for yourself, but also for the impact that you will have on others. Stay close to Me. You will need My power and My strength; you will need the Spirit's indwelling, for I call you forth from your Egypts, your places of emotional and psychological bondages, to set other captives free. As I lead you out, grab the hands of My other children whom I love, and draw them out with you. All those who will cross your path, I desire to overtake with love. Be My hands; be My feet. Be My voice and set captives free.

By My empowering, you too can make the blind see and the lame walk unhindered. Your words that speak of Me and My healing touch are My voice to the wounded around you. Be My voice. Love My children.

January 26

Remember these things, O Jacob. Take it seriously, Israel, that you're my servant. I made you, shaped you: You're my servant. O Israel, I'll never forget you. I've wiped the slate of all your wrongdoings. There's nothing left of your sins. Come back to me, come back. I've redeemed you. Isaiah 44:21-22 (MSG)

How I have missed you, My Child! It is as though you have gone to a more exotic foreign country and come no more to visit Me in My humble abode. Has your love for Me paled in the face of new affections that tantalize you with their promises of feverish excitement? Have you grown bored with My unchangeableness, My steadfastness, My immovability? Have the noises of the world overshadowed My still gentle voice so that you no longer hear it through the din that rumbles within your ears? Have you lost the fervor of your first love? Has the sight of Me on your pathways become so commonplace to you that you no longer view Me with pleasure and expectation? Child, there is nothing that will satisfy you that lies outside My hands. It is only **in** Me and **with** Me that you will find peace for your restless soul. Come back to Me, and dwell with Me again. I have missed you, Dear One. Your attentions have wandered to other lovers, but it is only I who can be the faithful provider for your heart's needs and your spirit's desires. I await your return with the same steadfastness that has sought after My people since the beginning of time. I will take your hand; I will lead you home.

January 27

For just as we share abundantly in the sufferings of Christ, so also our comfort abounds through Christ.

2 Corinthians 1:5

Indeed, sadness will come; it is woven into the very fabric of this earthly life. It wasn't meant to be this way, but when rebellion took over, it brought with it a host of other unappealing consequences. As the years peel off, the knowledge of sadness becomes more and more intimate; life is hard and sadness ... epidemic. In the answer of My Son, I not only settled for mankind the rebellion issue but all the negative hoard that accompanied it: sadness, loneliness, rage, anxiety, melancholy, confusion, apathy; all the pain that tortures mankind. In Christ, all these states of man are answered; whether it feels so or not Child, it IS truth. Turn your contorted soul toward Me; confess to Me all that afflicts you. As I mastered the waves of the sea, so My words can calm your stormy seas. Relinquish your oar; listen instead to My voice, and hear My instruction. I have and I AM your answer.

January 28

"Come, follow me," Jesus said. Matthew 4:19

Follow Me. Such a simple command and yet ... Follow Me. Leave what you know behind you, and come after Me, your unknown. Follow Me. Drop what you are doing; leave your tax collecting and your fishing, and go where I go. Follow Me. Walk out of your family's door, and be unsure how and when you will be brought back to them again. Follow Me. Leave what you have known and who have been religiously, and venture out into the great unknown of the spiritual world. Follow Me. It seems in My Word that those I called had no doubts, no second thoughts, no wonderings. Those things are not for you to know. My words compelled them; they spoke deeply into their hearts and found the tender places that had searched so long for the One and the Way that would make their life complete. They followed what they did not yet know, urged on only by what they could not yet describe. So too I call you: follow Me. Leave behind; venture forth; dare. Let your deep places hear My voice, and what you do not yet know will be eclipsed by the call that falls deep within your very bones, your every breath. Follow Me. Come!

January 29

For God does speak - now one way, now another - though man may not perceive it. Job 33:14 (MSG)
I always have something to say to you! It was My words that spilled from My mouth that created everything that you know and see. It was My words that I spoke through My prophets and followers to remember, pass down, and to pen that you might know Me and My ways for you. I am not a God of silence now, for My words pour forth through the Holy Spirit who indwells you. My creation cries out as well, if you will only see and hear. I whisper to you in your inmost being and speak to you in the watches of the dark night hours. As you fall asleep, I long to murmur words of love and protection into your ear as you drift off. When you wake, I am there waiting to converse. Do not attribute times of dryness and silence to Me. Those are the times when circumstances have caused you to lose your focus, and the noise of the enemy stops your ears from hearing My softer voice. I am a God who speaks. Seek My voice as you seek My face. Listen with the ears of your heart, and hear what I am saying to you.

January 30

"Follow me," Jesus told him. Mark 2:14
Follow Me. It's long been My word for My disciples: *'Follow Me!'* What are **your** nets with which I ask you to stop fishing for fish and fish instead for My men? What is it **you** do that I call you to turn and use in a new direction? Follow Me. It is not **your** course that you must follow that will bring you light and hope and peace. It is **My** course for you. My calling is radical, My Child. It asks you to leave what you have known. It asks you to leave the comfortable places. It asks you to sacrifice. You look in amazement sometimes at My original disciples, for that is what they did: put down all,

left all, and followed Me. You too, follow Me! I'm not talking about the pastor or someone else seemingly full of wisdom. I'm not talking about following him; I'm talking about following **Me**. I'm not asking you to follow your parents, or even your spouse, or your best friend. I'm asking you to follow **ME**! I'm not asking you to direct your own way, to lead on, to persevere, to push through … I'm asking you to follow … Me. If you don't know the difference, Child, ask Me, right now. Follow Me!

January 31

When I felt secure, I said, "I will never be shaken." O Lord, when you favored me, you made my mountain stand firm; but when you hid your face, I was dismayed. Psalm 30:6-7

My favor lasts a lifetime, your lifetime, but sometimes it is hard for you to see for it is mixed with the sin and the sorrow of this fallen world as well as My hand of loving correction and discipline in your life. How I long for you to call out to Me for mercy, for My love, for My presence when your days are sunny and easy. But often it is only in the hard and lonely darknesses that you stretch your hands out to Me. I have made your paths straight and built for you a secure fortress of My grace and protection, yet too often in that ease you forget who provides your strength and have reveled in your own shaky powers. It is in those times that I must show you who is Lord, and who holds the reins of your life. For it is not you who are invincible, but I; it is not you who have the strength to not be moved, but I who choose to make you immoveable. If My face seems hidden from you, seek Me. Acknowledge My ways; seek My mercies, that your day might be made bright by My light and your life made firm by My power. For otherwise discouragement and weeping, yea even dismay, lurk waiting for you to declare that your security rests in your own wisdom and strength rather than in Me.

FEBRUARY

February 1

Two are better than one, because they have a good return for their labor; if either of them falls down, one can help the other up. But pity anyone who falls and has no one to help them up. Ecclesiastes 4:9-10

Life is indeed a perilous journey. Even in the places it seems as if the trail is stable and the path clearly marked, at any moment the ground beneath can give way, and through no fault of your own, you have become one with the snow and ice hurtling down the mountainside taking all you have known with it. I deny not the violence, the fury, and destructiveness of these events. Events such as these are not as infrequent as you think, and for this very reason I admonish you to bind yourself to fellow travelers. Without them many have lost their lives, unable to turn in the rush, and thrust their ice-axe into something solid to slow their decent. If bound to others, when one falls, the others all can turn as one and strike for solid ground, helping the helpless to stop and find footing. Find your companions while the trail is safe and the sun shines; learn to tie your knots to others; there IS safety in numbers.

February 2

I have fought the good fight, I have finished the race, I have kept the faith. 2 Timothy 4:7

Follow Me. Kick off your sandals; wade past the shallows and push your way into the depths, My depths. You have stayed in the shallow waters far too long. My disciples are neither timid nor fearful, for they know it is My arm that keeps them safe and not their own. Let it be so with you, My Adventurer. Gather up your robes so you can run. Unencumber yourself from all that will either deter you or slow you down. My race goes not to the swift but to the willing. My prize is given not to the fearful, the timid, those slow to dare, but to those who finish the race, those who swim the course with Me by their side.

February 3

I love to speak to you. I love it when you listen, when you surrender yourself to Me so I can push your flesh out of the way and pour My words and My thoughts through you. Your world is full of words – of TV and song, of conversation, of books and work that is done, of emails and advertisements. I long to fill your mind and your heart with **My** words. Turn to My Scriptures. Tune in to My voice. Empty yourself that I might speak and fill you up. This listening to Me is more than just a notion – it's a commitment, a surrender, and a covenant. You are bound to Me through My death. You are one with Me by My creative power and love. I call you to listen as I walk beside you. You listen to a friend, why not listen to Me? You learn the life stories of those sisters and brothers I bring beside you, why not learn My Story more deeply? I know **you** so well; why not lean in and listen and know **Me** more? My Spirit will make your prayer a reality: **'Speak, Lord, for your servant is listening.' 1 Samuel 3:9**

February 4

I am the vine; you are the branches. If you remain in me and I in you, you will bear much fruit; apart from me you can do nothing. John 15:5
I do not dwell in vague perceptions; My home is not a passing cloud where I sit, ministered to by cherubs strumming lyres while I glance down at My paltry creation with disinterest. No, I AM the God of your daily reality. I dwell, as you dwell, smack dab in the midst of your mess. I AM a close-up God, an intimate companion of the daily grind. I know your concerns, your frustrations, your anxieties as well as your hopes, dreams, and faith-walks. This is where I dwell, but you must, in your own mind and heart, put Me there, imagine Me there, walking out each moment with you. This knowledge, this sacred imaging is as huge to faith in God as a baby's first breath is imperative to life. Without it, your day ends in shards of broken glass, with chaos reigning,

but with it, you can KNOW My embrace, My daily moment-by-moment presence with you … and by this knowing you WILL stand!

February 5

I wait for the Lord, my soul waits, and in his word I put my hope. My soul waits for the Lord more than watchmen wait for the morning, more than watchmen wait for the morning. Psalm 130:5-6

Wait on Me. Stand still and wait. Your cause is in My hands; your very breath concerns Me, so wait on Me. My hand is not too short to save, nor are My ears too clogged to hear your cries. Wait on Me. Deliverance comes from afar; victory hides behind what looks like defeat. Wait on Me. It is in Me that you put your trust, so wait on Me. I see; I hear; I know. There is nothing that concerns you that is outside My purview or devoid of My knowledge, so wait on Me. What you can perhaps change by your quick action today should perhaps not be changed; wait on Me today instead. In the silence and the interminable minutes while you look for the darkness to give way to the promised light, lift your eyes to the heavens and remember My faithfulness to you. There are times when I call you to swiftness, but when I instruct you to stand still, you must wait on Me. Be ready as the runner is poised at the starting line, but it is **My** starting gun that you must hear before you leap forward. Wait on Me!

February 6

"If you'll hold on to me for dear life," says God, "I'll get you out of any trouble. I'll give you the best of care if you'll only get to know and trust me. Call me and I'll answer, be at your side in bad times; I'll rescue you, then throw you a party." Psalm 91:14-15 (MSG)

You are Mine. Hear those words as a claim **on** your life, but hear them also as a promise **for** your life. Much of what you attend to in the hours of your days, both the blessings and the challenges, causes you to lose your true focus, for you so often forget both who you are and Whose you are. It is only in the settled in place of submission to Me, of seeing yourself confidently dwelling in the shadow of the Most High, that you can truly live your life contentedly and expectantly. Life is too full of turmoil to live it outside of My grip of grace. Wait on Me Child; seek My presence. Stretch yourself out of your days and your ways into the arms that hold the universe in motion. Those same arms hold all of your days, the doings of your life, your dreams, your fears, and your pain. Because you are Mine, all of those pieces of your life are Mine as well. Tremble not when faced by the details of your life. Those are safe and covered by My blood and My love. Tremble only when you forget that you are Mine. Turn back and renew your first love; hide yourself in Me, for you are Mine.

February 7

[W]hat is that to you? You must follow me. John 21:22
Go where I send you; be who I call you to be. Follow the path that is My path for you. Its way will not always be clear to you, nor will the ground be without obstacles. What I call you to will often be unheralded and unrecognized, even by those who know and love you the best. Yet it is **My** way that matters and **My** handprints on your life that are the important ones. Tremble in your own inadequacies but do not falter; I will fill you with what you need and give you My fearless strength as your inheritance. Walk the path I set before you, whether it is straight or tortuously crooked and whether it is flat or quickly climbs with no relief. It is My way that you walk in and My will for you alone that you fulfill.

February 8

No one can serve two masters. Either you will hate the one and love the other, or you will be devoted to the one and despise the other. You cannot serve both God and money. Luke 16:13

The world thinks and moves and has its being in the god of dollars and cents. Daily it bows to its precepts, adhering to its strict rules of profit. It is in love with its god who tickles its taste buds with fanciful dreams of glut and greed and selfishness. It lays itself down, body and soul to gain its god's favor, abandoning all that it is and all that it has to its dictatorship. Guard yourself Child; check your own mind and heart with frequency; determine if you too have not bowed your knee to this world's money god. The priests of the god of this world may have wealth, "things" enough for several lifetimes, but peace of mind and heart eludes them. They can "fix" many things in the world to suit their tastes, but they cannot buy themselves one more minute when the True God of the Universe calls their name. Then the folly of their wealth rises up, and in life's most fatally tragic, ironic moment turns on its disciple, and with a sneer of contempt, denies all knowledge of them, leaving its follower naked and poverty-stricken in God's economy. Mine the true wealth of life, the treasures of mercy, the gifts of peace, the Fort Knox of forgiveness, and the storehouse of My compassion. If you have these, then you truly can call yourself wealthy.

February 9

Beloved. Come away, my lover …. Song of Songs 8:14

Come away with Me, My Beloved. The hour awaits us, and I am eager to meet with you and pour My Spirit into you. Too often the multitude presses against you, and the clamor of the world keeps you from Me. In those times, when you come not because you hear not, you lose so much more than an hour's communion with Me. The distractions of the world rob your peace; they let your joy slide away like the sand in an hourglass. There is nothing left in you to prevent the mudslide that life in this world brings. So come away, My Child. Leave the world behind you and draw close. All of that world's concerns that touch you, even all that you do in My name and all those you love, will still be there when you return, but you will have been filled by your meeting with

Me, and you will be enabled tenfold to walk in grace and love where I have placed you.

February 10

Blessed are all who take refuge in him. Psalm 2:12
The earth is a terror-filled place. Even in the ease that it sometimes affords you, you know it for what it truly is: unreliable, full of despair, hounded by war and the rumors of war, frightening, and uncertain. Kings announce themselves - then rise and fall. Money multiplies - then vanishes like dust in the wind. All that once seemed sure becomes uncertain in a heartbeat; what provides safety on one day gives way to worry on another. How long will it take you to realize that the trappings of this world are fleeting, and the terrors they sometimes engender will last but for a night? The things that cause you pleasure here, as well as all that causes alarm, are but momentary in the ticking of the clock of My eternity. Don't build your hope on what this world can bring you; neither let fear about what it cannot provide cloud your vision. All that is in it will one day pass away, and I will return to take My children home. Hide yourself in the shadow of **that** promise.

February 11

Yet I am always with you; you hold me by my right hand. You guide me with your counsel, and afterward you will take me unto glory. Whom have I in heaven but you? And earth has nothing I desire besides you. My flesh and my heart may faint, but God is the strength of my heart and my portion forever. Psalm 73:23-26
Why are you bowed down, bent over? I have come to set you free from your burdens. I bring release from the weight that overwhelms you, the hardships that you endure, and the lack of health in your body and soul. Do you not see My face turned toward you? Lift your head, Child, and when you cannot, know that I am the One who lifts your head high that you may see My gaze of love and affection for you. It is My

shield of protection around you that guards you from so much that you do not even know. You feel overwhelmed, burdened with trials, and overtaken by the enemy's hand. If you only knew what My shield of covenant love protects you from: the unseen forces of darkness and the almosts that would have ruined you. I have bestowed My glory on you; it is under that mantle that I hide you, shield you, protect you. I desire your praise, Child, not just that you might bear witness to My saving mercies, but that in such praise you too might be grounded in My truths: forever I shield you, forever I lift your head, and forever I love you.

You, Lord, are a shield around me, my glory, the one who lifts my head high. Psalm 3:3

February 12

Ah, Sovereign Lord, you have made the heavens and the earth by your great power and outstretched arm. Nothing is too hard for you.... [G]reat are your purposes and mighty are your deeds. Your eyes are open to all the ways of men. Jeremiah 32:17,19

By My power has all been made, and by that same power I watch over it all. Creator and Ruler are bound together in My same strong arm of might. My creative ways are far beyond what you can understand. Why, then, would you think you would understand all of My purposes or My deeds? Trust that I see you; know that I both watch you and watch **over** you. Do not forget that I am the God of Deliverance and your Savior who loves you.

February 13

When these things begin to take place, stand up and lift up your heads, because your redemption is drawing near. Luke 21:28

'Ready or not, here I come.' It's a child's play call of attention. But Child, ready or not, here **I** come. As a tornado siren sings out across the land, so is the sound of heaven this morning. My alarm is being set off, My siren singing out,

'Ready or not, here I come!' It is like a football game, and the sound of the people in the stadium sounding out as one as the kicker is ready to kick the ball. Even without eyes, as the yell comes to a crescendo, one would know that the ball is about to become airborne. That's what it's like right now, Child; ready or not, here I come. It's time to bend your knee. If you need to break your pride, it's time; put your foot on the neck of pride; put your foot on the neck of sin in your life that you've let linger and linger. It's time to put your foot on the neck of arrogance and stubbornness that boasts, *'I will not change.' 'I will not bend.' 'I will not break.' 'I will not speak to that person.' 'I will not forgive.'* Child, time is short; it's time to break yourself so you can go out there and speak My word and speak My comfort and speak My love to the people that know Me not. Ready or not, here I come. You're saved. They are not.

February 14

Surely the arm of the Lord is not too short to save, nor his ear too dull to hear. Isaiah 59:1

My hand is not too short to save, nor are My ears unable to hear your cries for rescue. Today I give you provision … for today. I sprinkle your manna from My heaven for today on today's fields. Such is true not just for your food and your shelter and all your physical needs but for your emotional needs as well. I provide for your emotions and for all the complexities that rage in your heart, but only for today, only for right now; the heart needs of tomorrow must wait for tomorrow. I fill you one day at a time. What you see as a breach of My promise to take care of you is really you vainly and disobediently trying to gather both your spiritual and your emotional manna into storehouses for your rainy days of tomorrow, even though I have told you clearly that I will provide what you need each day for that day alone. Manna, your provision just for that day; offered, provided for today, one day at a time, not the measure for tomorrow. Remember, it is not that My arm is too short to save you nor My ears too clogged to hear you; this daily way is how I choose to provide for you so that you will lean on Me and stay close. Trust My saving, providing love for you in this.

February 15

Why, we even saw the Nephilim giants.... Alongside them we felt like grasshoppers. And they looked down on us as if we were grasshoppers. Numbers 13:33 (MSG)

All My grasshopper people, tremble before Me. Bend your knee. Bow your hearts. For it is I who is great, and it is I who uses you. I use grasshoppers; I don't need mighty kings. I make little Davids into mighty kings and mighty warriors. It is only your love for Me, and only your obedience to Me, that transform you into whom I have chosen you to be. What I have called you to is **My** work, and it rests on My greatness, not on yours. Who I have ordained you to be is **My** work, and it rests on My hand of strength. My arm is not too short. Yours is, but **My** arm is not too short. Reach toward Me. Stay in a position of praise, of surrender, of love for Me, and your great God will take care of the rest.

February 16

Then I acknowledged my sin to you and did not cover up my iniquity. I said, "I will confess my transgressions to the Lord" - and you forgave the guilt of my sin. Selah.... You are my hiding place; you will protect me from trouble and surround me with songs of deliverance. Selah. I will instruct you and teach you in the way you should go; I will counsel you and watch over you. Psalm 32:5,7,8

'Cover my sins, O Lord!' you cry to Me, and cover them I will. Acknowledge them, repent of them, expose them to Me, and the chains that bind you will be broken. My release comes for you when your honesty intersects My loving forgiveness. I cannot hide in safety the parts of you that you refuse to expose to Me. I cannot protect that which is not Mine.

Stand naked before Me and be unashamed, for there is nothing about you that is too sinful or too unholy for Me to love. Come away from the pretenders who surround you, from those who say *'Yes'* when the answer should be *'No,'* and those who say *'No'* when My answer is *'Yes.'* Find your truths in Me; find your limits in Me, remembering that My boundary lines for you fall in pleasant places. Let Me and no one else be your Counselor, your Guide, your Instructor, your Teacher, your Deliverer.

February 17

Praise the Lord, O my soul, and forget not all his benefits …. Psalm 103:2

Forget not all My benefits, My Child. Forget not **all My benefits**! Stay your mind on Me; still your heart before Me and remember. What is it that you're focused on right now? Is it what you have? Or what you have not? Is it what you lack? Or what I provide? My Word cautions you to not forget all your benefits, all the things that I have given you. The enemy of your soul would rather convince you of your lack. He would rather you focus on your pain. He would rather you focus on what you do not have. He would rather you focus on disease and illness and lack of money and lack of resources or problems in your family or tragedies with your children or all the tragedies in this world. And that, My Child, is what the world teaches you to look at and what it would have your eyes focus on. I say, Child, forget not all **M**y benefits to you. Stop watching the TV all the time and watch My movies of My faithfulness. Down through the years of your life and down through the years of all My people in My Bible are story upon story of My benefits. Come to Me with your needs, yes, but forget not all the benefits I have given you already. It is there in those memories, in those thoughts of My good gifts to you that you will find My provision for your spirit, for your mind. You will find **My** peace and **My** strength in the face of whatever the enemy has thrown in your face. Child, forget not My benefits to you.

I remember the days of long ago; I meditate on all your works and consider what your hands have done.
Psalm 143:5

February 18

Those who cling to worthless idols forfeit the grace that could be theirs. Jonah 2:8
I willingly offer all that I have to you; My inheritance is yours to claim. I have written My last will and testament and sealed it closed with the drops of My Son's blood; there is no chance that I will change My mind. All I have is yours. My creation sits at your feet, yours to enjoy and yours to claim for all eternity. Love, forgiveness, wisdom, power, righteousness are all yours through Me because of My hand and My standing in your life. You are surrounded by My grace, bound up in the gentle cords of My love. Rich Father that I am, you need never fear lack. But despite this, despite **all** this, you wander hopeless and lonely because you sell your inheritance. Prostitutes of the simplest sort woo you away with imagined splendors, and your lustful greed sweeps you away into the arms of lesser lovers. O prodigal Child of My heart, surrender your pride and return to Me. Your idols are man made, carved from the wood of the trees you fell, molded from the metals you yourself mined. They have no power; they offer no hope; they can neither love you nor keep you safe. Turn your back on them and return to Me, and I will once again enfold you in My grace.

February 19

I will give you the treasures of darkness, riches stored in secret places, so that you may know that I am the Lord, the God of Israel, who summons you by name.
Isaiah 45:3
Mine My treasure trove. My great gifts to you lie buried below the surface of your life. Take the time to dig for them. Take a break from your daily life; your have tos and your shoulds keep you living far too much in the superficial rather

than the deep. I am often below the surface of your ordinariness. You find Me and My gifts beyond your comprehension when you allow yourself to be consumed and overwhelmed by the pragmatics of your life. Stop; listen; reach out to Me. I will come and speak and draw close to your heart and you will find great treasure that you never suspected even existed. The world, **this** world, often holds too much sway over your heart and your spirit. Go deeper than the outward trappings and you will find Me waiting with a treasure map to point the way to the valuables in My deep, for precious to Me are the hearts of My children when they draw close to Me. I will reveal My great riches to them and invite them to share in My astonishing bounty.

February 20

In spite of all this, they kept on sinning; in spite of his wonders, they did not believe. Psalm 78:32

Come stroll with Me. Take My hand, and walk beside Me. I have so much to show you. Mysteries that you have not yet understood and blessings that you have not yet seen are poised at the fringes of your life waiting to invade the walk with which you have grown so comfortable. Release that comfort, surrender that which is known, and come, follow Me. Your obedience positions you, allows Me access to you, and prepares your heart for what I am eager to accomplish with you. That to which you allow yourself to remain shackled prevents Me from taking your life and your purposes to another level. Surrender, Child, and obey. Trust that what I have delivered you from, what I call you to complete, and the good work that I have been about deep within you will open doors and possibilities that you cannot yet imagine. But also know that your forward movement into these new things that I long to accomplish in your life and through your life is hindered by the shackles that you have not yet stepped out of. Step forth into My arms of love; leave the familiarity of your known bondages. Freedom awaits, and in that place of My liberty, I have much to show you and much I long to do with You at My side. Stay with

Me; commune with Me. Rest and grow in My presence. There is no time for shackles in what I am up to with you.

February 21

Be on your guard; stand firm in the faith; be men of courage; be strong. 1 Corinthians 16:13
Be still and know I am God. Not just for your own life, but for the lives and the hearts that I call you to treasure and intercede for. It is I who am God, I and no other. In your frenetic rush to ease pain and right wrongs and provide comfort, you sometimes forget that. Pursue **My** timing; give way to **My** purposes. Relax in the midst of all that you do not know, and trust that I know all. I call you to intercede and to love. Run the race with endurance, but be sure to follow My track and not your own. Your good intentions are little more than worthless if they are not encompassed by My great plan and My great love. Be strong in My might; steady your course; look to Me, and when you have done all, stand. It is in such standing that My power will come on your behalf and for those you cover in prayer.

February 22

But You are holy, Enthroned in the praises of Israel. Our fathers trusted in You; They trusted, and You delivered them. Psalm 22:3-4 (NKJV)
I inhabit the praises of My people. When you draw near to Me, you will find Me there, for I have already drawn near. Your attitude of adoration and your spirit of worship bring you close to My heart. When you surrender the turmoil of your life, lay your anxieties at My altar, open your very soul to My worthiness, and give Me glory, I march right into the midst of your life. Your praises are an invitation to My presence - a red carpet that invites Me close. It is when the enemy breathes fear ... dread ... confusion ... into your spirit that you lose sight of Me, your praises drowned out by your anxiety. Stand, Child. Lift your eyes from that which the prince of the air would have you see, and instead gaze on

My face, the crown of thorns on My brow that proclaims My never ending love for you, and My pierced palms reaching to draw you close. Praise Me for what you know to be truth, for My creating, My redeeming, for My breath of love on your life. And I will dwell close to you, inhabiting your praises.

February 23

No one lights a lamp and puts it in a place where it will be hidden, or under a bowl. Instead they put it on its stand, so that those who come in may see the light. Luke 11:33

I call you to shine as lamps in this world's darkness; I place you on a lamp stand so that many others can see and be drawn. Your light is not in how many bible verses you have memorized and can recite, nor is it in your resume of "do-good, be-good" attributes. Those things have little impact on this sin-sick, deeply-wounded, ravenously-hungry world. The light I call you to be is ...YOU! You ... in all your daily, with your sense of humor, struggling with your trials, bearing your heartaches, fighting your obstacles, showing your kindness. This changes the world ... all of **you** ... laid out, perfectly surrendered imperfection to Me. This is what it means to "BE" My lamp, emitting real light, authentic light, a shining reflection of the Light of the World. I AM the Light; I am also the lamplighter, and I will illuminate you as I purpose, and I will place you as I will, and I will call those about you to turn their heads and see. Surrender ... just BE.... I will cause you to shine.

February 24

He reveals the deep things of darkness and brings deep shadows into the light. Job 12:22

I have not invited you into My deep places and then left you alone and adrift. I have already explored all those unknown places long before you reach them. Even the hardship and the anguish that sometimes confront you are vehicles for My love for you to shine forth. If in the great darkness you can see and feel Me, how bright will be the light in your more comfortable days! Despair not, O Child of My heart, for great will My comfort be if you lean into Me instead of into your circumstances. Forget not that I have betrothed you to Me. I have taken you from the simple love of a child to the complex relationship of an adult bonded to another forever, like that of a spouse or a lifetime friend. It is there in such deep love and friendship with Me that you will find your great joy and contentment, regardless of your outward circumstances. Press toward Me; lean in and find Me!

February 25

Jesus wept. John 11:35
I weep for so many things, Child. I weep when My people see Me not and hear Me not. I weep when sin in your life masquerades as righteousness. I weep when you fall prey to the treachery of the evil one. I weep when you live in the midst of My bountiful protection yet feel yourself to be impoverished and adrift. It is My eyes and My eyes alone that you must desire. It is My ways that you must seek. How often you have seen or known what makes Me weep and yet gone about your business ignoring My heart. I weep, Child, because I am both holy and loving. I weep for your small faith and for your tolerance of injustice. I weep for your casualness, your indifference to your own sin and your disrespect for Me, the Holy One. But most of all, I weep when you are careless with My great love for you.

February 26

You are my hiding place; you will protect me from trouble and surround me with songs of deliverance. Selah. I will instruct you and teach you in the way you should go; I will counsel you and watch over you. Psalm 32:7-8
Quiet Child. Be still. You rush, but I urge you to slow down. Let the Spirit temper the pace of your footsteps.

Quiet your anxious heart. Seek Me first, and put yourself under My authority. Remain tightly held in the grasp of My grace. The plan for your life is Mine; the urgency for its completion is Mine alone. In your surrender lies your peace and your safety. In your obedience lies the quiet in the midst of the storm. I am taking you to deep waters, but do not be afraid, for I am right beside you. I have taught you what you need to know, and I will continue to teach you in the depths. Be attentive; stay focused; lean into Me. The enemy's plan to drown and to shipwreck will be thwarted by My Spirit. Be relentless in your turning to Me. Do not become distracted by the foghorns or the choppy waves, for there is nowhere that you can be that is not within My grasp.

February 27

The Lord is the stronghold of my life - of whom shall I be afraid? Psalm 27:1

Lift up your eyes. Gaze at your Redeemer; acknowledge your Liberator. See and believe that I have rescued you, and that in all the days of your life I will continue to rescue you. Be not surprised by that, for I am your Fortress; I am your Stronghold. I am the Safe Tower to which you can run. There is safety to be found when you position yourself close to Me as Protector and Defender. My stronghold is available to your life, but you must enter into it. My covenant with you will never force you to seek My protection and deliverance, but it will always offer it. Come then; run and hide yourself in My shelter. Crawl under the safety of My great, sheltering wings. Do not stand alone on the world's battlefield, afraid of all that sets itself against you and aims to destroy you. Come inside My stronghold, and find your fear transformed into safety and peace. Come, My Child, come.

February 28

There is no fear in love. But perfect love drives out fear, because fear has to do with punishment. The one who fears is not made perfect in love. 1 John 4:18

Perfect love casts out all fear; **My** perfect love casts out all fear. Child, I am captivated by you. When you stand in need, do not fear for I am truly captivated by you. Anything that you fear, any need you have - healing for your body, help for your loved ones - embrace My great affection for you. You never stand alone; My Spirit continually hovers close, drawing you to Me. Lift up your eyes of hope, for in that lifting I will pour out My grace upon you. I cannot leave you; and I will not forsake you. I am captivated by you My Child, apple of My eye, object of My affection. Feel My great love and affection and presence that literally cannot abandon you; hold it to you as you walk through this day. Fear not My Beloved.

February 29

Therefore, if anyone is in Christ, he is a new creation; old things have passed away; behold, all things have become new. 2 Corinthians 5:17 (NKJV)
I take the desecrated things in your life, and I purify them. Your lands of desolation I replant and rebuild. Your heart and mind I renew. If after three days in the grave I brought My Son, your Savior, back to life, can I not also bring this to pass in your life? It is My power that is at work within you. Stay no longer in the midst of the darkness and rubble of your life. That which the enemy has destroyed, I will restore; that which he has misused, I will repurpose. I am faithful and this I will do!

March 1

[T]he Mighty One has done great things for me .... Luke 1:49
Name them, My Child. Name those things that I have done for you. Recount them to others and recount them to yourself as well. Such rememberings are like weapons in your arsenal. When your enemy comes against you, your praise for even one of those great things that I have done for you will vanquish your foe. The way of this fallen world is to

focus on your have nots, to retell the stories of your tragedies, to live trapped inside your impossible situations. **My** way is to do great things on behalf of My loved ones and to watch how their lives, when bounded by the recollection of those great things, destroy that which assails them. You too, My loved One. Live on top of the mountain of the great things I have done for you. Your propensity to live in the shade of that mountain makes you vulnerable to those forces that seek to destroy you, that wander the plains of your life. Rise above them; live on top of the reminders of all that I have already done for you. Recall and praise Me, and your life and ways will be prospered.

March 2

Behold, the hire of the labourers who have reaped down your fields, which is of you kept back by fraud, crieth: and the cries of them which have reaped are entered into the ears of the Lord of sabaoth. James 5:4 (KJV)
Injustice is the vanguard of this age; millions upon millions of voices have cried to Me over generations - cried for justice, and I, the Lord Sabaoth, hear their cry, hear **your** cry for vindication. I, the Lord of angel armies, wield uncontrollable power, and in My time, I shall release this power on your behalf. I hate injustice; its stench is appalling to My nostrils and reeks of selfishness and cruelty and disregard of My Lordship. There is no need to plot your release, revenge, or resistance My son, My daughter. For I, Lord Sabaoth, hear your cry, hear your call, and note your faithful endurance. I shall recompense the oppressor in your stead, and you shall dine with Me in his presence, and each morsel shall be sweet as honey because of your faithful looking to Me. All generations find Me faithful.

March 3

So shall they fear the name of the Lord from the west, and his glory from the rising of the sun. When the enemy shall come in like a flood, the Spirit of the Lord

shall lift up a standard against him. Isaiah 59:19 (KJV)
I will NEVER leave you in the heat of your battles as the enemy plots strategic maneuvers against you; in the very moment of his evil conception, My standard is raised against him. My acceptance of you, My fervor for you is not only contractual but also familial. In Me are perfected paternal protection and affection, boundless maternal care and patience. My love also processes the spousal passion and pursuit that will keep your heart in constant anticipation of our time alone together. My heart, My life is seamlessly bound to you. I cannot, even if I willed it, **ever** leave you alone. The enemy rails against you; that is a fact of this earthly life, but your hope of survival, nay your hope of triumphant success is set in the concrete of My union with you. O tempest tossed, still yourself and think on these things; they are strength for the battle and light for the way.

March 4

Free me from the trap that is set for me, for you are my refuge. Into your hands I commit my spirit; redeem me, O Lord, the God of truth. Psalm 31:4-5
It is not just for My Son that these words hold power. They are truth for you as well. Commit your spirit to Me, and watch and see how I reverse the intentions of the enemy, dissolving his plans in the creative power of My own. Was I still a refuge for My Son, My only Son, as He hung on the cross, giving life for you even in His dying? So too I am a refuge for you, My Beloved. Even when things seem the most hopeless, there you will find Me, and there will I protect you from the traps that the enemy prepares for you. My safety and protection do not always come in the outward; sometimes they remain in the background, invisible almost in the face of circumstances. But release your spirit to Me; unclasp your grip on how you define refuge and safety, and there you will find Me. I will spring the trap that has been set for your demise; I will bring Spirit good out of the enemy's evil intent.

March 5

I led them with cords of human kindness, with ties of love; I lifted the yoke from their neck and bent down to feed them. Hosea 11:4

I wrap you in the cords of My loving kindness, for you My Child are My heart's desire. I have bound you to Me with strands that are like iron: My willing, invincible love. Think not that I will happily let you wander the wilderness fields of other gods; you are Mine and the price that I have paid for you was indeed high. Gloat not at your collections of idols. No matter how well crafted or how well fed, they will leave you lost and lonely. Break them and grind them to bits. As Moses instructed Aaron and My people, grind up the golden calf that you constructed to replace Me and be done with it. There is no other god that has life and gives life. There is no other that loves. All your idols will happily pretend to fill your voids, but they think nothing of you, My Child. They have neither created you nor cared for you. It is only I, with My limitless affection for you, who can bring you health and peace. If it is freedom that you seek, find it in Me. Think not that being bound to Me is a jail sentence; it is life and hope and peace. Be bound in the straight jacket of My love for you; there you will find safety and rest for your heart.

March 6

As the heavens are higher than the earth, so are my ways higher than your ways and my thoughts than your thoughts. As the rain and the snow come down from heaven, and do not return to it without watering the earth and making it bud and flourish, so that it yields seed for the sower and bread for the eater, so is my word that goes out from my mouth: It will not return to me empty, but will accomplish what I desire and achieve the purpose for which I sent it. Isaiah 55:9-11

You see only shadows of Me and My ways; the substance and reality of Who I am and how I work are far beyond your understanding. Do not trouble yourself on My behalf, and do not allow the enemy to trouble your soul either. The picture you see is only partially completed. My Word is still going forth accomplishing My purposes. Even when you think you see, you see through a glass dimly. Eternity will reveal what I have purposed all along, and how the "all things" that you didn't understand fit together into My good things. Be at rest. Trust in My ways, My thoughts, and My purposes, for they are higher than yours. Choose to let it be well with your soul.

March 7

The path of the righteous is like the first gleam of dawn, shining ever brighter till the full light of day. Proverbs 4:18

Fear has no place in this walk with Me, Child. I have called you, and therefore I will equip you. I have walked beside you through the long journey of it all. Even in the part that was in the darkness when you could not feel Me or find Me, I was there. Fear is the enemy's tool to keep you from your destiny, to keep you from purposes I have not yet even revealed to you. Cower not under the whiplash of his words, the taunts that he hopes will paralyze you. Focus on Me, not on him, nor on yourself nor the crowds that surround you. Let My gaze of love so capture your heart that you have eyes only for Me. When your gaze is firmly planted on Me, that is when My power will come upon you and My light shine like the noonday sun. Hear only the sound of My voice singing over you with My love, for when you hear Me and Me alone, that is when your victory will be won. Fear not, for My perfect love casts out all fear, and I will make you brave.

March 8

This is what the Lord says: "Let not the wise man boast of his wisdom or the strong man boast of his strength or the rich man boast of his riches, but let him who boasts boast about this: that he understands and knows me ...." Jeremiah 9:23-24

My plans and purposes for you have nothing to do with how much you have or have not. They are instead a matter of faithfulness to My calling of you. Rich or poor or somewhere in between, I use you as I see fit. Poverty is not My goal for My people; neither are riches and ease. I ask you to allow Me to use you exactly where I have positioned you and to be open to where and how I might move you, whether that be up or down on an economic scale. Your riches are Mine, but your lack is Mine as well. In the final analysis neither are important, only your malleability in My hands. Be used by Me.

March 9

About midnight Paul and Silas were praying and singing hymns to God, and the other prisoners were listening to them. Suddenly there was such a violent earthquake that the foundations of the prison were shaken. At once all the prison doors flew open, and everyone's chains came loose. Acts 16:25-26
Each human, even each of those called by My name is, at times, possessed by his woundings. Each hiccup in relationships is a jerk of the wheel of the possessor. Wives languish in loneliness; children act out in frustration; husbands and fathers busy themselves with work or sports or hobbies to still the possessor's voice. Generations of brokenness crash upon the shores of every single person's life; none is exempt; none escapes its tsunami waves. Even in the most godly, the broken and the wounded places call the shots much of the time. You, My Child, must recognize this possession, for only in its recognition can it be taken in hand; only when you see that when you react or do not act at all, it is because in your broken, in your woundedness you can only act out of self-preservation. Only the Triune God can exorcise your possessor. Let your **Abba Father's** heart of love for you move you to recognize the **Son's** sacrifice for your freedom. Then, join forces with the **Holy Spirit** in pursuing, in arresting, in binding, and finally in the healing of the broken, fractured, bleeding, and bruised places of your

heart. Only in the continual pursuit of healing can you become truly possessed by the One who has sacrificed Himself for your freedom.

March 10

Then he said to Thomas, "Put your finger here; see my hands. Reach out your hand and put it into my side. Stop doubting and believe." John 20:27
Let Me take the raw, the real, the honest of you, the parts that pain you, that scare you, all your broken pieces, and hold them safely in My hands. But before I do, take a close look at My hands. These are the same hands that reached out to touch and to heal, that wrote in the dirt as the woman's accusers slunk away, that broke bread with My friends, that took up My own cross and carried it. These are the hands that will forever display the reminder of My crucifixion. It was for the likes of you that My blood was shed, the temple veil torn, and death defeated. There is both comfort and power in these hands. What you relinquish to them will be held securely, safely. Accept My offering, and surrender what pains you. Then the heavy core of you will be replaced by My perfect peace.
Jesus reached out his hand and touched the man. "I am willing," he said. "Be clean!" Immediately he was cured of his leprosy. Matthew 8:3

March 11

Let us draw near to God with a sincere heart in full assurance of faith.... Let us hold unswervingly to the hope we profess, for he who promised is faithful. Hebrews 10:22-23
Come. Come Child. Come find Me. Draw near to My heart of love for you. Come away from the noise; come away from the ordinary distractions of your everyday life. Come. Come find Me now in the quiet places of your heart, along the deserted byways of your mind, within the sin-stained corridors of your spirit. In all those places, if you only quiet

yourself, you will find Me there. It is not I who hides; it is you who too often does not look. It is not that I am speechless but that you too often cannot hear Me over the noise of your ordinary. Come find Me in your dark hours; come see Me in your lonely, your complicated, your hopeless. When you are weak and needy is when I am most eager to show Myself. Empty your hands; bid your spirit bow prostrate before Me. I am waiting; I have come; I watch for you in expectation. Come find Me, for with My heart of love for you I have drawn nigh.

March 12

God's loyal love couldn't have run out, his merciful love couldn't have dried up. They're created new every morning. How great your faithfulness! I'm sticking with God (I say it over and over). He's all I've got left. Lamentations 3:22-24 (MSG)

I am the God of wonders, Creator of all things, even those incomprehensible, and Sustainer of all things by My might. Why then would you expect to know and understand My ways? They are far above you. Can you not trust the One who formed you, the One who sees the end from the beginning, to sustain you, to accomplish the right things in your life, to work My will and My way even in the circumstances that you do not understand? Have you forgotten My faithfulness? Have you lost sight of My love? Are not My mercies, like the sunrise, new every morning? Does not My world speak of My constancy and My enduring provision? Can you not hear the very rocks cry out in praise to Me? Why then is your soul cast down, your heart afraid, your faith uneven? Stand still and know that I am your God, and choose this day to believe.

March 13

The Lord looks down from heaven on the sons of men to see if there are any who understand, any who seek God. Psalm 14:2

Wise men seek Me. Sages study Me. Mystics follow Me into deserted places. And what of you? Will you drop your fascination with the things that you can see and collect and look for Me instead? Will you dare to face the quiet of the universe's farthest reaches in order to hear My still, small voice? Will you risk reputation, swear off possessions, do whatever it takes to travel beyond the allure of this world's kingdom in order to find My Kingdom's perspectives? You can only dwell in one place at a time, only live in one home each night. Store up your treasure in Me; hide the secret places of your heart under the shadow of My wing. I will keep you safe. I will be your Great Protector. I will be the Champion of your heart. Lose yourself in the finding of Me rather than in the vain worldly voices that surround you. Be like My disciples of old, and come away with Me.

March 14

If you follow my decrees and are careful to obey my commands, I will send you rain in its season, and the ground will yield its crops and the trees their fruit. Your threshing will continue until grape harvest and the grape harvest will continue until planting, and you will eat all the food you want and live in safety in your land. Leviticus 26:3-5

Spring has come early! Winter's grasp has released the land. Pull plow and disc from their slumbering place, gather seed saved from last season's harvest, and ready yourself for planting. My fields now choked with weed and hardened by neglect are broad and vast and cry out for till and seed. Anguish not at the size and scope of the task set before you nor lament over lost ground surrendered to the enemy last season. This is a New Season! And I, Creator of sinew and bone, will give you strength for the day, day by day. Labor, yes, but turn your face to the Giver of sun and rain and seed; this will keep discouragement from clouding your labors and fatigue from halting your progress. The beginnings of tasks are the hardest; dig deep into grace till faith becomes sight, and you will see a harvest beyond all expectation.

March 15

How great is the love the Father has lavished on us, that we should be called children of God! And that is what we are! 1 John 3:1

Matchless is My love and extravagant are My feelings for you. All that you can imagine is but a dim shadow of the reality of My great passion for you. My boldness makes your daring seem puny. My great strength on your behalf makes your efforts appear weak. The endurance of My love in the face of the sum of all your offerings reveals the fickleness of your own best efforts to be faithful and to love well. Although all this might lead you to despair knowing that you can never measure up or appropriately reciprocate, I intend instead for it to free you to know and accept My love for you in a new way. Be no longer constrained by the boundaries of your own ability to love, for My love for you is limitless. Begin to think in terms of **My** strength, **My** loyalty, and **My** persistence rather than your own. Dwell inside the circumference of My caring and My passion, for I only wait for you to accept My love, not match it.

March 16

He has done it! Psalm 22:31

My call to you echoes across the reaches of time. From before the first creative Word that I breathed into this world, from before time began, I called you forth and stepped with you into My purposes for you. None of this is new to Me; you, however, have been growing into it, moving into it, being placed within it. Not in spite of your sinfulness, not despite the dirt on your life, but because of it, I can use you and I will use it. I have claimed it all, and I have sanctified even this. Surrender all your *'I cannots.'* Relinquish all the pieces of your life that you feel hold you back. Surrender your past, your present, as well as your future to Me, and allow My hand to completely refashion you and lead you toward My purposes. I have done it and I will continue to do it For you; in you; with you.

March 17

As iron sharpens iron, so one man sharpens another. Proverbs 27:17

Iron sharpens iron. Choose your friendships carefully then. Some will not sharpen you at all, for they have no iron about them, only plastic that bends and is flaccid against the touch of another. Others are made of metal all right, yet it is metal of a different sort than yours, and the scraping of them against you will make sparks fly but hone you not. The ones that I would choose to sharpen you against may not be comely in appearance or erudite in speech or noticed by the world, but when rubbed against their life and their spirit, your edge will be made exquisitely sharp, your blade honed and ready for My intricate uses. Not many friendships will be like this. Count yourself fortunate if you have one that can sharpen you thus, without sparks, or rust, or breakage. And if there is no such friend in your life, ask Me to gift you with one, for it was My idea after all. I will apply the oil of My Spirit at the point where the two blades will rub together; My oil turns what is otherwise just friction into a catalyst for honing the kind of sharpness that I can use.

March 18

I tell you, open your eyes and look at the fields! They are ripe for harvest. John 4:35

My fields are ripe and ready for the harvest. Generations before you have sown and watered, and now you must reap. *'How do I reap?'* you ask. Go out into My world, Child, and listen and speak. Live your life in ways that are worthy responses to My calling of you. Reflect Me in all that you do and say. Be part of My redemptive Kingdom force in every situation. Bring My Kingdom culture into all the byways where you travel. Find new ways of living and doing, **My** ways. In these days that you call the end days, people are hungry for the light. Bring My light into situations with both your words and your deeds. Be ready to tell others the reason for your hope. Season all your conversations and your actions with My grace. I will lead you to the fields I have appointed for you to harvest. I will put the scythe into your hand that I would have you use and instruct you to claim the mature grain in My name. I will teach you to pluck My ready fruit from both vine and branch in such a way that nothing is bruised or lost. Be My hands. Be My mouth. Bring My harvest of souls, those who will be your brothers and sisters for all eternity, into the storehouse of My Kingdom.

March 19

Noah did everything God commanded him. Genesis 7:5 (MSG)

I asked of Noah some very wild things, you know. Nothing like what I called him to do had ever been done or ever even thought of before. He might have decided that he was crazy to even contemplate such notions, or, even worse, he might have decided that his God was crazy. Instead, he just did what I told him to do. You rebel sometimes at My soft, gentle voice asking you to speak of something of Me to someone who knows Me not, or only knows Me in theory. You ponder the possible repercussions that such a mention of Me might have on how people think of you. But Noah ... I asked Noah to build a crazily huge boat ... out in the middle of a floodplain ... with everyone he knew looking on ... and no one understanding ... and he did it. Why? Because he did everything I asked him to. He followed My crazy-sounding boat building plans down to the last measurement. He completed My animal husbandry plans down to the last pair. He obeyed My instructions about saving the people that I would use to repopulate My world. Preposterous, no? Unthinkable! Unheard of! Balk not then at the little things I ask of you, the little faithfulnesses. If Noah could build such an ark solely on the basis of My unfathomable command of it, what about you? Will you do what I instruct you to do? He saved the world as you know it by his obedience. What might I be planning to save through yours?

March 20

Whoever is patient has great understanding, but one who is quick-tempered displays folly. Proverbs 14:29
There is a savage energy that flows before a thing is done or said that blinds you from seeing the reality of what that thing will feel like once it's done or said. Words and deeds are like water flowing swiftly over a spillway; they flow quickly, faster and faster until they torpedo over the threshold of the ravine … it's done … it's said. Then, as the energy dissipates, and the pace slows, you come back to yourself and tremble at once at your words, your tone, your actions and ultimately … there is great regret. This is the way of humanity; jails and prisons, real and those of men's souls, are bursting with stories of passionate anger, jealousy, injustice, fatigue, failure, and folly carried out, then bitterly grieved. Among the casualties are marriages, broken and bleeding, relationships mauled beyond repair, churches, synagogues, their noble causes dusty and bloodied from the battles of words, skirmishes of action without love. Season your words, your actions heavily with salt, Child. Spend time and more time in My presence, receiving what you need, molding to My image so that when you walk the sometimes dark pathways of relationship you can truly be gentle as a dove. People are breakable, very breakable, and your words, your actions forcefully pouring over the spillway can dash so hard against another as to forever cripple both speaker and hearer. Gentle Child, gentle; tread gently; soften your words; temper your actions. Vent to Me; give Me the full force of your emotions; I will join with you in slowing your torrent.

March 21

**So if the Son sets you free, you will be free indeed.
John 8:36**
I have come to set you free; I have come with your freedom dangling from My hand of power like a key to a slave's shackles might have dangled from a slave trader's hand. Consider what your freedom cost Me, and do not take it

lightly nor neglect to take advantage of your hard won emancipation. You are free now from the tyrannies that have long run roughshod over your heart and over your life. You are free from the sin that has so easily beset you and entangled your footsteps. You are free from emotions that would clog your life in Me and your daring for Me. Now you are free from your past hurts and the losses that framed your childhood days. You are no longer bound by old pain and former lack, no longer chained in darkness. Your light has come; your new day has dawned. Hope rings like a clarion bell across the morning of this day. I have come to set you free, and whom I have set free is free indeed!

March 22

For the eyes of the Lord range throughout the earth to strengthen those whose hearts are fully committed to him. 2 Chronicles 16:9

I give you a glimpse, Child, of just how big I am and of how much I care for all My creation and all My people. I work among you and those you love, yet thousands of miles away you will find Me at work as well. Wherever you might go, My presence will meet you at the gate of your heart and life. In all those places, you will find once again that I am at work; once again I am about My business of redemption and of raising up My people to be proclaimers of Me in the places where I have planted them. Such omnipresence is incomprehensible to you; to Me it is just a reflection of My heart and My infinite love for all of My creation. You know that there is nowhere you can flee from My presence, no place that is outside My gaze. You know that I am with you always, without limitation, without constraint, even unto the ends of the earth. Let it not surprise you, then, when rivers of My Spirit flow and manifest My very Godhood in all places and at all times. Count yourself fortunate to be part of a generation who can see this truth with their very eyes. There is no place too far away, too remote, too different from what you are accustomed to, for Me to not show up and do My work. Be part of that work wherever I send you, wherever I plant you. Be My eyes that see Me in all peoples and in all places. Marvel at My bigness!

March 23

The thief comes only to steal and kill and destroy; I have come that they may have life, and have it to the full. John 10:10

Hearken not to the voices of other gods. Your enemy is not only loathsome but also mischievous. You recognize him in the obvious, but do you recognize him in his more subtle disguises? He hides his tactics behind screens of normalcy and nonchalance. Press into Me; allow My spirit to speak into your heart and your days. Discouragement, disease, disinterest and discontent are not from My hand, but from the hand of the avenger and his demons who are at war with the world as well as your heart. Although I will bring forth good from his ploys, I never applaud his successes in your life. Submit your ways unto Me; keep your eyes focused on Me. Gird yourself with the praises that you speak unto Me, and you will find that Satan's schemes no longer terrorize you and no longer cause you to lose your focus on Me or your faith in Me.

March 24

From the lips of children and infants you have ordained praise because of your enemies, to silence the foe and the avenger. Psalm 8:2

That's what you want, right? To have the foe and the avenger silenced in your life? To finally hear only My voice speaking truth to you and not have to listen to the prattle of your enemy whose words betray and destroy your heart? I have ordained praise to accomplish that. It's the solution to the equation: voice your praises of Me, and your enemy's voice will be silenced. His antics cannot stand in the face of the realizations of My power and My deeds that come as part and parcel of your praising Me. It doesn't take much; even the praises of an infant who is still without words and experiences has enough praise to close the mouth of Satan. Even as I closed the mouth of the lion that My servant David might not be injured by his powerful teeth, so is your foe's mouth shut and his power halted with your voice of praise. Join the chorus of even the least of these, My Child. Rout your enemy without even lifting a hand against him. Praise Me!

March 25

"Where is your faith?" he asked his disciples. In fear and amazement they asked one another, "Who is this? He commands even the winds and the water, and they obey him." Luke 8:25
When life is easy and you are in the flow of the jet stream, you can take your ease at the helm as the Wind fills your sails to capacity and pulls you along. But, as you know Child, life is easy most of the time, and when the sails sag and the boat slows in the doldrums of your life, there is only one thing to do; come to Me in this slow time, this seemingly useless time, this time when storms and doubts and currents capture your vessel and move you to places you didn't want to go for hunks of time you didn't want to spend there. Heave-to, son; lock your rudder, daughter; this will keep your vessel from drifting into undesired currents. What I am saying is … *'Find Me,' 'Lock onto Me.'* I, through My Word, through My Spirit will keep your drift to a minimum. Then, in this safe place, come dine with Me; take food; take drink; take rest. Arise and commune with Me. I am strengthening you for the next leg of this journey, one you would not have had the strength for had I left you in the jet stream. Take your rest in My time; the Master of wind and waves will tell you when it's time to loose your rudder and once again point into the wind. I alone know when it's time to trim your sail to once again catch My Spirit Wind.

March 26

True, God made everything beautiful in itself and in its time - but he's left us in the dark, so we can never know what God is up to, whether he's coming or going. Ecclesiastes 3:11 (MSG)

O My loved One, how frazzled you sometimes become because you insist on knowing My mind before it is time for you to know it. It is a huge promise that I have made to your heart: I will make **all** things beautiful in My time. Yet because your heart cannot yet understand My currency, you doubt My word. Just because you do not yet see such transformation, just because you cannot imagine how beauty can come from ashes or life from death or ease from misfortune doesn't make it any less so. I have set eternity before you, but there is much that you do not yet understand. How could it be otherwise with your finite mind? You have the mind of Christ, but that too is a promise that is not yet completed. Live on the near side of My promises; take hope in them and rest your heart in them. When you don't yet comprehend, find peace in the fact that their veracity is not determined by your understanding but rather by My faithful omnipotence. I **will** make ALL things beautiful in their time, in My way and by My power. Stand firm in that promise even when you cannot yet see its fulfillment.

March 27

You hem me in - behind and before; you have laid your hand upon me. Such knowledge is too wonderful for me, too lofty for me to attain. Where can I go from your Spirit? Where can I flee from your presence? If I go up to the heavens, you are there; if I make my bed in the depths, you are there. If I rise on the wings of the dawn, if I settle on the far side of the sea, even there your hand will guide me, your right hand will hold me fast. Psalm 139:5-10

When you think to run and when you are tempted to hide from Me, this question remains, *Where can you flee from My presence? Where will you not find My Sprit?'* Not only am I your All in All, I am **in** all. The world, as big as it is, the universe with the heavens and the darkness and the light of even other galaxies, is too small to contain Me. My dwelling places are so various, so all encompassing, that you can't even imagine. But imagine this My Child: My love for you so eternal, My plans for you so significant and so bold, that I would take charge of not just your creation, but also your development, and I would plan all your days before your days even began! My hand is laid upon you. I watch you; My face is ever turned toward you. I build up walls of protection around you. Let your soul take rest in My never-ending attention to you, for I know you as a lover knows His beloved, and in My love I keep you.

March 28

The generous soul will be made rich, and he who waters will also be watered himself. Proverbs 11:25 (NKJV)
You were created to have a generous heart. My design of you disallowed both the fear and the greed that would cause you to hold bounty close to you. Your Garden heritage proclaimed surfeit over your life - both provision and stewarding of a rich and plentiful world where there was no question of sufficiency. With the fall of mankind came the thorns and all that made work hard and plenty less than it was meant to be. And so your temptation now is to hold things tightly to yourself rather than sharing all that you have with a faith-filled and generous spirit. My promise is simple however; not only will I provide for you, but I will provide with the same measure as you bestow. Your giving is but a reflection of My giving nature and practice. I replenish what you pour out; indeed I resupply in an even greater measure what you offer to others with joy and thankfulness in your heart. Risk more in this that your recompense might be more as well. Walk in My ways - the way that led to the cross because I refused to give less than My very best to those I have loved. So sow into others' lives with a generous heart,

and pour out some of the waters that bless your life with a bountiful measure.

March 29

Shout Hallelujah, you God-worshipers; give glory, you sons of Jacob; adore him, you daughters of Israel. He has never let you down, never looked the other way when you were being kicked around. He has never wandered off to do his own thing; he has been right there, listening. Psalm 22:23-24 (MSG)
Renounce the things of the world that you lust for so that you might rejoice in Me. Honor Me with your praises and your loud exaltations. There is much in Me to be grateful for and many reasons that you should remind yourself of them. Today is a day of loud hallelujahs as you recognize who I am. Do not, however, let your praises die as the cares of the world engulf you. Let your expectations be tempered by My will; subdue your own desires that you might know Mine. Surrender both your hunger and your hurts to My omniscient hand. Remember that a thousand years is but a day to Me, and three days in a dark, dead tomb only made My resurrection seem more miraculous and more wonderful. So it is for you Child: the little deaths, the dark tombs that life brings you will give way to My exultant victory and My eternal light. Rest in Me as you praise Me, for I am the world's Risen King.

March 30

God, make a fresh start in me, shape a Genesis week from the chaos of my life. Psalm 51:10 (MSG)
It is time, My Child, that you let Me be your Great Physician. You no longer need to allow this world's cancer to spread through your heart. You no longer need to submit to the dictates of your heart of stone. For such a heart I came into this world, and for such a heart I paid the ultimate sacrifice. I have purchased a new heart for you - no longer a heart of clay, no longer a hard heart, but **My** heart. Yet your heart is

not like a Lego block; it cannot just be unattached and a new one substituted. It requires My intricate touch; it necessitates My physician's hand. In your surrender will come great victory; in the midst of your pain will come your healing. As I perform heart surgery on you, I will cauterize the bloody flow. I will complete what I begin. What I cut, I will mend. What I remove, I will replace with what is Mine, a perfected and holy heart of My flesh.

March 31

Behold, I have refined you, but not as silver; I have tried and chosen you in the furnace of affliction. Isaiah 48:10 (AMP)

You **are** My chosen one. Seed of My seed, it is not by chance that I call you My Child. Seasons come and seasons go. They change by My designing. The winters of your days impale you with their cold, harsh breath, but those times too are used by Me to refine you. It is in your pain and your hardships that I smelt you. It is there that I choose you and call you to come close to My side. Your affliction is My furnace, and there I make you hardened ore with strength that goes far beyond your weak-kneed human condition and purity that supersedes the fallen humanity that you inherit. Although your heart is troubled, even though your senses are overwhelmed by pain of so many kinds, even there I will not only bring you through, I will also refine you and bring you forth.

April 1

God is bedrock under my feet, the castle in which I live, my rescuing knight. My God - the high crag where I run for dear life, hiding behind the boulders, safe in the granite hideout. Psalm 18:2 (MSG)

I am your Refuge, the place where you can hide. When winds assail, I am the Rock upon whom you stand and you will not be shaken. When enemy armies march against you, when your foe gathers strength in the wilderness, I am your Shield and your Defender. My victorious right arm is lifted high in the midst of your battles. This same passion, this relentless strength and might, is the core of My love for you. You feel My tender heart for you and My Abba Daddy lap of safety and comfort. Feel also the strength of My Father love, the same victory displayed that rent the veil when I gave My life for you, the same power that brought Me forth from the tomb.

April 2

The words of the reckless pierce like swords, but the tongue of the wise brings healing. Proverbs 12:18
Child, allow Me to guard the gates of your mouth, for a great torrent arises from your belly, and the truth of the message will be lost in the chaos of energy that threatens to explode your levees. Truth must be spoken, yet so often these truths are wrapped in your own pride, your own hurt, your own self-righteous anger, and when pulled back like a slingshot the truth is lost in the slam of words. Your words, your truths must be wrapped in love, in grace, in kindness. The cost: a laying down of your selfish will, a headlock to your flesh, a determination to have the best for not just yourself, but also for the one I love as you. My Spirit alone can bring healing. Do you have the courage, Child, to truly let Me speak through you? Do you have the sacrificial bravery to STOP and roll your words around in your mouth and **truly** taste their flavor? Do they taste like Me? How would you feel being not the deliverer of this word meal, but the receiver? Would it encourage you to change, to see another point of view? Would it give you room to stretch, yet encircle you with arms of security and assurance of relationship? Or, as so often happens, would the waves of hurt and angry words leave their hearer battered and broken, left like flotsam on the sand? Truth, My truth, is spoken with kindness and gentleness; it is how I speak to you, and it is your snap-line.

April 3

You are not your own, for you have been bought with a price. The Prince of Darkness held you captive, for your forefather Adam sold your birthright too when he indulged in his own desires in the Garden instead of following hard after His God. You were lost then, caught in the thrall of both sin and suffering, even before you were born. You were doomed to recreate disobedience and defiance time and time again all through your life. And no matter how much I loved you, you would still own a bloodstained, guilty heart that by My own perfect nature I would have to abhor. But no ... the story does not end there, for I loved you past life itself, and in My Son I laid down all My rights that you might be able to pick up your own life and dwell with Me. Don't treat this casually, My Child, for it is indeed the limit of love, this sacrifice of My all for those who are both unworthy and unloving. It is no small thing to have Me, the only God, give up My very self so that life might be offered to you. Because of this, you do not own yourself. Satan tried to pawn you in the economy of the universe, but I bought you back, paid for you in full, and will always be in the process of cleaning and polishing you so that your pure gold might shine forth. Never forget the price that I paid for you, the blood that I shed for you, the life that I traded for yours. Never take your freedom lightly. Never treat that which is of the greatest consequence with anything other than the wonder and thankfulness that it deserves.

For you were bought at a price; therefore glorify God in your body and in your spirit, which are God's.
1 Corinthians 6:20 (NKJV)

April 4

I ask - ask the God of our Master, Jesus Christ, the God of glory - to make you intelligent and discerning in knowing him personally, your eyes focused and clear, so that you can see exactly what it is he is calling you to do, grasp the immensity of this glorious way of life he has

for his followers, oh, the utter extravagance of his work in us who trust him - endless energy, boundless strength! Ephesians 1:17-19 (MSG)

Victory has come; the price has been paid for your redemption; garden-variety friendship between Me and thee has been restored. The veil between heaven and earth, between holy and common, has been forever rent, never to be resewn or rebuilt. Resurrection comes in the morning and along with it hope forever, life forever, and Me forever walking and talking with you. Do you not yet know what you have so often heard? The power that raised My Son from the dead is the power that is at work within you. Why then do you dwell in the lands of fear, of lack, of despair? You live in the dark day between the crucifixion and the resurrection knowing My promises but not able to believe that they are true. Why do you dwell there, Child? Why do you hear My words of promise and of power but not believe? Why do you so often ignore the power of My Spirit at work within you? Why do you clutch the dark of the tomb when the light of resurrection glory has already been revealed and passed on to you? Take up the mantle of the Holy Spirit. Gird your loins with the truths that I have spoken in My Word. Take your stand in the power of My revealed and resurrected might. The Day is coming when your victory will be complete because Mine is, but Child know this: that Day has also already come! Live in that truth, My truth!!

April 5

I pray also that the eyes of your heart may be enlightened in order that you may know the hope to which he has called you, the riches of his glorious inheritance in the saints, and his incomparably great power for us who believe. That power is like the working of his mighty strength, which he exerted in Christ when he raised him from the dead and seated him at his right hand in the heavenly realms.
Ephesians 1:18-20

My son, My daughter, My Child of the new covenant, you are one of My true worshipers, for you worship Me in spirit and in truth. I have come to be with you! The stone is rolled away; the garments are discarded; the tomb is empty. I am not there, for I have indeed defeated death; I am ALIVE! And now, Child, you need to learn this truth: that very same power that took Me out of that grave and conquered death is yours to claim and live within today! Right now, **right now**, right here, name the tomb that you live in. Is it an addiction? Is it fear? Is it pain? Is it hurt? Is it your past? Is it your present? Is it your future that is yet unknown? What is it Child? Look at that tomb right now. Look at yourself bound up in that tomb. You have the power that I gave you; because I am resurrected, that power lives and works and breathes within you! So take off those grave clothes; roll that stone away. You do not need to be in that tomb anymore. I have come to set you free, and where the Son is there is freedom indeed! So take My message, and let it seep into your heart. See with your mind's eye right now the tomb that Satan, the enemy, would have you live in. It does not need to hold you. Do not **let** it hold you. For I have come today, for you, for whatever it is; I am here, for you!

April 6

In love he predestined us to be adopted as his sons through Jesus Christ, in accordance with his pleasure and will - to the praise of his glorious grace, which he has freely given us in the One he loves. Ephesians 1:4-6
All grace is given unto you. It is a gift freely bestowed upon you that you might be a victor as you run the race that I have set before you. Lay down your striving and pick up My grace. Run with the endurance that I have given you and not with your own strength. Grace it is that sustains you, grace that makes you holy in My sight despite your sin-stained soul. The finish line will not be achieved by your striving; it is I who has already crossed it and I who goes both before you and with you. My grace is sufficient for all your todays and tomorrows. Get yourself up on the starting block; be

attentive; be ready. Run with Me in the grace that is My gift to you.

April 7

Abraham fell facedown; he laughed and said to himself, "Will a son be born to a man a hundred years old? Will Sarah bear a child at the age of ninety?" Genesis 17:17
I am the Dream Giver; age, circumstance, and status matter little to Me. I birth dreams that you cannot even conceive of yet, but the seeds are there, Child, planted when I designed all that is you. On the day of My choosing, I will reach out My hand and by divine destiny touch the dormant seed, and life will quiver within its core. Soon it will grow enough to make its life known to your senses, a small tug, a tiny kick within, spelled by time. As knowledge of its life settles in your spirit, more and more of your focus will be taken with its health, its vitality. Your preparations will increase as faith prepares to become sight; until, finally, in the fullness of time, our dream comes forth, a dream that personifies our oneness, a dream that brings glory to Me and delight to you. Be not as Sarah who laughed at the dream she thought long dead ... *'Is **ANYTHING** too hard for the Lord?'* **(Genesis 18:14)** I, the Lord your God have declared it.

April 8

It stands to reason, doesn't it, that if the alive-and-present God who raised Jesus from the dead moves into your life, he'll do the same thing in you that he did in Jesus, bringing you alive to himself? When God lives and breathes in you (and he does, as surely as he did in Jesus), you are delivered from that dead life. With his Spirit living in you, your body will be as alive as Christ's! Romans 8:11 (MSG)
Come forth! My passion for you surpasses the boundaries of all your previous loves, and My courage defies all reasonable expectations for a battle on your behalf. You need cower no longer, nor fear war against your flesh, nor assault from the

enemy of your heart. It is My triumphant walk to Calvary, My submission to sin's victory in man's heart, My once-for-all payment that looses all that binds you and sets you free in Me to win all the battles that assail you. Do not let your heart be overwhelmed by what you see, what you feel, or what you hear. My truth is deeper than all that. It hovered in the darkness of a closed tomb for days that felt like eternity before hope and truth and triumph sprang forth. Satan's last chance is gone now, his strongholds ultimately conquered, innocence and hope restored. The tomb will never hold back My life again. The circumstances in your own life that cloud this truth are only the enemy's dying breaths. Come forth from your darknesses, your tombs, your sin. Your time has come!

April 9

I am making a way in the desert and streams in the wasteland. Isaiah 43:19

I am the Way Maker. Whether through the arid desert or the high mountain passes, it is I who goes before you to make a way. It is I who guides you and I who protects you. There is nothing that you can do on your own to keep your path safe or to ensure a safe landing for your feet on My shore. I see ahead of you as well as behind you. I surround your flanks with My legions of angels. When you stumble I keep your foot from falling into harm. Take a map; pack supplies; be watchful and alert, but know that in the final analysis that it is only I who makes a way for you. There is danger in the presumption that your watchful preparedness is what keeps you safe and leads you home. I am the Good Shepherd of your soul; it is I who goes before you and leads you forth in all the days of your life.

This is what the Lord says - your Redeemer, the Holy One of Israel: "I am the Lord your God, who teaches you what is best for you, who directs you in the way you should go." Isaiah 48:17

April 10

For your Maker is your bridegroom, his name, God-of-the-Angel-Armies! Your Redeemer is The Holy of Israel, known as God of the whole earth. Isaiah 54:5 (MSG)

Reluctant bride you often are, but Mine nonetheless. Shed blood, poured heart, I ransom you and pursue you with the tokens of My love. Once you have noticed My affection, attended to My sacrifice, and lifted your gaze of shame to finally meet the eyes of My compassion, it will be hard for you to not continue to hear My voice. Even when you only sense a whisper, an echo of My heart of love for you, pay heed. Do not take My sacrifice lightly, nor ignore the price I have paid to open doors, break down walls, and build bridges between holiness and your fallen creatureliness. I stand at the door of the bridal chamber and knock. Only you can give Me access; not even the power of Holy God will crack through the gate of your heart that you have not opened. Be neither afraid of My pursuit nor undone by My relentlessness. My intentions are as pure as My Garden creation, My heart the only model there is of sacrificial, eternal love.

April 11

All praise to the God and Father of our Master, Jesus the Messiah! Father of all mercy! God of all healing counsel! He comes alongside us when we go through hard times, and before you know it, he brings us alongside someone else who is going through hard times so that we can be there for that person just as God was there for us. 2 Corinthians 1:3-4 (MSG)

Whose tears do you cry when your heart breaks, My Child? Recognize that sometimes your tears are selfish tears, born of your own needs, your own desires, and your frustrations when those feel as though they haven't been met. But often your tears are **My** tears, and your heart is **My** heart. I have caused My love to grow deep inside you, My love for others in the places where you live your life. Planted deeply, your heart beats as if it were Mine. I dwell in the midst of the life you lead; I see what you see, feel what you feel, and fall in love with My pieces of creation seen through your created eyes. All of it is Mine, and your feelings are Mine too. Relax into the truth that the tears that you cry are My holy tears falling as yours. I bend your heart as it breaks with My love for My people.

April 12

God, King of Israel, your Redeemer, God-of-the-Angel-Armies, says: "I'm first, I'm last, and everything in between. I'm the only God there is. Who compares with me? Speak up. See if you measure up. From the beginning, who else has always announced what's coming? So what is coming next? Anybody want to venture a try? Don't be afraid, and don't worry: Haven't I always kept you informed, told you what was going on? You're my eyewitnesses: Have you ever come across a God, a real God, other than me? There's no Rock like me that I know of." Isaiah 44:6-8

Pick up the end of the thread that is your worry, and hold it in your hand. Walk with it around and around that thing that causes your worry. Circle it with your prayers, forgetting not to praise Me along the way. Praise Me for all that I am - that I am God, even in the face of your realization that you are not. Praise Me that I hold the other end of each of your worry threads, and I will not let go. As you walk your circle, pound out the drumbeat of My faithfulness. Sing the songs of your past deliverances. Feel the touch of the thread in your hand, and know that this thing that you care about, that you worry about, is important to Me as well. Circle it with your prayers and your strong confidence in Me like My people circled Jericho over and over again, for day upon day, before the walls tumbled down. Do not be afraid to hold the thread of your worry in your hand as you pray and as you circle. Your worry will soon be tightly bound up in your prayer-wrapped faith, and the other end of the thread will lead you straight to Me.

April 13

A very large crowd spread their cloaks on the road, while others cut branches from the trees and spread them on the road. The crowds that went ahead of him and those that followed shouted, "Hosanna to the Son of David!" "Blessed is he who comes in the name of the Lord!" "Hosanna in the highest!" Matthew 21:8-9

King I am; Lord I am. **Your** King of Kings; **your** Lord of Lords. It matters not whether I ride in humbly on a donkey or charge in on My steed with a crown on My head; King I am; Lord I am. Throw down your cloak; throw down your privileges; throw down your name and your reputation that I might walk over it, that I might take possession of it. O My Child, you know what comes in the days ahead. You know; you've seen; you know the end of the story. You know My resurrection light; you know My eternal love for you and the fact that there is nothing that stops Me. Nothing that takes My life away; nothing that takes My love for you away. Do not be fickle like the long ago crowd that threw its cloaks down and then grabbed them back up and put them back on to protect themselves from what they did not know and from what they did not understand. I let My friend Lazarus die that I might raise Him up. And sometimes, My Child, I let hard things into your life, too, that I might raise you up in a way that you don't understand. Do not leave Me; do not forsake Me. Do not be like Peter who denied Me because he did not understand. You know the end of the story. You know that My tomb will be empty. You know that I will be raised. You know that I will come again, so live in that hope; live in that truth. Do not be fickle and do not let your heart lead you astray. Do not listen to the lies of the enemy that say that I am **not** enough, that all the circumstances prove it, that I should be betrayed, that I am not deserving. O My Child, I am your King; I am your Lord - King of Kings and Lord of Lords! Pick up those palm branches; lay down those cloaks, and do not desert Me even when the dark days come, even when you stand in the tomb that is closed off for days

on end. My Child, My light will come. Resurrection is
around the corner. My Second Coming is nigh.

April 14

Be merciful, just as your Father is merciful. Luke 6:36
Mercy is My name! And I walk the highways and byways of
sin, of illness and brokenness, severed relationships, broken
marriages, crime, pornography and shame. Open your mind
and heart to Me, for I AM the only One who can free you
from the chains of these burdens. I AM the only One who
can break the handcuffs. Mercy is My name; and mercy is
also your name when you reach out to a brother or a sister
locked in the grip of sin. Mercy is your name when you go
into the highways and byways and call them, reach out to
them, touch them, speak to them, hear them, listen to them.
They have a story to tell, and they need My mercy. Mercy is
My name; I give you My name. Be mercy for them.

April 15

Waiting ... the earth holds its breath. Its God-made-flesh is
dead and lies buried. Though earth has cracked and split and
moved and thunder has raged in the heavens because of it,
today the sun is shining and the earth waits. Quietly.
Expectantly. Waiting.... We might fear that the story is
done, but Creator-made earth knows better. The Saturday
after is the Saturday before. Sandwiched between grief and
untamed expectation. Caught between the loud wails of
Friday's mourning (the Friday that really wasn't so Good at
all it seemed) and the incredulous gasps of wonder and
tentative joy of Sunday's could-it-really-be resurrection day.
And you? Created and much loved One, what of you? Do
you too hold your breath and wait? Honoring Me with barely
restrained joy beating hard in your heart because you know
how this story ends? Because you know Sunday is coming
and you know what Sunday brings? Is that glee I see in your
eyes, childlike glee that expects the unexpected and believes
in the unbelievable? Oh, I hope so Dear One. For tomorrow

crashes into your world, that stone-rolled-away Sunday where heaven's hopes meet earth's defeats and forever wins! Take joy, dear heart. Sunday comes and with it your heart beats finally free, for I have risen, and I have come, and I will come once again and then forever, forever!, you will be Mine in bliss.

Applause, everyone. Bravo, bravissimo! Shout God-songs at the top of your lungs! Psalm 47:1 (MSG)

April 16

I pray to God - my life a prayer - and wait for what he'll say and do. My life's on the line before God, my Lord, waiting and watching till morning, waiting and watching till morning. Psalm 130:5-6 (MSG)
You who wait with baited breath, with something precious to you closed behind the tomb, dark, seemingly hopeless, dead. Whatever it is: a dream, your health, your relationships, your hopes, your prayers, if you are waiting for good news, today I am here to say, *'I have risen! The tomb is empty. The stone is rolled away. There is no dark where dawn does not come. There is no night where I have not promised day.'* You, who wait with baited breath, count not by earthly days. Count, in the most secret places of your heart, the moments that I accompany you as you wait in that dark place. For I have come ... and I will come ... and I will come again. And there is no place that is too dark; there is nothing that is too hopeless; there is nowhere that My light will not pierce. So today, My Child, take hope, for I bring you more than just My risen self all those many years ago; I bring you hope for every tragedy, for every death, for every sickness, for every perversion, for every hopeless relationship. I bring you the power of the Light of My coming. I bring you tombstones rolled away. I bring you death brought back to life. I bring you ... Me!

April 17

This is my command: Love one another the way I loved you. This is the very best way to love. Put your life on

the line for your friends. John 15:12-13 (MSG)
Speak kindness from your heart to My children. Speak truth, but speak it gently. Take your role of friend seriously, for I have placed you in that role. When you speak to one of My children, do so only to edify, not to cut down or destroy. Your words have the power to heal and encourage. The choice is ultimately yours. Remember your own imperfections, the logs that impair the vision of your own eyes. Go gently, carefully, into the territory of friendship, for the enemy encamps there, endeavoring to kill and destroy, while I would have you bring peace and hope.

April 18

So what shall I do? I will pray with my spirit, but I will also pray with my understanding; I will sing with my spirit, but I will also sing with my understanding.
1 Corinthians 14:15
Child, do you want to rout the enemy? Are you tired of being under his thumb? Are you tired of the enemy flaunting in your face? Child, where's your prayer language? When I came at Pentecost, I could have given any gift to mankind. What gift did I give? I gave the gift of tongues. It's the sword in My mouth; it's the sword in your mouth. It brings My angel warriors and causes them to swing their swords in directions you know not. Use your prayer language; and if you have not a prayer language, seek Me for it; it is time. Enemies are coming that you know not of; what better weapon than to have the Father who knows all to speak the words through your mouth to rout the enemy before he shows up at your doorstep. Children, I speak not lightly; I speak with fervency; find your prayer language. Use it daily; pray without ceasing, your finite mind loses words very quickly; My mind loses no words. I can speak continually: when you are driving, when you are sitting alone, when you are working, when you are playing, all times you can be praying through the Spirit. Constant prayer. Constant prayer while still being present in the moment. I speak not lightly. Find your prayer language.

April 19

I will ransom them from the power of the grave; I will redeem them from death. Where, O death, are your plagues? Where, O grave, is your destruction?
Hosea 13:14

Come into My tomb, Child, and see that it is empty. I am not there. I have flown the proverbial coop; I have conquered death and taken all the limits off of life. Your tombs are empty too, Child. The places of all your defeats, the deaths of all your hopes and dreams, the limits of your reach ... all those tombs are empty, the stones rolled back, and your grave clothes also now left lying empty and unused. Do you know what that means My Child? You look for Me in all the wrong places when you expect Me to be boundaried by the limits of this world. You set limits on yourself as well when you do not live in the truth that through Me your impossible is also possible. Such dark and fractured places of death and defeat hold Me no longer, and I remind you today that they shouldn't hold you either. I have won! My love has defeated hate, and there is no end to what I will do with and for those who allow themselves to love Me back.

April 20

Oh, the utter extravagance of his work in us who trust him - endless energy, boundless strength! All this energy issues from Christ: God raised him from death and set him on a throne in deep heaven. Ephesians 1:19-20 (MSG)

This is your new year, Child. This is the day where I've drawn the line and paid the price, so **this** today is your new year to celebrate. You might suppose that it comes at the end of December, or when the New Year's Eve ball drops in your city. But nay, Child, **today**, today is your new year; today I offer you grave clothes tossed off and new life because of **My** new life. I offer you a renewed heart, mind, soul, and spirit because today I have made all things new. I am your Lord; I am the Giver of all. And I ask you today to make this day new, to stand and proclaim, '*This is my new year. In my spirit, I will live anew.*' Because of Me you have the power, the same power that raised Me from the dead, and today that Power lives in you.

April 21

My lover spoke and said to me, "Arise, my darling, my beautiful one, and come with me." Song of Songs 2:10

It makes Me sad for you when you put limits on what coming to Me can look like. If you could only hear My covenantal heart for you, you would know that there is freedom in My love for you. Ours is not a relationship bound by prescriptions so much as it is relationship formed by deepening trust and growing intimacy. Put My love for you inside a box with the boundaries of either format or religious tradition, and you will quickly lose the staggering potential that our love covenant holds. You would never think to confine your intimacy with spouse or best friend to a daily half hour slot, or perish the thought, just a five minute morning check in - but too often you do exactly that with Me. Why Child? Do you not think Me to be big enough, or kind enough, or eager enough to match your ebb and flow of desire and connection? Do you fear that the quick turnings of your mind toward Me throughout the day do not give Me pleasure because they don't fill some self-determined time slot or follow some prescribed discipline? No Child. I want you to come often, stay long, stay short, come playful, come serious, come despairing ... come in all the seasons of your heart and whenever your mind turns toward Me. Wear your dress up clothes or wear your work clothes; come in your leisure, or come in your crowded busyness; as long as you don't costume yourself in make believe, it matters not to Me. As a lover would say to the loved one, *Just come!*'

April 22

I saw the Lord seated on a throne, high and exalted, and the train of his robe filled the temple. Above him were

seraphs .... And they were calling to one another: "Holy, holy, holy is the Lord Almighty; the whole earth is full of his glory." At the sound of their voices the doorposts and thresholds shook and the temple was filled with smoke. "Woe to me!" I cried. "I am ruined! For I am a man of unclean lips, and I live among a people of unclean lips, and my eyes have seen the King, the Lord Almighty." Isaiah 6:1-5

My holiness is beautiful. Too often you think it only terrible or alarming in its reality. Yet it is My holiness that conquered the enemy, withstood temptation, and defeated sin and death on the cross and in the tomb. Look My holiness straight in the eye. See if you can recognize it for all it is worth, for all that it calls you to, for all that it causes you to lose and all it causes you to gain in your life. Remember it is the theme song, the anthem, of the elders in heaven, for Holy, Holy, Holy am I. Fall on your face before that beauty and before all that that My beautiful holiness brings to your life. Worship Me; worship My holiness.

April 23

God's now at my side and I'm not afraid; who would dare lay a hand on me? Psalm 118:6 (MSG)

Hear My heart for you. Even after so many years, after so much healing and redemption, you still need to draw close and hear My heart. Others who should have had a heart for you abandoned you, but I did not leave you. I walked beside you each step of the way. I cried more tears for you than you cried for yourself. I tried, always, to speak into the unspeakable places of your heart and mind, to bring light to the darkness in which you sometimes dwelt, to bring hope whenever despair set up camp around you. Sometimes you heard Me and felt Me, and sometimes you didn't, but I was always there. I am there now - ready, able, and willing to clear away the cobwebs in those closed off, unused spaces, the places where abandonment caused you to close the door and walk away. Some of those places you don't even know about or don't remember, but I do. Trust Me; let your deepest self mold to My embrace and I will show you. I will open you up to new possibilities, new pieces of yourself. I will thaw what was frozen and suspended in time. I will reveal who I created you to be. Your abandonment did not change that, nor did all that you became in the face of that. It is all part of you, and all of you is Mine. Let Me begin to complete it now. Be not afraid for there is only joy to be found in the discoveries, new growth where the old was razed to barren soil. Trust Me in this; it is abandonment payback time. The weeds that the enemy planted have been uprooted. The deadly fruit that he so cavalierly, so daringly caused to grow has been burned to ash in My holy flames. Your tentative postures of surrender have become full-blown, and I have stepped in boldly to reclaim for you that which was lost. Lift up your gaze; wipe your tears; watch and see what I will now do, for the time has come.

April 24

Forget about what's happened; don't keep going over old history. Be alert, be present. I'm about to do something brand-new. It's bursting out! Don't you see it? There it is! I'm making a road through the desert, rivers in the badlands. Isaiah 43:18-19 (MSG)

The sacrifice that I desire is a broken and contrite heart. Let your walls down; in place of the strength you feel you must grasp and produce, let there be surrender. Where you think you must have wholeness, allow your brokenness to show. I cannot heal what you do not voluntarily reveal. I cannot make strong what you claim is already strong. I will not push or force My way into your heart or your mind. You must open doors to Me willingly; you must let down your guard and unbarricade your entrances. The pain that you have felt and boxed and stuffed, you must release. The strength that you have manufactured in order to continue to live, you must relinquish. Allow Me into the old places that were dark, the lonely places where you imprisoned your hurt and your pain. Allow Me to see your brokenness, even the brokenness of years and years and years ago. Entrust Me with all that you felt but did not share: the wounds, the sin, the holy desires, the godless desires, all that has never, ever seen the light of day. Allow Me to see your brokenness, for I have already known it and already been present in it. Now I need you to invite Me into it and share it with Me as you would a friend to whom you have entrusted your life. I am that Friend, that Keeper of your heart, the Faithful One who has preserved you. It is time to see Me as your place of safety where all things can be made known, acknowledged, felt and healed. Give up your self-protection so that I can be your protector. Give up your own attempts at strength, so that I can be strong for you.

April 25

Do not be anxious about anything, but in everything, by prayer and petition, with thanksgiving, present your requests to God. Philippians 4:6

I have cautioned you in My Word to not be anxious about your food or your clothing or your care. I remind you to be anxious about nothing but to let your requests meld with your praises as they pour from your heart to Me, mindful of the fact that I already know what you need. Do not allow the enemy's spirit of anxiety and fear to take up residence in your heart. You are My cherished possession. What do **you** cherish that you do not also take care of, My Child? Do you think My care is somehow less than yours? Or do you believe My ability to provide and protect somehow inferior to your own? How could that be? I am the one who loved you first; I loved you before you even came into being, and My hand of love is also a hand of power. I spare you from so many things, things that you know nothing of because I have prevented them from coming to pass. Take refuge under My wings of protection and love. Live within the fortress of My promises. Remind your mind of My attitude toward you by raising your voice with *'Yes!'* and *'Amen!'* in acknowledgement of those promises to you. Look about My world and see how I have cloaked even the lesser parts of My creation with beauty and majesty, and know I will care for you as well. Cast off your anxiety, for I take care of My loved ones, even when they see it not.

April 26

It will be a shelter and shade from the heat of the day, and a refuge and hiding place from the storm and rain. Isaiah 4:6

I AM the bridge over troubled water; why do you work to walk through the waves and dangers of the turbulent waters gasping and choking through each step? This is not My will for you, for any of My children. My will for you, Child, is to view the angry, violent waves from far above them with a grateful heart that beats thankfulness that your God asks you not to ford such waters. The seas are dark and awesome in strength and terror, no doubt, and you question your ability to make it through safely to the other side; as well you should. Let us settle that question now; you cannot. If you choose to walk into the wake instead of over it, you will be lost. You must make the decision on this before you walk. I cannot comfort; I cannot guide; I cannot whisper to you over the chaos and clamor of sound created by the trouble if you're in it. Walk above, Child; I've created this bridge of safety for My children. Walk over dry; walk over safe; walk over being able to hear and talk and sing. I have not forsaken you; I have not forsaken those you love. Sing and praise and give thanks as if they already rest in My arms of mercy, as if they already acknowledge Me as their one and only God, as if the day is already here where they hear and listen and rejoice in THEIR God. I will honor such faith and move with such praise. Satan works hard Child right now, bloodying your face with blows and whispering of the terrors of the sea, but … grasp My hand Child and walk with Me; I have a plan … I have a plan.

April 27

Stop trusting in mere humans, who have but a breath in their nostrils. Why hold them in esteem? Isaiah 2:22

Rejoice My Child; this morning let praise rise from your very soul. And for this reason: I am the God of the comma. I'm the God of the comma! Where even your own spirit has put a period, I replace it with a comma. That dream that feels dead in your own soul, remove that period with praise and worship and let Me put My comma there. Your health, your children, your marriage, there are so many periods where I wish to put My comma. Because that's what I'm all about; I'm all about the comma in your life. Where the world says, *'No!';* where the world says, *'Stop!';* where the world says, *'Period!';* I say *'Comma!'* Believe in that comma this morning. Believe in the God of the comma because He wants to bring a comma to your life, to your spirit, to your broken dream, to your broken health, to your broken marriage, to your broken children. I am the God of the comma.

April 28

You will not have to fight this battle. Take up your positions; stand firm and see the deliverance the Lord will give you, O Judah and Jerusalem. Do not be afraid; do not be discouraged. 2 Chronicles 20:17

You forget who you are. And you forget who I am. You forget the power that I have bequeathed to you, the power and authority that are yours because of My sacrificed and risen Son. You stand immobilized in the face of your strong enemies, but I tell you, stand, stand firm and watch, waiting for the victories that come through My strong hand of power and might and love. Do not stand as though you live in darkness, for My light has come and it can never, ever be subdued by the power of darkness again. Do not stand as if waiting for a captor to click shut the last of your chains and handcuffs, for your freedom in Me is permanent, and you need never be captive to anything other than Me again. Health, finances, relationships … all are in My hands. I lose sight of nothing that concerns you. Come to Me with an expectant heart. In My Name, raise your sword, cast down your enemies, forge through the darkness into My victorious light. Forget not whose you are My Child, for you are Mine, and My victory comes on the wings of dawn.

April 29

I, even I, am he who comforts you. Who are you that you fear mortal men, the sons of men, who are but grass, that you forget the Lord your Maker …?
Isaiah 51:12-13
You run willy-nilly, scimper-scamper down the roads of life crying, *'Kiss it and make it better!'* when you skin yourself against the rough patches. But you always ask the wrong person for that comfort; friend or lover or mentor or confidant or parent, yes there is ease there and love, but it is **I** who holds the only balm that really provides relief. Just because I am invisible in the ordinary sense of the word doesn't mean that I'm sightless or voiceless. I see; I hear; I speak; indeed, I even touch. But if you fill your horizon with help only from those around you, and heap your storehouses full of only the tangible offerings of this world, then there will be neither room for nor need of My provision. True healing comes from Me; all else is but a band-aid that protects the wound but doesn't heal. You must find Me in the forest where all your other comforts and idols and mini-gods dwell; find Me, and then choose Me instead of your others. If you would heal your wounds, if you would find ease even in the midst of the roads' rough risings, then it is I who you need and not another.

April 30

But as for me, I watch in hope for the Lord, I wait for God my Savior; my God will hear me. Micah 7:7
You wait, in the stillness, in the quiet, in the midst of the hours when it is still dark. Stay there, Child, for as long as it takes for you to finally hear My voice, and see My face, and feel the touch of My hand stretched out to you. If you move from your waiting too soon you will miss what I have for you. The frenetic pace of the world will catch you up and

wash you away, far from the quiet of My heart beating for you, far from the place where you can gather your strength as I reach out for you. Do not rush My coming, for I come in My own way and My own time. Do not grow impatient in the stillness. Am I not worth waiting for? Am I not worth even these few moments of your day? I call you to community, to love and to union with others of My family. But they too must wait. Their call upon your life must take second row to **My** call to you. The voices of family and work and obligation must be silenced for just these few minutes while you wait for Me, while your eyes and your ears turn toward your true Home.

May 1

My heart is not proud, O Lord, my eyes are not haughty; I do not concern myself with great matters or things too wonderful for me. But I have stilled and quieted my soul; like a weaned child with its mother, like a weaned child is my soul within me. O Israel, put your hope in the Lord both now and forevermore. Psalm 131

Concern yourself with Me, Child, not with things that are too wonderful nor those that are too difficult for you. I will reveal Myself to you, uncover understanding, and bring forth healing. You need only to be still before Me, to wait on Me, and to stay unbusied, unhurried, and undistracted in My presence. Lean into Me like a weaned child on her mother's lap. I will speak, show My heart, send flashes of insight, and reveal feelings long unfelt. If it seems that you do not know and do not understand, don't be alarmed. Your job is not to figure things out, but to position yourself, plant your feet, stand firm, and listen. My job is to speak, to teach, to tutor, to instruct. Wait patiently, Child.

May 2

But when you give to the needy, do not let your left hand know what your right hand is doing, so that your

giving may be in secret. Then your Father, who sees what is done in secret, will reward you. Matthew 6:3-4
Let Me remind you of My caution, that you not let your left hand know what your right hand is doing in matters of giving. You know your own intentions, but it is ever so easy for misplaced pride to take over your heart and convince you to preen about your goodness and generosity. Even when such preening is only for yourself to notice, it is bad news for your heart. Perish the thought that such self-congratulation might make its way into your talking with another, dropping mention of your kindness that notice might be taken by another. And I tell you the same thing about your generosity in serving another one of Mine: beware of the pride that leads you to flaunt such love and turn it from a private act to a public display. O Dear One, how very quickly you forget the Source of all your bounty. It is not such a big thing to have given away when you realize that what you give isn't yours in the first place. When you sow into another's life, whether that giving is of your time or your talents or your treasures, let it be done in the closet of your heart that I alone might know and I alone might applaud.

May 3

David said it all: I saw God before me for all time. Nothing can shake me; he's right by my side. I'm glad from the inside out, ecstatic; I've pitched my tent in the land of hope. Acts 2:25-26 (MSG)
In both your sorrow and your angst, acknowledge Me as the gatekeeper of your heart and the guardian of the entrances to your soul. The night has been dark; how dark you never knew, for I stood there, My pure light shining forth into the darkness, keeping despair at bay, shedding My light into the shadowy corners of your life. Now I allow you a taste, a glimpse, of what that darkness was truly like. The tears you cry are a dim reflection of the tears I cried for you. Painfully you feel them now; strong as you are, redeemed and restored as you are, an earlier entrance into your heart of such bottomless grief would have demolished your tender self. In

that dark night of your soul, I spared you from the enemy's plans for your heart. I stood close to you and took the blows from his mallet of hatred, stood in the streambed of a river of destruction and let it not overtake you. Feel a taste of it now, that you might know the depth of My love for you and My willingness to protect you and keep you safe. The ground you stand on and now revisit with Me beside you is holy ground, for it bears the bloody stains of My fight for you.

May 4

You have hedged me behind and before, and laid Your hand upon me. Psalm 139:5 (NKJV)
I've got your back; I've got your front; I've got your flank sides. Even better than when I escorted My people through the wilderness with My cloud by day and My pillar of fire by night, I have placed My Holy Spirit within you. No longer do you need to be guided by the externals, for I live inside you and speak to you as a father speaks to his child. As you go forth, as you move in your day, I dwell within you with My presence and protect you with My strong right arm of power. Nothing that crosses your path, nothing that enters your life escapes My notice. And there is nothing that I am not prepared to deal with on your behalf and for your benefit. It is to your heart's detriment that you see yourself as a solitary soldier fighting an invincible army alone and unaided. That picture could not be farther from the truth. From within you I guide and protect and counsel; from without I set up legions to war on your behalf. You are not alone, and your ultimate victory is sure.

May 5

I greet you with the great words, grace and peace! We know the meaning of those words because Jesus Christ rescued us from this evil world we're in by offering himself as a sacrifice for our sins. God's plan is that we all experience that rescue. Glory to God forever! Oh, yes! Galatians 1:3-5 (MSG)

I am yours. Not in the same way as you are Mine, but nonetheless I offer you claim to Myself, to My power and My love. As I willingly offered Myself to you on the cross, My death for your life before it was even conceived, so I offer Myself, covering each of your hours and all of your days. Claim My gift, My offering of self to you, for I cannot **make** Myself yours. I can only wait, life outstretched toward you, hand of fellowship and miraculous power offered to you. Allow nothing to interfere with your image of Me, not the enemy's voices and distortions, neither your own sense of self-sufficiency nor your long-held disgust with your own heart. Push away those emotions, break through the shadows, and see Me for who I am; see My offering and My love for you for what it is. I have covenanted with you, betrothed you, and made you Mine for all eternity. Relish the truth that there is nothing that will change that, for I am yours!

May 6

Therefore if you have any encouragement from being united with Christ, if any comfort from his love, if any common sharing in the Spirit, if any tenderness and compassion, then make my joy complete by being like-minded, having the same love, being one in spirit and of one mind. Philippians 2:1-2

Do you sense My presence? Do you sense the deep well of love that I have toward you this morning? The great grace that I pour into your life? I know what happened last night, but here I am this morning showing up in your heart, in your mind, in your spirit. I open up to you a deep well of forgiveness, and acceptance, and peace. Child, the people outside My presence know no such thing. They've never experienced true safety. They've never known a true safe place; it's cold, it's hard, and it's mean outside, and the meanness grows meaner, and the hardness gets harder, and the hatred digs deeper. Take what you get here in My presence this morning, and open your arms to those outside these walls: the discouraged, the destitute, the disenfranchised, and embrace them. Be My child; be My arms; be My voice; be My help to those outside your walls.

May 7

If you are pleased with me, teach me your ways so I may know you and continue to find favor with you. Remember that this nation is your people. Exodus 33:13
As I stretched My arms wide and willingly died for you on the tree, stretch yourself wide and willingly. Count all else but loss, and dive deeply into the knowing of Me. I have walked before you and shown you My way. Make of yourself a servant who willingly follows My example and who walks inside My footprints with joy and abandon. Like Moses, refuse to move from where you are without My sure presence going before you and with you. Know Me well enough from your time in My Word and in fellowship with Me that I will be pleased to answer the requests of your heart, for they mirror My own longings. You are child of My heart and breath of My breath. Although you have been stained by fallenness and sin, yet you still are My created and chosen one, and I take great pride in you as you allow Me to transform you. I will teach you My ways; I will reveal to you some of the secrets of My heart. Things that I do not share with everyone, I will share with you. For you have sought Me out and made yourself My willing servant and My trusted friend.

May 8

Be strong and very courageous .... Have I not commanded you? Be strong and courageous. Do not be terrified; do not be discouraged, for the Lord your God will be with you wherever you go. Joshua 1:7,9
Over and over again My refrain rings out: *'Be strong! Be daring! Trust Me! I will neither leave nor forsake you. Never give up, for I am your Abba Father, and I take care of My own!'* Whether an army massed against you or problems with no end in sight, what you see matters far less than you think. Do you believe Me?

Do you trust Me? Are there reasons beyond counting for your heart to know that I am faithful to you in My love? Why then do you sit at the side of the road you travel with your head slumped and tears of fear and despair overtaking your heart? I am with you **wherever** you go. Your courage and your strength come from that truth. Lift up your head; strengthen your weak knees with My promise. Let My proclamation lift the discouragement from your spirit; let My breath blow terror away on the winds. And with a lightness of heart that comes from My presence, your strength and courage will flow.

May 9

Living then, as every one of you does, in pure grace, it's important that you not misinterpret yourselves as people who are bringing this goodness to God. No, God brings it all to you. The only accurate way to understand ourselves is by what God is and by what he does for us, not by what we are and what we do for him.
Romans 12:3 (MSG)
Think not too highly of yourself. Neither hold yourself in such low regard that you block My use of you. If you see yourself as invaluable or important, then you are likely standing in the way of My purposes rather than in the shadow of them. Yet if you argue with Me about what you cannot do, you also end up restraining My hand in your life. How slow you are to learn, Child. When will you realize that I can use you in spite of yourself? That it is I in you that moves you forward to accomplish great things for My Kingdom, and that nothing you can do on your own holds either significance or power? Part of being made more and more into My likeness is your invitation to My indwelling, your surrender of self that I might overtake all that you are. There is no limit to what I can do through you or what I can make of you. But it comes at a great price: the relinquishment of yourself and your pride. Do not stand in My way, Child, for I have great plans for you, and great is your role in My

Kingdom if you sacrifice your own ways and allow Me to have Mine.

May 10

I pray that out of his glorious riches he may strengthen you with power through his Spirit in your inner being, so that Christ may dwell in your hearts through faith. And I pray that you, being rooted and established in love, may have power, together with all the Lord's holy people, to grasp how wide and long and high and deep is the love of Christ, and to know this love that surpasses knowledge - that you may be filled to the measure of all the fullness of God. Ephesians 3:16-19

Child, I want you to feel My pride for you this morning. In the hard places where you have walked in the last months, in the last weeks, in the last hours, you've looked for My handholds. You've tried to reach out to Me in the tough and the hard places, and I've been there for you. But Child, this morning I want you to feel My pride. As a mother feels pride for her children and their accomplishments, even in their failures if they're looking up and trying, know that I feel the same for you this morning. I know you've walked in hard places, and know that there are more hard places to come, but know as a mother reaches out to her child, so I reach out to you. Feel My pride for you this morning; open your arms, and receive My mercy into your heart. Help Me to help you soften the hard places. Help Me to help you in all the things that you face. I am there. I am the Great Parent. And I am merciful.

May 11

And the Lord said to Gideon, "The people who are with you are too many for Me to give the Midianites into their hands, lest Israel claim glory for itself against Me, saying, 'My own hand has saved me.'" Judges 7:2 (NKJV)

The laws of **My** battlefield are different than your world's.

The world sees the one with the most as the winner ... the one with the strongest ... the one with the best. But in My Kingdom those rules are often changed. Might is not always determined by physical prowess or mathematical quantities. The I AM who dwells within you breathes might and power the way you breathe air. And so My battles in this world are waged and won in different ways than you might expect. There are chinks in your own armor, but despair not, for even so I will protect you and through you I will win My battles. I use you not because of your own goodness or your own strength but because you are Mine. The world needs to see Me, not you. Those children who are not yet Mine need to see you accomplish the impossible so that they might know exactly who the Accomplisher is. So, do not be afraid of your weakness or your inability; it is precisely those lacks that become the vehicle for My greatest victories so that others might raise their hopeless eyes and finally see ... Me.

May 12

The Lord is my shepherd, I lack nothing. He makes me lie down in green pastures, he leads me beside quiet waters. Psalm 23:1-2

Quiet yourself; slow your breath; like floating on a still pool when the water muffles all sound, let the noise of this world become muted. Come still yourself Child; life has slammed into you for too long now without you setting yourself aside for rest. Breathe ... feel My presence come behind and pull you back against My strong, warm Self. Feel My arms of strength and compassion wrap about your body pulling you into Me. Yes ... deep sigh ... this is the proper response; let go for a time the worries and ways of this day; be a child embraced in the safety and certainty of your loving parent's embrace. Feel My breath rise within My chest, and mimic your breathing to match My own ... no rush ... no hurry. You may be CEO, pastor or teacher, caregiver or chef, but here Child, you are simply Mine. Your only responsibility is to release your woes, let them drop to the ground, while letting My favor, My kindness, My influence saturate your being. I know what this day holds beyond your knowledge, beyond your imaginings, and I've got it! Nothing is beyond My knowledge or My ken; no shock or surprise to you moves Me in the least. I have the answer before the crisis arises; before the day turns bleak, before the mistakes are made, I've planned redemption for each situation. So Child, today, when that "thing" happens, return in your mind to this place, this moment, and feel again My strong, competent arms, and remember My all-wise, all-knowing presence, and embrace My words of encouragement and hope. It will make a difference in your day, in the troubles that cross the path of your day. I am with you, Child, so much closer and so much more involved than you imagine.

May 13

For you did not receive a spirit that makes you a slave again to fear, but you received the Spirit of sonship. And by him we cry, "Abba, Father." Romans 8:15

Offspring of My heart, child of My youth as well of My old age, My child for all of eternity ... that is who you are. Do not take lightly that the King of Heaven, yea the Lord of all the Earth, calls you His beloved One, for indeed I call you that and so much more. Ours is not meant to be a relationship of formality and distance. You are not the subject of an inaccessible king who enthroned himself in a distance palace and who keeps himself far away from your daily affairs because He finds them somehow too undignified. Nay, My love for you is like that of a father who dreamt of your birth for years before your conception and who provides for you, protects you to the ends of his might, and stays up late at night fantasizing about and planning for the good things he will give you. Mine is a love that invites you not only to dine at My tables of bounty, but also to climb onto My lap and find Me not just great and strong but also eager to hear of your little daily things. There is nothing that enters your life that doesn't concern Me. There is nothing about Me that doesn't invite you close. It is good that you recognize My holiness and bow before Me on bended knee, but good it is as well to know the depths of My fatherheart and draw close to its beat of constant and unchangeable love for you.

May 14

We live and move in him, can't get away from him!
Acts 17:28 (MSG)

Make your home with Me, homeless, orphan waif. Your head knows that you are none of those, yet your heart screams *'foul'* in its inmost parts and chants *'alone … alone … alone.'* You know Me to be in you, dwelling, taking up residence; now learn to know yourself to be Mine in a fresh way. Actively make your home in Me; dwell in Me; live in Me. Not homeless, not orphan, not alone - rather, **in** Me. Being "in Me" calls for intimacy: a bridal chamber, acts of love in the bedroom of our home, continued, daily sharing, intimacy in the private and hidden moments, and familiarity in the daily stuff of life. Join yourself with Me; allow yourself to become one with Me; let there be a union. Deep calls to deep; I am deep and I call to your deep. Be at home in My love. Let My love rewire your need and your heart's cry; let Me fulfill and fill up all the empty broken spaces. My love is a home that will not be repossessed; it is an intimacy that will never abandon. My home for you is a safe place where you can dare again, a place where promises are kept and never broken, where intimacy grows even deeper, where trust is built as a sure foundation. Creator God's covenantal love, irrevocable, unchangeable: Home.

May 15

As a father has compassion on his children, so the Lord has compassion on those who fear him. Psalm 103:13

My compassion toward you springs forth. Feel it now in the stillness of your heart; see it come. Know My Father heart of love for you. My mercy toward you, beloved Child, is new every morning, fresh as the dew, faithful as the daily manna I send for you. You cannot wear down My mercy nor use it up. Know this Dear One: My heart beats **for** you, as My heart beats **in** you. What the enemy intended for evil in your life, I have redeemed for good. Fear his footprints no longer, for I have come both before and after him, to reclaim My territory in your life. I have chosen you as My treasured possession. Know My care for you and hear My voice today: be not the enemy of your own soul.

For the Lord has chosen Jacob to be his own, Israel to be his treasured possession. Psalm 135:4

May 16

There is no one holy like the Lord; there is no one besides you; there is no Rock like our God. 1 Samuel 2:2
'There is no one …. There is nothing ….' Hear the words that rip out of the depths of your anguish and your fear. They are words of hopelessness and despair that ooze out of you like blood from a wound when you are cast on the brutal shore of circumstance. I understand those words, My little One made of dust. I understand and I have come to finish those sentences in your life. I am the Holy, Omnipotent One who counters all the other realities in your life; I am the great But. There is no one but Me! There is no way but through Me. I hold all the promises in My hand, and I will deliver on each one. You cannot, but I can! You are weak, but I am your strong arm of protection. You are nothing without Me, but with Me you are My powerful, invincible instrument. You are shifting sand, but I am the Rock on which you can stand. You are sinful and selfish and unable, but I am the propitiation for your sins and the restorer of your broken walls. You are hopeless, but I am your Hope. There is no one besides Me, no "but" beyond Me, and nothing that concerns you that is beyond My reach.

May 17

No one born (begotten) of God [deliberately, knowingly, and habitually] practices sin, for God's nature abides in him [His principle of life, the divine

**sperm, remains permanently within him]; and he cannot practice sinning because he is born (begotten) of God.
1 John 3:9 (AMP)**
I lay My seed in you; I impregnate you with My promises. Hold yourself ripe and ready for My entry into the deepest and most hidden parts of you. Make sure that I am your one and only. Offer yourself to no other. Let Me glory in your nakedness and revel in the fact that you expose and open yourself to Me. In your unflinching vulnerability to Me lie your safety and your freedom. I deposit My seed within your willing spirit, and there it will grow and soon bring forth fruit of the most amazing kind.

May 18

**Therefore, since we are surrounded by such a great cloud of witnesses, let us throw off everything that hinders and the sin that so easily entangles, and let us run with perseverance the race marked out for us.
Hebrews 12:1**
Run with endurance the race I have set before you. Circle your goals with diligence. Be unflagging in the strength of **My** might. Be unafraid of even the night watches, for I will run beside you even then. Be tireless for I will give you strength to complete your circuits. Know that it is My love that carries you. Although there is lap upon lap for you to run, you do not run alone; I run beside you. And just like runners training for a race, I tell you, bring your friends with you to run alongside to spur you on when your spirit grows faint and your heart grows weak, to speak words of encouragement as you run. Run without flagging, My Child. Run with **My** strength; run with My Spiritwind blowing behind you, blowing My breath to give you strength. But know this Child, the race does not go to the swift. The race goes to the one who has endurance; it goes to the one who stands in My strength and when the weather gets bad and the days get cold and things get tough, the one who continues to run no matter how slowly, no matter how painfully … that is

the one to whom the prize will go. So I call you, My Child, to heed My words and to run the race that I have set before you with endurance, with Me beside you forever leading you home.

May 19

Surely God is my salvation; I will trust and not be afraid. The Lord, the Lord himself, is my strength and my defense; he has become my salvation. With joy you will draw water from the wells of salvation. Isaiah 12:2-3

Do you hear Me? I call to you, day and night, trying to reach your ears. But, the enemy of your soul, of your very life holds you in rapt attention. His hand is wrapped around your throat, squeezing, choking as he spits his hateful, fearful words into your ear. You are under his spell, held by ignorance of who I AM and what I've accomplished for you. Your head spins and whirls with thoughts conceived by the enemy, spoken into your ear and birthed by your faithless imagination. This life is a war; each and every moment your enemy prowls and seeks the weak; he culls them from the herd and wreaks havoc into their hearts and lives, instilling panic where there could be peace, anxiety and anguish where there could be trustful waiting. I have not changed; I stilled the angry waves in times of old, and My strength has not wavered. I came not to just provide for you an eventual heavenly home, I came to provide LIFE ... more abundant life, a life cut free from the enemy's web of destruction. You, Child, have much to do with your own freedom; you must CHOOSE Me; moment-by-moment **you must choose**. Do you trust Me with your health, with your children, with your stresses and anxieties? Search your heart, and hear Me; you cannot trust one whom you do not know. Would you hand over your life's savings to a stranger, trusting him to safeguard it? Of course not; neither can you hand over to Me those people, those troubles, those questions you hold closest to you when you do not truly KNOW My character. Learn of Me; unlock the richness of My ethos, for in that richness your peace emerges, in that God-understanding your will to throw off the enemy is revealed. My people are ruined because they do not know what is right or true; seek Me with all your heart while I may be found, and peace will become yours, for I AM peace.

May 20

Then everyone will know that I, God, have saved you - I, the Mighty One of Jacob. Isaiah 49:26 (MSG)
I am Lord of the impossible. I am Restorer of the broken down and Creator of the new. I bring life from death and hope from the darkest doubt. Where there is nothing, there I am. Even from the blackness of the deepest night, I will bring forth My light. When your enemy assails you, I will be your Victor. I will remain faithful when all others desert you; I will never leave nor forsake you. It is in those situations where there is no earthly recourse that My power and My might, My strong and loving right arm, will be most visible. Turn to Me when all hope is gone, when all seems impossible, when any chance of rescue has steadily dwindled to nothing. There, precisely there, and then, precisely then, I will stride purposefully in to show all who watch exactly who I am. In those moments and places will My might be made known and My love be seen.

May 21

Be strong. Take courage. Don't be intimidated. Don't give them a second thought because God, your God, is striding ahead of you. He's right there with you. He won't let you down; he won't leave you.
Deuteronomy 31:6 (MSG)
Come Child; come near and rest. Memories are a hard and heavy burden. Your darknesses give way to My light, but even in that lightgiving and in the healing, there is still much pain. You are not alone. To feel that even for a moment is the lie of the enemy, his mallet held over your tender heart. The truth is that I never left you. In the fearful nights, in the long lonelinesses and the many questions, in all of those days

and nights when you wondered and feared, I stood with you. I was both your rear guard and your front guard. I was there, standing watch and protecting you from the fiery darts of the enemy. There was no changing of shifts, no moments when I was inattentive, no days before I was assigned to watch over you. Even when you thought you no longer needed Me, still I stayed, and even now I remain. I am here to walk beside you, out of the darkness and into the healing light. My beloved Child, you have endured much. I have sifted you, separating what the enemy intended for evil from all that I have repurposed for your gain and My glory. Do not brood; do not wonder; I have turned and will yet turn your sorrows to rejoicing.

May 22

[S]o David inquired of the Lord, "Shall I ...?"
2 Samuel 5:19

All power, wisdom, and strength come from Me, Child. Why then do you forget to seek Me for specifics about the decisions that cross your path each day? Is it that you think I am too busy to care? Or that I don't concern Myself about the ordinary details of your life? Perhaps you think that if you are neither prophet, preacher, king nor president, principal nor CEO that your decisions are not important enough to be of value to Me or to My world. How wrong you are, Child, on all those counts. For the least of these I came; for the least of these I died. There is no one who is not of consequence to Me and no one whose life and choices do not have Kingdom consequence. Ask of Me and I will lead. Seek Me and I will guide. Turn to Me with your *'Should I?'*s and your *'Or should I not?'*s, and I will direct your course. I will never stay My hand from touching your life; it is only you who can keep Me away. Let those who have ears hear Me and those who have eyes see Me. Turn to Me and I will answer; ask Me and I will lead.

May 23

The Lord will keep you from all harm - he will watch over your life; the Lord will watch over your coming and going both now and forevermore. Psalm 121:7-8

I speak to the desperate of heart. I speak to the depressed. I speak to the beyond downcast this morning. I am still the light in the darkness. I am still the help that comes from the hills. Many of you face situations where hope has evaporated, and indeed, in this world, there IS no hope. But I am still the comma, and I am still the hope. Bend your knee in surrender, for I alone know the path through this darkness; I alone know the path to the heart that you want to be touched by My hand. And I alone am the one who can keep you and make you strong in the midst of the battle. I know you are beyond despondent. I know that you are beyond depressed. I know that you feel there is no hope, but there is. I am still the light in the darkness, and I still come to the aid of those who call upon My name.

May 24

Since we live by the Spirit, let us keep in step with the Spirit. Galatians 5:25

You have stepped out; now I tell you to step up. Invisible no longer, you are one of My Truth speakers; born of My love for you and fashioned from My great mercies, your life and words carry Me forth into My world. I have instructed you to be fearless, and finally you are beginning to walk in the peace that such obedience brings. Now comes the thrill of daring: daring to position yourself to be used, daring to get your hands dirty in the mud of My world. Step up into My vision, My mountains of hope; see My world from the perspective of My Holy Hill and not the confines of earthly indignities. Awesome are My deeds, and to you I have passed My baton; you are heir to the workings of My power. Step up into My promises, and you will scarcely recognize yourself. Take wind on **My** strength, and I will send you where you are yet unknown to do My bidding and to heal the inhabitants of My land. There is no end to what My light through you can bring to this dark world.

May 25

The Life-Light blazed out of the darkness; the darkness couldn't put it out. John 1:5 (MSG)
Like lightning pierces the storm-blackened sky bringing light where there was no trace of it, so does truth spoken into the days and places where the enemy's grip holds tight reign. Darkness is the ploy of Satan. Keep things locked up and unspoken, and his bondages will remain intact. But when My children choose to dash fear and shame to the ground and awaken hope with their voices of truth, My light can flash in and overcome the darkness. Knowing that such words can break Satan's thrall does not make the speaking of them easy, but nonetheless My Holy Spirit will have sway over the hearts of those who will let Him. My dawn hovers over the night waiting to break forth and crack the horizon open with its light. In like fashion, I too dwell at the edges of each of your darknesses. Invite Me to come and My strong power will pierce the blackness and take it by storm. Light will prevail in all the places where truth is spoken; I will take up residence everywhere I am invited. My light will clear away the mirage that makes darkness both impenetrable and unchangeable, for I will make all things new just as I do with each day's dawning.

May 26

But now the Lord my God has given me rest on every side, and there is no adversary or disaster. 1 Kings 5:4
The drumbeat of war has been your cadence for too long, My Child. There is a time for war, but there is also a time for peace. Even in your "rest," you bring knife and sword to your bed, alert to every sound and ready to jump to battle. Over time, this posture will suck every tendril of joy from your heart. Trials come; battles must be fought and won; the enemy tires not, and his ways are devious and persistent. But,

he has trained you to never let your guard down, to stay in battle formation, shield raised, muscles straining to hold weapon and defense, taking no time to rest, or eat, or drink. Yes, your path has been full of bloody battles; skirmishes of all kinds have trained your eyes and ears to pick up the coming clash of swords quickly. This is good; this is needed. But needed, too, is to know there are times to put your weapons down, bathe your bloodied self, change into your civilian clothes, and come away with Me. Even in the midst of your wars with the enemy, this must be done, and done often. You need the time in My restful presence to remember why you fight. You need the insight I will give you to know where next to set up your defenses when the battle lines are drawn again. You need to lay your weary head in My lap, and let Me sing My love songs over your exhausted spirit. In this place, battle-axe and maul are not needed; in this place you can once again take a deep breath unhindered by the stress of battle. Here I meet you; here I calm you; here I minister, and here the river of peace that passes all understanding begins to flow. Battle weary Child, come.

May 27

I am not a God of stops and starts, or one with limits and boundaries. Although it is hard for your finite mind to conceive, one of My favorite words is "all," and My promises to you are full of it. In ALL things I work for the good of those who love Me. **(Romans 8:28)** My plans stand through ALL generations. **(Psalm 33:11)** I forgive ALL your sins. **(Jeremiah 33:8)** Nothing in ALL creation separates you from My love. **(Romans 8:39)** Seek Me first and I will give you ALL the other things you need as well. **(Matthew 6:33)** How is it then, Child, that you worry? If you know that My reach is without boundaries and My love without limit, can you not trust My care for you? Is there anything more that you can do with your own power that I have not already planned to accomplish on your behalf with Mine? My ALL for you is one intricate, tightly woven promise that stretches back long before you were born, back before My people were called, back before even time as you know it began. Rest then, My much-loved One; find your comfort in My ALL that surrounds your life like a battalion of sentries guarding your walls.

May 28

For the Lord gives wisdom, and from his mouth come knowledge and understanding. Proverbs 2:6
I have not left you adrift in a canoe without paddles or on a sailboat without sails. I have not created you and then left you alone to see where I would have you go with only your own eyes. It is not with your own mind that I expect you to guide your ways. I am the great I AM, the one who creates and redeems but also guides and directs. I am the one who wrote the story of Revelation even before Genesis was penned. Had I desired to leave you alone to plot your own course and find your own way, I would not have sent My prophets or My Holy Spirit. I have not left you to your own devices. I have spoken down through the ages, and My Word has come forth. In your todays, I still reveal Myself; I speak to those who are willing to quiet themselves enough to hear. Although there is much knowledge in your world, little wisdom survives except as My people seek it from Me. Through My Word and My Holy Spirit, I teach those who desire to learn and speak to those who care to listen. Do you seek wisdom? Then seek Me. Do you desire truth in your inmost parts? Then empty yourself of all that the world would convince you that you know so well, and surrender to My Spirit's touch and My Spirit's voice. Into the space that such admitted ignorance reveals, I will be able to pour My wisdom and My truth.

May 29

So he got up and went to his father. But while he was still a long way off, his father saw him and was filled with compassion for him; he ran to his son, threw his arms around him and kissed him. [The Parable of the

Lost Son] Luke 15:20
O My Precious Child, know that your return in no way disappointed Me. Know that I did not, not even for a moment, harbor anything in My heart for you except joy, compassion, and eager expectation. I did not care about your sin, your defiance, your disregard. I cared only that you came back. I offered you no cloak of shame, emblazoned no scarlet letter on your forehead, did not wait for you to speak words of penance or even for you to ask for My forgiveness before I ran to you and embraced you. Such is My heart for you, always and eternally My heart for you: love with no strings attached, love and compassion that is not earned - that only is. When you have spent all and come up empty in the world's economy, there you will find Me, running to meet you, full of compassion and eager to take you into My arms. Do not think of your unworthiness; think only of My love for you that waited for you to think to return. My gift to you, Child: to see you, to have compassion on you, to run to you, to embrace you.

May 30

Ah, Sovereign Lord, you have made the heavens and the earth by your great power and outstretched arm. Nothing is too hard for you. Jeremiah 32:17
Child, hear My voice for you; hear My heart for you today. What in the depths of your imagination is the worst thing that could happen to you? The thing that you fear most? About money. About relationship. About loved ones. About your health. What is that thing? The worst thing that could happen? Or, My Child, My beloved Child, the worst thing that has **already** happened? Put it in your hands now, and lift it up to Me. Offer it to Me, Child, because I love you more than you know. And I am a bigger and more thorough Victor than you have ever seen in this world. There is **nothing** that is beyond My sight. And **nothing** that is beyond My arm of strength and might. And **nothing** that is beyond My heart of love for you. You hear the world's voices that tell you that I am **not** enough; that I do not care

enough and cannot do enough. They are lies. I am Victor.
The enemy's words are lies and hold no truth. Come before
Me this morning, Child. Don't be afraid to admit to Me
what it is you fear, what it is that you hear right now even in
the midst of your praise and your devotion. What is it,
Child? Lift it up. Offer it to **Me**. Break the power of the
enemy and the strength of his lies **right now**. Because
whatever you can imagine that is horrible, I am stronger than
that. I am more loving than that. And I will make that too
bow before My knee.

May 31

**The Lord does not look at the things man looks at. Man
looks at the outward appearance, but the Lord looks at
the heart. 1 Samuel 16:7**
I look not on the outward. What is seen matters far, far less
to Me than the unseen. Appearances are much less important
than you realize, for truth often hides in less obvious places.
Far into the depths of your heart I see. There it is that the
real you dwells, hidden from most but never hidden from
Me. Like a surgeon performing open-heart surgery with
scalpel and patient persistence, I carefully open you up. It is
only when you are exposed and vulnerable before Me that I
can do My work. Your outward calm and competence have
for years belied your inward, hidden turmoil. Your put-
together face and ways hide the empty holes within you that
have long dwelt unnoticed. I am in the business of
restoration, but such healing comes with a price. You must
be willing to invite Me close, to allow Me to cut and peel
back the surface layers in order to expose that which only the
Master Surgeon has the wisdom as well as the power to
repair and make whole.

June 1

**'My heart is overwhelmed; Lead me to the rock that is
higher than I!'** you cry. **(Psalm 61:2 NKJV)** And so My
Holy Spirit will indeed lead you, for your tender heart is full

of just a small measure of the pain of this world of yours. Yet even such a small measure can overwhelm a faithful one with a heart open to the pain the enemy plans for those whom I love. If He can turn a beloved one of Mine into a sniveling one, then he wins on two counts; he destroys you, and at the same time the strength that you provide others vanishes. Fear not the feelings that ravage your heart, for those are the precise feelings that make you Mine and give you a Christ-like heart. To feel for another, even sometimes to carry another's feelings as your own, is part of My plan. Be My strong tower, a place where others can run with flesh and bone and skin and speech. Be willing to be a cross bearer, a burden bearer in My name and for My sake. In losing yourself I will find you, and I will lead you to My Rock where your heart will be secure.

June 2

Now I know that the Lord saves his anointed; he answers him from his holy heaven with the saving power of his right hand. Some trust in chariots and some in horses, but we trust in the name of the Lord our God. Psalm 20:6-7

I will tutor you in the ways of your heart and teach you to see life and the pretender's ways with **My** eyes. I will not leave you adrift in stormy seas, nor fail to come to you in the dark watches of the night. There is nothing that is beyond My understanding and nothing beyond My power to overcome and to heal. Don't be alarmed by the unexpected skirmishes with the enemy of your soul. You may be surprised by them, but I am not. I will instruct you in the way you should go and transform your mind so that it is more and more like Mine each day. I am not a God who stands afar off. I come near and eagerly abide with you and in you. When you are blinded, take My hand; when you are lame, lean on Me; when you are heart sore and overwhelmed, know both My love and My life's resurrected power for you.

June 3

Even in the times of your streams flowing at floodwater stage, Satan can break you and make it seem as though they are running lean and almost dry. He can take bounty and convince you that it is lack; he can cause you anxiety even in the midst of joy. His is a loud and insistent voice, and you must learn to fight against his lies that masquerade as truths that you might begin to better hear My own words for you even when your cisterns are full and hope fills your horizon. But now your feet are clay, and your heart is broken. This time it is not Satan, the Great Pretender, who twists the truth and veils your eyes so that you see lack where there is plenty or grief when there should be joy. This time your sadness is real; tragedy has walked full force into your midst and must be acknowledged. So what will you do with those realities, Child? How will you handle the times when there **is** reason to weep and wail and wonder what on earth My hand of love is up to? Will you run to the dark forests of fear and anger and hide yourself away there to lick your wounds and bemoan your dark days? Or will you pursue Me even when your heart is broken, even when you have to forge through thick and painful brambles to make your way to My side? Will you remember that even in the valley of the dark shadow of death that you need not fear, for I walk beside you? Whether your pain is but an illusion of the Master Trickster or a real touch of misery that is the fruit of this fallen earth, I will never leave your side; I will never desert you. Even though you walk through great darknesses, nonetheless it is I who goes with you and I who will carry you when you no longer have the strength to go on.

Be strong and courageous. Do not be afraid or terrified because of them, for the Lord your God goes with you; he will never leave you nor forsake you.
Deuteronomy 31:6

June 4

And you, my child, will be called a prophet of the Most High; for you will go on before the Lord to prepare the way for him …. Luke 1:76

Hear My Holy whisper; at the place where your knee bends, at the place where you see that all that stands between you and a Righteous God is the sacrifice of My Son … there is where you hear My Holy whisper. What do you know, Child, of My Holy? You forget that a Holy God covered Himself in the cloak of humility, debasing Himself for the sake of all the world. My Holy whisper has one purpose, to create a humble spirit within; the heartbeat of one humble servant brings more Godliness to the world than a whole congregation of moralists. The world travails, moaning and anguishing; let its affliction bring forth in you, not a screaming, selfish brat consumed with its own appetites, but a humbled child who knows his life depends on the daily goodness of His Heavenly Father. This humble child, this smitten bride will change the world. Be not discouraged; I orchestrate each tick of the clock; each injustice, every kingdom reigns only with My permission. I am molding My child-bride, making her ready for her bridegroom, and when this beaten, battered, disenfranchised world looks upon her unpretentious beauty, then revival will sweep the land. My perfect storm is in the making; the cold, brutal front of humanity is soon to be overwhelmed by the passionate heart of My child-bride called from the womb of humility. Look up child; see My face of compassion shine upon you; the story's not over … in fact, your most jubilant chapter is about to begin.

June 5

The Lord your God is with you, he is mighty to save. He will take great delight in you, he will quiet you with his love, he will rejoice over you with singing. Zephaniah 3:17

I rejoice over you with singing, Child; can you not do the same? Bring Me your sacrifice of praise, a sacrifice that costs you nothing except perhaps your high view of yourself. It is when you name all the reasons you have for praising Me that you begin to realize just how great I am. In that position, you see how very little you are responsible for in the affairs of your life. It is I who order the heavenlies and I who keep the planets in orbit and cause the rising and the setting of the sun everyday. Rejoice that it is with a hand of love that I accomplish all these things that you cannot even begin to imagine much less control. Be glad that I love you so, My Child, for without My love, where would your life be? Indeed, where **could** your life be if My hand was one of indifference to you? A boat adrift with neither sail nor paddle, such a horror life would be even as you travelled through river canyons of beauty. But Creator God is indeed the Lover of your soul, full of kindness and mercy, intimately involved in all that concerns you, and eager to draw close to you. Rejoice that it is so! No dark taskmaster am I, no unconcerned king blinded by his own power. Turn your eyes toward the Savior who died for you; you will see My love for you pour forth - a love that has no end and that always yearns to comfort and protect and draw you close. As I rejoice over you with My singing, bring forth your voice, and join Me in a duet. Rejoice in Me; sing My praises, for then you will have seen Me and known Me, and the glory that you ascribe to Me will transform both you and your ways.

June 6

He had pity on his people .... 2 Chronicles 36:15

I look with pity on My creation, for I have given them everything for life and peace, and they use it not. Instead all too often My children wallow in the filth that still lives in this world and fall prey to the hopelessness that days without My truths bring them. Do not be ignorant of all that I offer you; My Word is rich with promises, and to walk in its ways is to walk with Me. How hungry and needy My children are; how sad it is to not have those hungers and needs filled when My bounteous storehouse sits close by with doors swung open wide. Seek Me and you will find Me; My peace I give unto you. Come drink of My Living Water and you will thirst no more. By the world's accounting there is great lack; resources are indeed insufficient to meet your needs, and uncertainty knocks on the door on a daily basis. But I am the Great One; I am the All-Sufficient One. I am the Alpha and Omega, the Overcomer, El Roi the God who sees. The Great King of the earth offers you all that you need, provides for your lack, and tutors you in the ways of the True Kingdom. Let My pity for your ignorant avoidance of Me and My bounty drive you to My outstretched hands full of peace and provision. Accept what I will happily bestow upon you My much-loved Child, and you will be satisfied.

June 7

The righteous cry, and the Lord heareth, and delivereth them out of all their troubles. Psalm 34:17 (KJV)
Yes, praise Me, My Child, for contrary to popular belief, I am not dead! Contrary to popular belief, I still move in this world, and contrary to popular belief, I still move in this country, and I still move in you. Be not discouraged. Lift up your voice; loose your feet; loose your heart, for contrary to popular belief, I am still the God that runs this world, that heals the sick, that helps the lost, that lifts the downtrodden. Contrary to popular belief, I AM GOD and I still rule. Loose your tongue today, Child; loose your tongue, for in that praise, I move!

June 8

Sometimes, Child, you lack peace, answers, direction and wisdom because you praise Me not. I do not hide My face from you; you, My Child, turn your back on Me in your anger and anxiety, and you refuse to see Me and My love for you. Like your own children, you forget what you have, what I have already given you, and what I have already done for you because you focus on what you want. And I, like you with your children, love you no less because you forget to thank Me, because you forget to praise Me for all that I have already done. But Child, you limit what I can do if you live only in the land of your needs and your wants and your concerns. Your praise releases Me to be God, to be powerful and effectual in your life. Your praise positions you to receive what I cannot give when your back is turned in torment. So even when you lie curled in your bed with tears streaming down your face, praise Me. Even when you sit in the darkness of not knowing why and not knowing what to do, praise Me. And I from Heaven will hear your cry and hear your words of surrender, and I will respond because I love you far more than you can ever imagine.

I will praise you, O Lord, with all my heart; I will tell of all your wonders. I will be glad and rejoice in you; I will sing praise to your name, O Most High. Psalm 9:1-2

June 9

Those who escape will remember me - how I have been grieved by their adulterous hearts, which have turned away from me, and by their eyes, which have lusted after their idols. Ezekiel 6:9

You trade one addiction for another, one idol for just another lover. Your sin is that you settle for pleasures that you can bring to yourself rather than the comfort that only I can give and only I can bring. Whatever your earthly gratifications, they fall short of what I long to provide you and even stand smack dab in the way of what I can give. Do you not trust Me to bring you joy and pleasure? I am the Lover of your soul - who could love you better than I? I am the Bread of Life - what food or drink can fill your hunger better than I? Release your propensity to fill your own needs and find your own pleasures. Stand still and listen and wait, long enough that I might bring you the pleasures that I intend for you. You fill yourself with counterfeit contentment, and then I cannot bring to you the contentment that I plan for you. You see only that which you have settled for and claimed for yourself; you do not even know the good that I have to give you. Set down your own pleasures; stop grasping the shreds of ease that you can find, and wait for Me to reveal the bliss that I have for you.

June 10

But there's far more to life for us. We're citizens of high heaven! Philippians 3:20 (MSG)

You sin against Me when you do not trust Me. You wrap yourself up in your own short cloak of comfort, but you find no real protection, for too much of you is still exposed to the harsh elements to be at ease. You claim your earthly citizenship without thought, knowing that the country you were born in is **your** country and home, knowing that you will never be denied its passport. But what of Me Child; what of My Kingdom into which you have been reborn? You have citizenship rights there now, yet you act like you are an alien and a stranger. Despite the fact that My shed blood has purchased your citizenship, you doubt My love for you. Oh, I know you would argue that that is not so, that of course you know that I love you. But Child, your lack of trust speaks otherwise. Your heart worries that I am not really for you - not really, not if I allow **these** particular hard circumstances in your life and the lives of your loved ones. You sin against Me when you claim that your understanding of your needs is better than Mine. You bring Me sadness when your mouth says you trust Me, but the actions of your heart reveal that you trust Me only when there is ease and comfort and bounty. I call you My Child, and My children are the inheritors of My great love and nurture. Think not that there is any circumstance that can intercept My powerful hand of grace upon your life. Think not that anything I do or don't do will ever make Me untrustworthy. You are indeed a citizen of My Kingdom. Travel this world as you will; your passport will always give to access to My promises for you. So trust Me with your hard situations and with your impossible circumstances. And trust Me in this most of all: I will always lead you Home.

June 11

Yea doubtless, and I count all things but loss for the excellency of the knowledge of Christ Jesus my Lord: for whom I have suffered the loss of all things, and do count them but dung, that I may win Christ …. Philippians 3:8 (KJV)

Child, do not take yourself so very seriously, for even at the height of your resolve, at the pinnacle of your self-discipline, when you manage, for a moment, to get all your ducks in a row, you are but a heartbeat from the opposite of those things. I say this not to discourage you, for goals are needful and discipline is a good thing, but I say it to keep you mindful of the brevity of this life and the folly of human striving. I call you to peace with God and with man; does that goal mirror your goals? If I call you today to surrender that "thing," that position, that pet project, that desire that seems rooted to your very soul … would you do it, or do you feel your heart clench at such a request? Could you, would you drop the tools and trappings of your strivings and lay them at My feet in surrender if I asked you to? Paul said of his position and place in society, *'I count it all as dung, for the knowledge of Christ.'* Test your heart, My son, My daughter; see whether it willingly offers up to Me, as a sacrifice, that "thing" that you clench so tightly to your chest, that dream, that person, that goal. Will you, Child, count it as but dung and lay it at My feet in humble submission? Not with half a heart, expecting Me to grant you permission to pick it up again tomorrow, or assuming I'll give you what you want if you make the attempt, but with unadulterated stubbornness lay it down with the assumption that it's the end of that dream? Harsh? Remember, Mine, what I laid down for your sake, what I gave up to come to your aid. I remind you of these things for your welfare; lay that "thing" in My hands, and trust Me with the outcome.

June 12

Why would you ever complain, O Jacob, or, whine, Israel, saying, "God has lost track of me. He doesn't care what happens to me"? Don't you know anything? Haven't you been listening? God doesn't come and go. God lasts. He's Creator of all you can see or imagine. He doesn't get tired out, doesn't pause to catch his breath. And he knows everything, inside and out. Isaiah 40:27-28 (MSG)

I stretch forth My hand, and I give power to the powerless and love to the unloved. Come before Me in surrender, for it is in your lack that I can fill you. It is in your acknowledgement of what you do not have and who you are not, that I can be your able God. Stretch forth your hands now, My Child; stretch forth to Me as I stretch forth to you. I have everything that you have need of. The world would speak of other things, but I know what you need, and I bring forth good from even what the world calls evil, even what the world calls lack. Here I stand, My Child. There is nothing that is too hard for Me. There is nothing that is too powerful for Me. There is no hole that is too deep and no pit that is too difficult to climb out of, for My hand is the hand of power. Reach out for Me now, Child. Whatever it is that you lack, speak of it to Me, and watch what I will do. It may not look like what you think it should look like; it may not be what it is that you have asked for, but trust Me in this: I am able - and I am loving. I will give you what you need and I will bring forth good from everything that the evil enemy intends against you to harm you. Stretch toward Me, Child; reach for Me; surrender to Me; speak of your lack to Me, Child, for then I will come in.

June 13

My command is this: Love each other as I have loved you. John 15:12

Are you willing to be broken for Me? Are you willing to lay down your rights and your needs and your feelings so that I can use you to bring healing and life to some of those who surround you? Are you willing to give away what isn't yours anyway? What sacrifices can you possibly make that would be even a speck in the face of what I have given for you, given **to** you? Be mindful, Child, of both My claim and My call on you. I call you to sacrifice; I call you to bend your knee that I might use you. It is only when your spirit is submitted to Me that your heart and your mind and your soul can follow suit. There are those of Mine that will never have what they need and never know Me as they should unless you, Dear One of Mine, touch their lives with yours and live out your surrender to Me in tangible ways with them. My claim on you is thorough and deep; you are **Mine**, to be used in remarkable ways that only I see and know. Give up your rights to a life that is just your own, and watch with both amazement and joy how I will use you to change and impact your world.

June 14

For the Lord takes delight in his people; he crowns the humble with salvation. Let the saints rejoice in this honor and sing for joy on their beds. Psalm 149:4-5
Breathe deeply My truth for your heart. Who you are and who you're not, know that **both** are beautiful in My sight. This truth is freedom, My Child, freedom! Hear My voice calling loud shouts of emancipation. You are free, so do not let your freedom shrivel and fall off like a dried up grape on a vine. Hear My truth for you, and cling not to the past, neither the pain nor the guilt. Step forth into the light of My day for you. Step out of the chains so long sundered. Good soul you are, **My** soul. Good heart you have for Me, My heart in you. No pride about it all, no, but joy to be used, joy that I have transformed pain and abandonment, sin and misjudgment into the God glorifying you that everyone sees - everyone except yourself. I have given you My joy, My satisfaction, My pleasure in you and about you. It is all yours, Child - claim it! You have denied yourself that for far too long. You are not just redeemed, reclaimed, and rescued; you are also well beloved inside and out, beautiful in My sight,

inside and out. Hear the cry of My heart to you, '*I am well pleased with you!*'

June 15

You are the salt of the earth…. You are the light of the world…. Matthew 5:13-14

Lonely. My children are lonely. They cry out for want of Me. Often they do not even know that it is I that they want, the touch of My hand, the promise of My grace, the forgiveness of My sacrifice, the limitless love of My heart. But there is no other - no thing and no person - that can fill the great cavern of their need but Me. You Child, you know Me. You know My touch, My grace, My forgiveness, My love. Do not hoard that like a miser would hoard the wealth that he thought might not come again. There is more than enough of Me to go around. Indeed, the more you share with others, the more of Me you will experience for yourself. Do you remember, Child, when **you** were lonely? When you went to bed with nothing but sorrow and hopelessness filling your heart? Have you forgotten who **you** were before I came and rescued you from the bottomless pit of yourself? I have come not to take you out of the world but to make you salt and light to the pit dwellers still in it. Your loneliness has been assuaged. Think not that that is a gift that should be kept to yourself; all My gifts to you are for more than just you. Open your eyes, Child, that you might see the lonely that surround you and the want of those who still live outside of My embrace. Let your life and your words speak love to them, My love. Give them hope by how you live, by the certainties in Me that mark the boundaries of your life and provide safe harbor for your soul. There is no greater sacrifice that I desire than to be the hands of My love and kindness stretched forth into this still tumultuous world. Be friend. Be gifter. Be truth teller. Be My vessel.

June 16

Praise be to the Lord, to God our Savior, who daily bears our burdens. Psalm 68:19

Burdens Are Lifted At Calvary; this old song of the church is as true today as it was the day it was penned. *"Days are filled with sorrow and care, hearts are lonely and drear. Burdens are lifted at Calvary, Jesus is very near...."* Child of Mine, this world passes out trouble like a dealer of playing cards. And you are as a child, small hands trying to hold on to the fistful of cards you already have while the dealer of woes just keeps flinging the cards your way. This is a sad truth of this world and the great tragedy of those that find My sacrifice a folly. They, because of their unbelief, will look for meaning, and like one trying to grasp water in his fist, the harder he tries the quicker he is disillusioned. Without My sacrifice, this life quickly becomes a place of hopeless, mindless, meaningless repetition, devoid of charm and grace; troubles devour joy at a breakneck pace leaving its victims angry and intolerant. This should not be the path of My children; your life is the same as theirs in all aspects save one ... Me. It is I and only I that sets you apart from a life of meaningless gestures. It is in knowing that I created you, breathed life into you, save you, rescue you, call you, daily knowing each thought, each situation, each encounter that you experience that gives you hope in this life. Burdens **are** lifted at Calvary because there I took your place; if you let Me, I will take your unmanageable fistful of troubles, and you, unburdened, may go out and play. Be not shocked at My words, for in truth it is your unburdened self that attracts this woe-laden world and begs the question ... HOW!? Come, I have a spot for you at the foot of My cross; unburden yourself.

June 17

Now that we have actually received this amazing friendship with God, we are no longer content to simply say it in plodding prose. We sing and shout our praises to God through Jesus, the Messiah! Romans 5:11 (MSG)

Friend. You are My Friend! I, the Holy God, the Maker and Sustainer of the entire universe, call you Friend! How almost unimaginable that should feel to your heart. How amazed your mind should be, for it is indeed no small thing. Its import is of great significance to you, for it breaks the bonds of all else that would frustrate your days. Sin is conquered, and shame is banished if you choose to dwell in the presence of My bond of love and sacrifice for you. There is no greater hope and no reality full of more promise than this: I am your friend and will be unwaveringly so through all that comes in your life. Break out into song, and declare the import of this friendship gift! Let your heart acknowledge that God your Maker and Christ your Savior is friend of your heart! I enter into the deep places of who you are and share the dailyness of your life. My acceptance of you will never waver so spread out your mundane and your real before Me. Speak in earnest; count on My attentiveness; know My interest; feel My like of you. And let your soul quiver with joy that the best kind of friend you could ever have is indeed eager to be **your** best friend.

June 18

Finally, be strong in the Lord and in his mighty power. Put on the full armor of God so that you can take your stand against the devil's schemes. For our struggle is not against flesh and blood, but against the rulers, against the authorities, against the powers of this dark world and against the spiritual forces of evil in the heavenly realms. Ephesians 6:10-12

I have given you My armor. You know what it is: My truth, My righteousness, My peace, faith and salvation which come through Me, and My Word. All those protect you and guard your inmost parts. It is to your peril to take off any of that armor, for without it the powers of the dark world that stand against Me will overcome you. The forces of evil are busy about you, prowling even now as I speak to you. Do not be ignorant of this; hear My voice and heed My words. It is not sensationalism that I speak but truth. Your only hope this side of the New Kingdom is to be armored and shielded by Me, the Lord Most High. Take your refuge in Me. Do not consider yourself immune to such notice by the enemy, for you **are** noticed. Do not get complacent; do not take off the armor even when you lie down to sleep. He who seeks to kill, steal and destroy comes in the darkness and in the hiddenness. He sneaks up to your fences and slips in unnoticed unless you are vigilant and mindful. Be aware; take heed; stand ready. Child's play is done; the war in which you are engaged is the real thing. Fear not, but do not forget My instructions and do not dare to neglect them. The battle is **not** done; relax your defenses and you will be attacked, surprised in the darkness, overcome, bloodied, and wounded deeply. Hear My warning and stand prepared, for your enemy prowls.

June 19

"Come now, let us reason together," says the Lord. Isaiah 1:18

Come, My Friend, let us put our heads together and reason this out. *'How can I reason out anything?'* you rightfully ask. *'I have no wisdom, and **You** are the Great God who **is** Wisdom.'* You are right in that, Child, for without Me you are blind and dumb and unfeeling. But know this: with Me you have all knowledge and understanding, for I have made it so. When you seek Me you will find Me, for I am the finder of the lost. Too often you hide yourself in one corner or another of your own mind and dwell there, tossing and turning your thoughts fitfully, trying to find pattern and sense, trying desperately to figure things out enough to make a wise right choice. Stop Child; you have left Me behind, and without Me there is no wisdom or rightness. I'll say it to you again: *'Come, let us reason together!'* for this is one of the roles of My Holy Spirit. You allow Me to hold your heart and to pray with you and for you with My indecipherable groanings. Allow this too; nay, **seek** this: let Me overtake your thoughts and your imaginings as you surrender them to Me. Then I can reveal **My** thoughts and **My** imaginings. Then I can help you find your way through both confusing choices and dead ends that seem to hold no path forward. Will not the God who has promised to make your paths straight also speak to you of which path to put your feet upon? Will not My counsel which brings peace to your heart also teach you what to do and guide you in all your decisions? Come in, surrender, and reason with Me.

June 20

Give ear and come to me; hear me, that your soul may live. Isaiah 55:3

My Child, My beloved, beloved Child, here I am. **Here I am!** Set aside **your** heart that you might hear Mine for you today. Come with your abandon; leave your presumptions behind. The presumptions that say, *'I'm unworthy,'* or *'I've already heard from God. I don't need to hear from Him again.'* Leave behind your tiredness. Leave behind what you already expect because I'm coming today with the unexpected. My Holy Spirit is here with you. Do you feel it - the brush of the wind, the wind of My Holy Spirit, the fire that I long to ignite in the innermost parts of your heart? I have something for **you,** so don't think that today is for someone else. Don't imagine that you're too tired or too preoccupied or too unsure to hear Me, for I have come for **you!** I ask you again: set aside your own heart that you might hear My heart, and come to Me with abandon. I will fill you and touch you and speak to you in ways that you have not yet imagined, for you are My beloved Child.

June 21

You adulterous people, don't you know that friendship with the world is hatred toward God? Anyone who chooses to be a friend of the world becomes an enemy of God. James 4:4

What will you put down that you might pick up Me? You say that you are ready and willing to be Mine, but your hands are full, and there is no room for Me. Are you willing to lay things down that your heart and soul might have room to welcome Me? Or have you grown too comfortable with what you have, the trappings of wealth, the comforts of flesh, the fullness that things of the world can bring? I only reveal Myself to those with hungry hearts, for the satisfied are not able to recognize their spirit's dissatisfaction. What are you willing to surrender, to sacrifice, in order that I might be more real to you, in order that you might fill yourself up with Me? Choose carefully, Child, for I ask you to choose today: Me or something else. What is Mine or only what is your own? What **I** see and know or only what you can see with your impaired sight and know with your incomplete knowledge? Today will not come again. Tomorrow I will ask you to choose again, but there is only one today, and who and what you make room for today will have an effect on both your own tomorrows and on the tomorrows of those whose lives you touch. Like ripples on a pond that last long after the pebble has disappeared beneath the surface, such are the results of your choices today. Lay down what you must in order to make room for Me.

June 22

And he was in the hinder part of the ship, asleep on a pillow: and they awake him, and say unto him, Master, carest thou not that we perish? And he arose, and rebuked the wind, and said unto the sea, Peace, be still. And the wind ceased, and there was a great calm. And he said unto them, Why are ye so fearful? how is it that ye have no faith? Mark 4:38-40 (KJV)

The ship is beginning to pitch and roll; if you keep your eyes on the things around you, the people, the events of this realm, you too will pitch and roll. Unable to find stable footing, your guts will churn, your equilibrium will desert you, and your heart will scream: *'Don't you care that the ship is going down?'* You, My Child, must find your sea legs. The chaos of the sea, with its angry, churning foam is still in My control; its might, though impressive to you, is still infinitely less powerful than I, and it rages only with My permission. I control the stars and planets, speak light to dawn upon the earth, set all physical laws spinning with a mere thought and a word of command. Do you really think Me impotent in the present state of this world? Because things, through your eyes, look bleak and man's selfish, willful arrogance pollutes the earth, do you feel I'm left with no choices, beaten by the arrogant, smooth-talking, demigods of this age? You know Me not, Child … all things, ALL THINGS exist and have their time only as I allow it. My plan encompasses every breathing being; I use them all with or without their consent or understanding. Rest in this knowledge; look to the hopeful horizon; it will calm the nervous seas of your heart even as turmoil rages all about you. If you turn your head around, you'll see Me resting in the stern of the boat, smiling … asking you the same question I asked My disciples 2,000 years ago, *'Why are you so fearful?'*

June 23

You, however, are not in the realm of the flesh but are in the realm of the Spirit, if indeed the Spirit of God lives in you. And if anyone does not have the Spirit of Christ, they do not belong to Christ. But if Christ is in you, then even though your body is subject to death because of sin, the Spirit gives life because of righteousness. Romans 8:9-10

Desperately lonely child, isolated from life and love and connection, your beating heart crying out, hungering for acceptance, for deep, connected, ecstatic, all-encompassing love. Yes, My Child, this hunger, this great need is the throbbing heartbeat of all mankind, today, yesterday, as far back as man and woman have walked this earth. This unquenchable thirst for connection, this drive for "oneness" has moved kingdoms, written a hundred thousand love songs, propelled mighty feats of honor and bravery, and joined countless millions in union. Tragically, this same hunger unmet has sired despots bent on punishing the world for their broken-boy hearts, written a hundred thousand works of hate, propelled heinous feats of anger, and separated countless millions in dis-union. Young, old,

Western, Eastern, married, single, politician, carpenter, teacher, criminal, Muslim, Christian, Hindu, invisible, celebrity, bully, victim, gay, straight, soccer-mom, businessman, the haves, the have-nots, the forgotten, and the unforgettable … one thing binds … the hunger for love, for connection, for "oneness." Seven billion beating hearts today desperate for deep, connected, powerful, protective … love. Who, My Child can fill such a void? None, save Me. Surrender your wanting heart to My Great Love; let Me fill your cavernous need, your endless want with My deep love and affection; connect with Me, Child, through music, written word, nature, quiet, and worship; be amazed how I calm, how I fill, how I satisfy your wanting soul. No man, no woman, no companion, no lover can still the crazy, seeking heart-need of mankind; I alone know its secrets, and I alone bring it to peace. Ask, Seek, Knock … I will answer.

June 24

Find rest, O my soul, in God alone; my hope comes from him. Psalm 62:5

'*Hope springs eternal*' the saying goes, and so true that is, especially for those who call Me both Savior and Abba. But hope pales if your heart does not stay close to Mine, for this world is still oft times a terrible and a terrifying place. Ease and wealth and comfort do not erase the terrors of the night and the worries of the day; only My peace can do that. So be careful what you put your hope in. Be cautious of laying it in the arms of something or someone that holds no promise of security in an eternal sense. Lay it not at the feet of chance or fairness or circumstance. Hope is only hopeful when it is rooted and grounded in Me and in My promises. When you truly know My love, you will have the offer of My hope. Perpetual, unchanging, undefeatable is My love for you; your hope springs forth from the eternal truth of that and nothing else.

June 25

Scorn has broken my heart and has left me helpless; I looked for sympathy, but there was none, for comforters, but I found none. Psalm 69:20

How long I have desired to bring you comfort where your pain is deep and haunting. How long I have wanted to pull you into My arms and have you sob against My shoulder. You have carried your hurt alone far too long. Even though I have periodically broken through and given you tools to empty it from the cavernous places within you where it grows, still it lives and still it builds. Hurt without acknowledgement, without apology, is a hard and heavy burden, for there is not much that can be done with it that won't damage either yourself or another. But you do ofttimes forget that My embrace is close, My arms always open and eager to gather you up and reveal My love. The story is never too old, never too many times retold, for you to fear speaking it again to Me. Come close, Child. My comfort is near. And someday all your tears will be wiped away by My hand, and there will be no more crying. Someday all wrongs will be made right. Someday you will dwell as one with the kind intentions of My husband heart of love for you.

June 26

Here I am! I stand at the door and knock. If anyone hears my voice and opens the door, I will come in and eat with him, and he with me. Revelation 3:20

I have always felt this deep love toward you. Strong or broken, mindful or sinful, My love toward you is forever constant. Your actions can pull yourself far from the place that you call home in My Kingdom light, and your sin can cause terrible havoc within your own heart, but My stance of love toward you will never change. I love you through the good times; I love you through the bad times. Your choice always is whether or not you will know that love, receive it, hold it, and let it minister to you. I sit here today with you, gazing into your eyes, knowing that you know that I can see it all, see all of you, and holding that love and forgiveness out to you in outstretched hands. Oh how beautiful My love gift is! But even wrapped, offered, and presented to you, it is still your choice what you do. Will you take it, Child? Open it and allow it to minister to you? Let it touch your deepest parts? Or will you choose to accept it but place it somewhere on a knickknack shelf in your heart, telling yourself that it is too pretty or too good for the likes of you to open? It is yours, Child, **yours**; no strings are attached, except your decision as to whether you accept My love or not. Your sinfulness is not gone, but it is covered by My love, My grace and My blood poured out for you. Blood that I shed for your present and your future, poured out to give you a future and a hope. There is nothing too big, nothing too shameful, nothing that can keep you from My cleansing love. Forgiven Child, My Father heart always runs and meets you on the roads of your returning. I grab you up in an embrace, twirl and spin and dance with you in joy that we are together, and trade the filth that you still clothe that piece of your heart with for My robe, clean and white and beautiful. Step into **My** portrait of you Child.

June 27

[L]ive as servants of God. 1 Peter 2:16

Under the shadow of My wings will be found many who do not yet know Me well but nonetheless need My protection. It is to those that I call you today. Love them even when they are not deserving of your love; love them, for so too have I loved you in your ragged and unappealing state. Serve them even when it seems too much work and too much trouble or a waste of your time that seems so precious to you; serve them, for so have I become the Servant of all even though I deserved to be known as King of all. To all those wandering wayfarers, to all those lost and lonely, to those still trapped in sins and addictions, to those who fall short of your standards of respectability and usefulness … it is precisely to those I came and for those I died. Do not think yourself above them. Be honored that I call you to ones such as these. Remember that you too were once like this, but still I eagerly invited you to shelter yourself under My wings. Banish your own pride, My beloved One, and live for Me, caught up in My ways and not your own, loving as I have demonstrated to you how to love.

June 28

"For I know the plans I have for you," declares the Lord, "plans to prosper you and not to harm you, plans to give you hope and a future." Jeremiah 29:11
My plans for you, not yours. You don't see, at least not fully yet. But you can trust, believe, and claim My promise that I know My plans for you and that they are good ones. Have I not proved Myself dependable and faithful in My love for you? Have I not guarded you, protected you, and preserved you? Can you not see My footprints scattered within all the days and the steps of your life? Would it not be somehow foolish to trust yourself instead of Me? To fear instead of believe? To assume the worst instead of My best? I never leave you, I never forsake you, and I have plans for your prosperity, your future, and your hope. Believe, Child.

June 29

The people rubbed their eyes, incredulous - and then also gave glory to God. Awestruck, they said, "We've never seen anything like that!" Luke 5:26 (MSG)
Find your amazement in Me, My Child. Turn your eyes and behold My wonder - all that I have done, My faithfulness to the generations before you and My faithfulness in your life, past, present and future. There is nothing and there is no one more worthy of your awe than Holy God. All that I am deserves your praise and adoration. And yet, you turn your heart toward others. You marvel at their power to destroy; you focus on the pain, the injustice, and the complexity of life in a fallen world. And in those imaginations you give power to the enemy of your soul; you step out from under the veil of My protection and strip yourself of the armor that

your spirit needs. You stand exposed and defenseless. Come back, Child; return your gaze to Me. Ground yourself in praises of who I am and all that I have done. Saturate yourself in the hope that I bring, for I am Mighty God and I will prevail. I am the First and the Last, as one day the whole world will recognize. Worshipful amazement is My due. Bow before what you do not understand but know to be truth. For I am the only truth and life and the only True Love that you will ever know.

June 30

Are you tired? Worn out? Burned out on religion? Come to me. Get away with me and you'll recover your life. I'll show you how to take a real rest. Walk with me and work with me - watch how I do it. Learn the unforced rhythms of grace. I won't lay anything heavy or ill-fitting on you. Keep company with me and you'll learn to live freely and lightly. Matthew 11:28-30 (MSG)

Don't look for answers; just walk with Me. Take your sad and your mad and walk with it; walk it out into the embrace of My presence. Cry out; weep your tears; stomp your feet. There is nothing in your heart or your inability to handle the hard things of life that alarms Me. Have you forgotten that I too wept tears for My friend Lazarus? That I swept tables and commerce to the floor in My anger? I know your emotions, for I created them and fashioned you in such a way that you would feel them. You so often seek understanding of situations or look to change either the circumstances or your feelings quickly, permanently. But I ask you instead to seek Me in the midst of it all. Shift your sore and recalcitrant heart so that you walk with Me close beside you. It is in that position that I can enter your moments, hold your pain and disappointment in My hands, and begin to bring good out of such frustrating feelings and situations. Change only comes through Me and with Me. There is no profit in walking alone, no value in trying to either ignore or walk away from what troubles you so deeply. Stop looking for answers and look for Me; you will find Me already beside you waiting.

July 1

He sent his servants to those who had been invited to the banquet to tell them to come, but they refused to come. Then he sent some more servants and said, "Tell those who have been invited that I have prepared my dinner: My oxen and fattened cattle have been butchered, and everything is ready. Come to the wedding banquet." But they paid no attention and went off - one to his field, another to his business.
Matthew 22:3-5

The marriage feast is prepared, and you are invited. I implore you to come, but I will not force you. Messenger upon messenger have I sent you to speak of the wedding, to lure you with words of bounty and endless feasting and celebrating. Yet you have too often turned a deaf ear and gone back to your dailyness, thinking perhaps that there was still time or that such a wedding was not as important as the next thing on your to-do list. You work hard, but too often you work wrong, focusing on the incidental while the important passes you by. Do not be deceived, My little One. Things of little importance often masquerade as things of consequence. You can only sift through all that seeks your attentions by tuning your spirit to hear My voice and seeking My words about your life. Do not go your own way until you are sure that it is **My** way. Do not make light, either by word or deed, of anything that I speak to you. I will wait; I will speak multiple times; I will send word upon word and messenger upon messenger, but I will not, indeed I cannot, wait forever. The feast will take place with you or without you. Do not make light of that which has great import to Me … and to your own soul.

July 2

Let this be written for a future generation, that a people not yet created may praise the Lord: "The Lord looked down from his sanctuary on high, from heaven he viewed the earth, to hear the groans of the prisoners and

release those condemned to death." Psalm 102:18-20

It is My compassion that saves you, My great love that releases you from your bondages. You have no power on your own; your very best strength is not enough. Your willpower is insufficient, and your pleas are useless; if it were not for Me and My interventions, there would be no hope for you. I have spoken truth to you through My prophets and My people for centuries, and that truth is yours to know and claim: I have released you from death itself; I have broken all the chains that have bound you; in My power there is nothing that can change the truth of your freedom. This is no small offering, My Child, for the footsteps of that Garden serpent Satan dog your footsteps to trip you up. He speaks half-truths in order to convince you of his self-serving lies. He ties your heart and your life in knots knowing that you will be unable to untangle the conundrums that he creates. He dresses up his prisons to trick you into thinking that they are beautiful fields of freedom and comfort. There is no recourse without Me, Child. You have neither the wisdom nor the power to set yourself straight or to keep yourself safe. But I, your very best Friend, your soul's Savior, your Tower of Strength … I have the wisdom … I have the power … and I will set you free. Rejoice My Child, for I will pursue you in your prisons even to the ends of the earth and the end of time.

July 3

I don't want Isaiah's forecast repeated all over again: Your ears are open but you don't hear a thing. Your eyes are awake but you don't see a thing. The people are blockheads! They stick their fingers in their ears so they won't have to listen; They screw their eyes shut so they won't have to look, so they won't have to deal with me face-to-face and let me heal them.   Matthew 13:14-15 (MSG)

Foolish child you are ofttimes.   Adolescent in your self-righteous, self-centered ways, you cut off your own nose to spite your face.   Why do you insist on acting as though you don't even need Me? Turning your head away, averting your gaze, acting as if I can't see you if you refuse to look at Me? Why would you persist in not listening when you know that I not only know what is best for you, I love you more than you can ever really conceive is possible. I hold your healing in My hands. I hold your health in My hands, body, soul, mind and spirit. I hold the hope for relational wholeness instead of disaster. Why then do you turn your back and walk away from well-being rather than toward it? Unstuff your ears; open your eyes and see. Listen as I speak; your Redeemer comes with healing.

July 4

To Him Who ever loves us and has once [for all] loosed and freed us from our sins by His own blood ....
Revelation 1:5 (AMP)

Your sin-streaked life, your sin-marred heart, is not abhorrent to Me. I have seen it, and it is no surprise to Me; long before you recognized it, I died for it and forgave it. My shed blood pours over you; miracle of miracles, it washes your sin away and turns filth and stain into pure white righteousness. My forgiveness is permanent, and the freedom I bring for you is a forever kind of freedom. No more slavery; no more servitude; no more indentured work for an unfair taskmaster. Your sins do not need to entangle you any longer, for My road runs narrow but true, and My forgiveness positions you to walk in My ways with the surefootedness of a gazelle. But, Child, for that to happen you must confess; you must relinquish your tight grasp on what feels like your entitlement - to pleasures, to indulgences, to self-centeredness. There can be no restoration or forgiveness when sin lurks behind the closed doors of your private heart and life. You are entitled to freedom, My freedom, not to sin; no matter how attractive it appears or how unavoidable it seems, sin will only enslave you and never meet your needs. Sin-streaked, sin-marred, come as you are, but come! Surrender and breath My clear air again.

July 5

Let the redeemed of the Lord tell their story - those He redeemed from the land of the foe. Psalm 107:2 (TNIV)
Lay your past down at My feet. Surrender what your heart clings to so tightly. Some of it has become nothing but rotten garbage with a stench that stinks to high heaven. Yet you have clutched it to your breast for so long that you are unaware of either its rottenness or its noxious fumes. Enough, Child; you have born shame and sadness for far too long. Your still festering wounds are not ones I have given you. Rather, I have long desired that you come to Me and crawl up in My daddy arms of love for you. Allow Me to embrace you and wipe your tears away; let Me give you a new song to sing. That song will transform the plaintive notes of your dirge into a melody that sings of My forever presence, of the light and love and joy that draws you, of a new creation that springs forth. Lay down those memories at My feet and see what I can do - see what I **will** do. Release your bitterness, your despair, and your defeat; offer them to Me as a sacrifice that is pleasing in My sight. Let Me be the keeper of all your memories and of your past.

July 6

Behold, God is my salvation, I will trust and not be afraid; "For Yah, the Lord, is my strength and song; He also has become my salvation." Isaiah 12:2 (NKJV)
Your strength; your song.... Do you know what that means, Child? Do you know what it means that your weaknesses do not matter because I am your strength? That your horror and your sadness will always be cushioned by the songs that I sing over you? Salvation. Strength. Song. What else is needful? In these promises I have wrapped up all you need into a bundle and offered it to you with open hand and heart. There is nothing left to fear if you trust Me; no terror by night or day will torment you if only you believe. I, your Lord, your Yahweh, your Adonai, your strong, holy, faithful,

powerful One is the one who also sings over you with great love and father heart affection.

July 7

You are all children of the light and children of the day. We do not belong to the night or to the darkness. So then, let us not be like others, who are asleep, but let us be awake and sober. For those who sleep, sleep at night, and those who get drunk, get drunk at night. But since we belong to the day, let us be sober, putting on faith and love as a breastplate, and the hope of salvation as a helmet. For God did not appoint us to suffer wrath but to receive salvation through our Lord Jesus Christ. He died for us so that, whether we are awake or asleep, we may live together with him. Therefore encourage one another and build each other up, just as in fact you are doing. 1 Thessalonians 5:5-11

Gird your loins; ready yourself for battle, for the fray is not in some distant land but comes nigh to your doorstep. In truth I tell you that a man's enemies will be those of his own house, those along his own street, those with whom he hangs his cloak where he works. Be wise as a serpent My Child, yet gentle as a dove. I said gird yourself, not "arm" yourself. Violence begets violence, and as much as it lies within your power, you are called to be peacemakers. This is the way the world must bend; Satan's time is short, and he hones his people emboldening them with self-righteous arrogance, grooming them in narcissism, fitting them for their role in passing down judgments in the name of humanity while ignoring their own cruelty toward humanity. Be not moved … BE NOT MOVED, for such have walked this earth since the beginning. Fear not the hate mongers, for throughout the ages they live and breathe and spout their trifles. Some gain wisdom in their journey; they repent and are among the most grateful of Mine. Most do not; they stammer and squeal, and belch their bravado until their breath stops within them. Be not fearful of the day in which you live, nor of the things they say. Let your words be few; remember as I stood accused, I was silent knowing all My words would be twisted and used against Me, against My beloved. I chose instead to silently speak to My Father and to hear His words of comfort and strength and assurance back to Me. A raging bull cannot be stopped by becoming a raging bull yourself; quiet yourself; still yourself; you will win some by this means; you will win none by slamming yourself into them for that is **their** game. Worry not My Child; I have overcome the world; let them sputter and spout, what matter? Truth shall, indeed truth has ALREADY prevailed; the details are just working themselves out by My Divine will.

July 8

[H]olding on to faith and a good conscience, which some have rejected and so have suffered shipwreck with regard to the faith. 1 Timothy 1:19

In all the suffering waves of life, My mercy is the lifeline that takes hold of the drowning heart. Your life, shipwrecked by pain, has bottomed out by choices made in folly, in ignorance, in abandon that have joined together, and the weight of those choices has sunk your soul to the deepest depths of regret and remorse. Your life is held by a thread, a golden thread that is strained and stretched beyond the breaking point ... yet it breaks not. My mercy holds the thread, holds your life, holds your future. Look into the face of your Savior; know Me for who I am, Giver, Sustainer, Benevolent Father. Here I stand, hand stretched forth, fingers waiting to grasp, eyes staring into yours. Will you reach forth and grasp My fingers? Will you look into My eyes of truth and abandon your self-cure, seeing it for the folly it is? My Word, My life, My sacrifice are the only truths that stand the test of time, and the only truth that has and will continue to sustain My chosen, My called-out ones. Seek Me today while I may be found, for time is short and the door closes.

July 9

What happens when you pour your heart out to Me in submission and surrender and your skies get darker and the distance between your supplication and My ears seems to grow ever further away? What happens when you are sure I have spoken and called you to something but doors close instead of opening and your heart feels ever strangled and frustrated in the face of My non-action? What happens when a promise I have made you isn't true in your life today, even when it comes straight from My Word? What happens when you think you know My heart for something but it appears that you must be wrong? What happens when you step out in faith and all you see and hear are the jeers of your watching peers making fun of you and your faith in Me? What happens when Omniscient Almighty God does not fulfill your hopes and expectations and even seems to dash them to the ground with little regard for your feelings? Can you still find Me, Child? Can you still trust Me? Can you still believe that I am for you and not against you? Can you still believe that My love for you is deeper, wider, longer, and broader than anything you can imagine and never, ever changes? Can you trust that there is more to this story of yours with Me than you can see? Can you stand and wait, firm in your truth that I will never leave or forsake you? Can you believe the preposterous notion that even this unbelievably, impossibly hard thing will bring good to both you and to My kingdom, even if you can't see even a sliver of that good right now? Will you bow your knee in surrender and then lift your head in praise despite it all, nay, because of it all? Will you dare to trust Me and take Me at My word and see what I will bring forth from such daring surrender? Will you let Me love you and make you Mine, in My ways and in My time, not yours?

"For my thoughts are not your thoughts, neither are your ways my ways," declares the Lord. Isaiah 55:8

July 10

Now then, stand still and see this great thing the Lord is about to do before your eyes! 1 Samuel 12:16

Stand still, small child, and see what I will do for you. When you have done all, prayed long, prayed hard, and relinquished yourself, it is only I who am left to do the work. Does it alarm you that you have no real power outside of Me and My power? It shouldn't dear little One, for what tragedy you might fall headlong into if you had enough power to contrive the answers to all your wishes. The same I, who loves you best and knows you better even than you know yourself, am the One with the power to do as well as the power to prevent. How sorry you would really be, My Child, if I did indeed give you everything you asked for exactly as you asked it. Trust Me to sift like wheat your desires and your dreams. Those that are Mine will grow deep and strong as you stand and await My strong right arm of victory. Those that were never really yours to ask for or to claim will blow away like the chaff in the wind that I might have room to plant and grow the dreams that are Mine for you and the desires that will satisfy both you and My Kingdom. Stand still; wait; see what I will indeed do.

July 11

No one's ever seen or heard anything like this, Never so much as imagined anything quite like it - What God has arranged for those who love him. 1 Corinthians 2:9 (MSG)

Crouch no longer in the darkness that descends; don't be overtaken by words that overwhelm you in the midst of the deepest despairs of your heart. Your mind has not yet understood, your eye has not yet seen, your ears not yet heard what it is that I have prepared for you, but My Spirit reveals it to you piece by piece. Do not be alarmed by what you do not yet know, but live and grow in the places of My revealed presence. Feel My heart for you and My Lover's touch. Turn toward My light that bombards its way into the darknesses of your world. There is none other than I. None that can save, none that can give you the true desires of your heart. Choose the One, the only One.

July 12

It wasn't so long ago that you were mired in that old stagnant life of sin. You let the world, which doesn't know the first thing about living, tell you how to live. You filled your lungs with polluted unbelief, and then exhaled disobedience. We all did it, all of us doing what we felt like doing, when we felt like doing it, all of us in the same boat. It's a wonder God didn't lose his temper and do away with the whole lot of us. Instead, immense in mercy and with an incredible love, he embraced us. He took our sin-dead lives and made us alive in Christ. He did all this on his own, with no help from us!
Ephesians 2:1-5 (MSG)

It was I who hung naked for you - exposed shamefully before all the eyes of My time. Though sinless and undeserving, I bore their unmerited hatred and scorn. I bore that for you, that your sin would need no recompense except what had already been won. There is no tit for tat because of your sin, nothing that you will get that you deserve because of your brokenness. Step boldly in freedom, proclaiming My forgiveness and My redemption. There are many who must hear, and who can hear only from another fallen one. Those who appear perfect in their faithfulness to Me cannot provide the comfort of those who know the evil intentions of the Pretender and the sinful actions of their own hearts and lives. Be My truthteller for them.

July 13

Today, please listen; don't turn a deaf ear …
Hebrews 3:15 (MSG)

Hear Me, My Child. Hear Me, for I have much to say. You have squelched My voice. You have deafened Your ears and hardened your heart and know it not. Your contentment with the things of this world, your search for ease and prosperity have made you easy pickings for the enemy of your heart. The day is coming when your inattention to My Spirit will lead to permanent spiritual deafness. I have shown Myself, revealed Myself in your days, and you have seen Me not. I have spoken to you, cautioned you, admonished you, and you have heard Me not. Today I plead with you, while your heart is softened by My presence, while your praise has made you sensitive to Me, while your fellowship in the midst of My people has cracked open the door between your ways and My ways that too often remains locked from your side ... today I plead with you to hear Me. Surrender your heart. Tear down the idols of this world that you have unknowingly raised in worship. Allow My Spirit to make you tender toward Me once again. Mine is a heart of love, full of compassion toward you; I am eager to lead you back toward My will and My ways. If you let Me, I will restore your soul.

July 14

For the Lord gives wisdom; from his mouth come knowledge and understanding. Proverbs 2:6
Mankind has been suckled on the milk of egoism; from the Garden's fall his goal, the aim of his life has been ... himself: his comfort, his satisfaction, his will, his way. Knowing this, Child, gives you the information you need as you daily walk in this world ... wise as a serpent, as you see, you acknowledge, you understand man's "bend" toward narcissism. Walk with this awareness, for without it you are exposed to many dangers. Be not deceived; open your ears; open your eyes; let My Spirit give you wisdom, for there are times I will say 'No' and your natural mind will not understand, and all your heart and eyes will see are green lights, your will closing off My warning in your wanting. Child, be not stubborn in your wanting; if you could hear what My heart hears every second of every hour of every day ... *'I knew he was not right for me, God.' 'My partner embezzled everything; he said he was a Christian; how could he ...?' 'You told me not to move God, but, it all just fell into place, and I thought ....'* The

heartbreak, Child, the years of fighting back, the loss, the pain of regret … none of it is lost in My economy, but to hear, to know when to … "not" are priceless gifts, treasures beyond all wealth. Come; seek My counsel, I who knows the true hearts of all men, I who knows what doors to open and which to not touch; I will give your heart true wisdom. You may not know why "not" this day, or this year, but one day, Child, your heart will overflow with gratitude for what I saved you from and saved you for. Be not as the stubborn mule that cannot be moved, for I desire to bring you the best of My gifts not the leftovers.

July 15

He provided redemption for his people; he ordained his covenant forever - holy and awesome is his name. Psalm 111:9

Little child, wanderer on this small patch of earth that you call your home, do not be confused by your place in My universe. It is not you who is the center of it, nor is it your earth or your sun. I, the Creator God, the Redeemer, am the universe's center. Around Me all things live and move and have their being. Through Me all things are held together. By My love, through My covenant, comes the only hope for mankind. Do not be deceived by a world that would convince you money is your all; I am your all. Do not be led astray by those who preach happiness as your ultimate goal; I am your happiness. Do not be overwhelmed by the circumstances that would lead your heart to fear and cause you to doubt that there is anything that is kind or caring that lasts; I am your compassionate Redeemer. Be small rather than huge in your own eyes that I may show Myself to you as the great and mighty covenantal God who has bought you and who seals you with the high price of My own blood, My own trustworthiness, My own love. You, Child, are held in the safety of My forever embrace, for I have redeemed you with My love.

July 16

Hear, O Lord, and answer me, for I am poor and needy. Psalm 86:1

I know your poverty and your neediness. I see all that you truly lack and all that your spirit needs. While the world around you corrals your desires and convinces you that your poverty lies in the physical realm, I see you completely and know what it is that you truly need. You were created for unity and wholeness in Me. You were designed to fulfill My purposes and to joy in bringing Me glory. Your spirit yearns for holy oneness with your righteous God. Yet your soul, your heart, mind and body, all too often waylay you with their own hungers, their own versions of neediness. You store up riches, but too often they are the wrong kind of riches. You seek comfort and abhor poverty, filling your soul with what you think is the choicest of meats only to find that your spirit still starves. You clothe yourself, and pleasure yourself, and doctor yourself, convinced that your needs have been met, unaware that you are still pitiful and poor and blind and naked. Like a mind controlled by an endless progression of TV commercials leading it to crave what it really needs not, your soul is made drunk by a steady diet of the world's intoxications. Be still, Child; be still long enough to hear Me speak to your spirit. You will know your poverty, and you will seek Me. You will feel your neediness and come to Me with your hands outstretched to receive from My bounteous storehouse.

July 17

I am my beloved's and my beloved is mine; he browses among the lilies. Song of Songs 6:3

"Castaway" … despised of all words; broken hearts, broken lives sit under the burden of this most hated of all words. Lives bought and sold, evils beyond description, lost innocence, lost hope, desperation of all kinds birthed in the aftermath of "castaway." You cannot run away from castaway; you cannot suddenly become "found"; you cannot remove the heavy burden this word cements upon your being. The truth of a parent's rejection, the inappropriate sexual invasion by a trusted relative or neighbor, the cutting assault of violent words from peers, teachers, loved-ones: these all drive the human soul out to sea finally to find itself alone, on an island of isolation. All the "haves" in the world cannot make up for this one "have-not." No thing, no treasure, no education, no social standing, no achievement, no adulation of man can restore belonging to a heart castaway. There is only one hope for the castaway ... rescue. There is only one place a heart castaway can find home, and that place is I. I come for the broken; I search for the castaway; My glory is in their deliverance; My joy is in their restoration. These castaways, these rejected, these disenfranchised, these are those I seek; these are those I rescue from their lonely quarantine. Do you see the castaway, Child, in the reflection of your own daily mirror? My Own, called already by My name, have you acknowledged your own castaway-child heart to My Spirit? Do you still feel alone, forsaken, odd, left? Oh, dear Mine ... call out to Me; send out your S.O.S.; strike the flint, and light your signal fire. I know where you are, Child, but to be rescued, to be healed of castaway, you too must acknowledge your desert island heart and call out to be saved.

July 18

But I, yes I, am the one who takes care of your sins - that's what I do. I don't keep a list of your sins.
Isaiah 43:25 (MSG)

You are My dearly beloved Child, born of My heart and imbued with My Spirit. My patient pursuit follows you through your hours, lures you in the empty minutes, and draws you to Me when fires surround you and the enemy encamps against you. Often you wear your guilt, your disease, like a hairshirt, but you need not. My every look, My every word, is filled with forgiveness and love. I want the best for you always, not the worst. My heart is not to punish you, but to draw you close. As you long for family and companions to fill your heart holes, so **I** long for you, but tenfold. Rest in the fact that I have first loved you; it is that love to which I call you.

July 19

[B]ut God did say, "You must not eat fruit from the tree that is in the middle of the garden, and you must not touch it, or you will die." "You will not surely die," the serpent said to the woman. Genesis 3:3-4

Dear heart, child of Mine, oftentimes it is not that you have not heard and do not know or remember My instructions to you, My commands for your living. No, like Eve you know and remember My words with enough exactitude to be able to follow My intents for your heart and your life, and I know that your aim is to please Me, at least with part of your being. The bigger problem in this fallen world that Eve left you is that Mine is not the only voice you hear, and My words are not the only ones that compete for your attentions. The enemy of your soul, that crafty plotter Satan, also speaks and twists My truths. He speaks lies in order to lure you into places that He knows will destroy you. He bats away My safe arm of protection that falls around your shoulders and replaces it with his own. But there is no protection in his arm, Child, for he will taunt you with the consequences of falling prey to his plans. He will provide neither comfort nor peace in the long run. He will neither rescue nor redeem you from your sin and only revel in your journey in the hard, cast off wilderness place where it will take you. Satan is here to stay and bound to live near you until I take you home, but he only has the power you cede to him. I have reclaimed you, fought and won to own you soul and spirit once again. Your ears will continue to hear his voice, but you no longer need to believe him. Your soul will continue to be tempted by the great latitude for pleasure and comfort that he seems to offer you, but you no longer need to fall prey to his plan for you. You have learned My voice; you have known My love. Each day if you listen closely in the stillness where you make room

for Me, My Holy Spirit will guide your ears to hear **My** voice
and your feet to follow **My** ways.

July 20

**My hope is in you. Save me from all my transgressions;
do not make me the scorn of fools. Psalm 39:7-8**

You have a will like iron. *'Move me if you can,'* you say. *'Change
me if You know how, for it appears that I cannot. Not really. Not with
any lasting power.'* And right you are about that, Child. You too
are caught in that vice grip of too often doing exactly what
you don't want to, no matter how hard you try not to - as
well as not being able to force yourself to do what you know
you should. Welcome to the land where flesh meets spirit.
Such a war comes as no surprise to Me; the same battle plays
out in the hearts and spirits of all My people. Remember this
though: you do not fight this battle alone, and you do not
fight it in your strength. Your relinquishment is your only
hope; your willingness to say, *'Indeed, I can **not** do this!'* is your
only recourse. It is not in might that you are strong or in
determination that your hope lies. It is I who am strong, and
I am your only true hope. Even your will cannot be budged
without My help, for your flesh will always fight your spirit.
Why do you think that I have cautioned you to guard your
heart? Why would I tell you that sometimes you must fast as
well as pray? Why would I admonish you to stand still
instead of hurling yourself headlong into the fray? I know
who you are, clay child: fragile, strong-willed even in your
surrender, too much at home in this world to yet be
completely of My world. And yet, though I will not take you
out of this world, I will walk beside you and empower you
within it.

July 21

**See, I am doing a new thing! Now it springs up; do you
not perceive it? I am making a way in the wilderness
and streams in the wasteland. Isaiah 43:19**

Reinvent; this is not a time for a speedy re-do; this is not a time for stubborn status quo; this is a time for reinvention. For a long time My church has held to a stubborn insistence of its own interpretation of My precepts; this interpretation will not influence today's people or its policies. For too long My People have scrambled onto the Christian bandwagon speaking platitudes into the crowd, screaming their strict adherence to the Law, while ignoring the rabid sin leaking from the pores of their own hearts. This should not be so, My Child. This reinvention that must take place makes you ONE with the sinner … as in your heart of hearts you know you are unable to stand before **any** crowd with raised head or fist, but only bowed knee and contrite heart recalling My daily mercy over your sin. Anger will not sway the tide of the enemy horde on the horizon, neither will your judgment. The only weapon that can dampen the battle cry of the Beast is My Love reinvented in the breasts of My own children. Love must start in My House, love that crumbles My Own's prideful hearts, that breaks their own wounded foundations and then rebuilds them with My acceptance, affection and redeeming grace, turning the acid water to sweet. The times are perilous, and I know you quake at their sight, but the thing that seems right in your eyes shall not prosper unless you lay down your hard traditions and begin to move by the breath of My Spirit. You are rudderless, appalled by the wantonness but impotent to intervene. But, Child, in the laying down of your toy weapons and your useless rants against the black tide, I shall arm you; I shall teach you My Songs of Victory; I shall make inroads into the enemy camps and assemble "Stands of Righteousness" that will rock the ungodly, shake them to their hollow cores, open their eyes of self-righteous arrogance, and melt their broken and wanton hearts for MY Name's sake and for Its own Glory! Release yourself to Me; reject the old ways, and behold a New Day shall dawn, and the "real" and the "authentic" and the "humble" of My People shall herald it!

July 22

But avoid all empty (vain, useless, idle) talk, for it will lead people into more and more ungodliness.
2 Timothy 2:16 (AMP)

Watch your words, for in many ways they steer the ship that is your heart. Talk may indeed be cheap in the world's vernacular, but it is also insidious. Before you know it, your words have boundaried your life; even if you don't know it, your words create either high vistas revealing hope and splendor or pitfalls that will trap both you and others. Choose wisely when you speak. The world would have you feel that loose lips are your right; freedom, after all, is yours to make use of. I would teach you, though, to measure your words, and I send My Holy Spirit to breathe a reminder into your listening ear that gossip harms both those who speak and those who listen, as well as the one being spoken of. Although My grace is always sufficient and I freely dispense forgiveness, you are far too liberal with yourself about those things that seem small to you in sin's economy. Gossip and backbiting are **not** small; sin they are, and sin they will always be to My people - no worse than other sins but also no less significant. Choose carefully your conversations; season your words with My salt and not the enemy's poison. Be mindful. Remember that someday you will be required to give account for every idle word. That, Child, should give you pause. **But I tell you that men will have to give account on the day of judgment for every careless word they have spoken. Matthew 12:36**

July 23

Therefore, I urge you, brothers, in view of God's mercy, to offer your bodies as living sacrifices, holy and pleasing to God - this is your spiritual act of worship.
Romans 12:1

Surrender to My holy fire. Bind yourself as an offering in My holy flames. What you think you will lose, you will in fact gain, purified, sanctified, and redeemed. What you do not offer willingly will be become your downfall and will in time be ripped from you anyway. There is freedom in the offering, My victory in the burning. The only power the enemy holds is over all that which you refuse to relinquish. What you sacrifice will be restored, encased in the 14 karat of My pure love. Trust Me in this, for My economy is not the world's. What feels like sacrifice in fact turns out to be the only way to retain anything that is of value, anything that is of Me.

July 24

I will lead the blind by ways they have not known, along unfamiliar paths I will guide them; I will turn the darkness into light before them and make the rough places smooth. These are the things I will do; I will not forsake them. Isaiah 42:16

You are not alone, My Child. My Spirit breathes in cadence with your breath; My heart beats its rhythm and causes yours to match Mine. Not one tear have you cried that I have not cried with you. Not one word have you called out to Me that I have not heard. Not one thing has happened that has escaped My attention. Where you find yourself - without companion and devoid of wisdom - that is exactly where you will most easily find Me. What you see as your weakness is really your strength, for it is in what you think you know that your trouble comes. Indeed, it is only when you admit your hopeless ignorance that My grace and truth flow in, filling your caverns of need and ministering to both you and what concerns you most. Do not be afraid, My alone One, for I am here. I dwell both within you and beside you. I never leave you alone, not for a second, and I never leave you without hope. Bury your face against My shoulder. Feel My strong arm wrapped around you. Cry your tears; bemoan your losses; weep for your inadequacies. It is into such a heart-hewn carved out place that I so eagerly come. Your desperation has made room for Me, and I will fail you not.

JULY

July 25

I love the Lord, for he heard my voice; he heard my cry for mercy. Psalm 116:1

I hear the cries of your heart. Even when they are unspoken, I hear. I have created your deep places for Mine, and so it is from within the very depths of My own creative heartbeat that I hear your longings. There **is** balm in Gilead, for it is My balm, the healing of the Great Physician. There **is** power, for it is My power, the might of the only Creator. Rather than just **you** knowing yourself, let **Me** know you. Open the floodgates of your soul to Me. Let My spring runoff fill you and overcome the flotsam of your past. What I have purified and made holy, let no one - not even you - call unclean. You are Mine, and forever it will be so. My voice echoes down the corridors of time calling for you, reaching out to you. Out of the shadows I bid you come. Stand tall before My love and My purposes for you, and cry out for Me with the voice I have given you.

July 26

Each of you should look not only to your own interests, but also to the interests of others. Philippians 2:4

It is a terrible and a holy thing to hold another's soul in your hands. And so I have called you to do with those whom you love. It is not that you are responsible for them, nor that you own either them or their singular worlds, but rather that those who live and breathe close to you are yours to cherish and protect in ways that mirror My care of you. Whether they are young or old, you have a certain responsibility - to think of them and their needs as much as you think of yourself and your own. And yes, Child, I know how impossible that sounds to you. Called to be selfless and sacrificial like your Savior I know is no small thing in this fallen, fleshly world. So stay close to Me; invite Me to your side in fellowship; surrender to My transformative power. It is the only way that you can handle the care of the souls around you with diligence and mercy.

July 27

He will call on me, and I will answer him; I will be with him in trouble, I will deliver him and honor him.
Psalm 91:15

I speak to the forlorn, to the broken hearted ... beaten ... grieving ... hopeless. I AM still the God of hope, the great I AM, that came to Earth to rescue and resolve, whose very name **Emmanuel** shouts **'GOD WITH US!'** In this broken place, turn your head and face the only One who can change the color of your sky. I am calling you, Child, calling you to Myself in this dark place that seems to have no shape or form, but hovers relentlessly over your heart. How your heart yearns to rewind the clock to a happier time or rush it forward to a place where your heart feels less broken. This cannot be, Child, and for good reason ... you would always rush ahead or rewind back, missing the blessing of ME in your present moment. I know these moments feel not blessed; in this hard place, time drags and is filled with heartache, but you will not know Me as Faithful One who **never** leaves nor forsakes if you do not know Me here. Reach out in your darkness, and you will find Me right there standing with you. Sing praises in your pain; spill your healing tears; you will find refreshment for your tired soul and a spark of joy even in the grief to carry you in your day. Neglect it not, Child, this daily meeting with Me, for like manna in the desert, you have need of a daily gathering, or your spirit growls for nourishment. I AM the bread of life, daily sustenance for your bleeding, broken self.... Lay down the distractions that only serve to draw you away from the true needs of your spirit, and drain your energy for anything that takes effort. Come, Mine; come lay your head upon My lap; I AM safety, and in My presence you will discover rest for your soul.

July 28

I know, O Lord, that a man's life is not his own; it is not for man to direct his steps. Jeremiah 10:23

In obedience is a surfeit of peace. Yours is not always to reason why; sometimes that is My role and Mine alone. This is foreign territory for you, My Child, I realize that: the doing when it has not passed through your own brain. But I call you to a life of the heart surrendered to the Spirit. Reason and logic are not gods; yet sometimes they dictate too much of your life as if they were. No one knows the spirit but the Spirit. There is caution in that, for you often fly too far afield of the Spirit with your mind and feelings. Yet there is also peace and rest to be found there, for Spirit obedience puts Me on the hook rather than you. You cannot reason your way to some kind of protection of My purposes and reputation. Do you not think Me Spirit-wise enough to take care of Myself? Once again I call you only to surrender, to a standing still, to an open spirit, and a humble heart that will wait and listen to Me. Yours is to be a life of obedience; Mine is to take care of the rest. Never forget that I can, and I will.

July 29

But he said to me, "My grace is sufficient for you, for My power is made perfect in weakness." Therefore I will boast all the more gladly about my weaknesses, so that Christ's power may rest on me. 2 Corinthian 12:9

I have created you; I have made you; I have called you by name and brought you forth from the darkness and from the floodwaters. In My hand are both your victory and your strength. Nothing else sustains you outside of My right arm of power and might. Stand still and see what I will do. Let the redeemed of the Lord bring forth praises, for you know the battles I have fought for you and won on your behalf. All that you have surrendered to Me is now My possession. I continue to mold it; I continue to mold **you**. I call you forth into your glory. I change your name, and I rewrite your life's story. You are no longer Stumbler, for I have made you Firm Walker on My Paths. You are no longer Shame, for I have made you My Pride. Be strong; be of good courage, for I have overcome the world, even the world within you. The past that frames you and the insufficiencies that rage against you all have been overcome by My blood and the power of My hand. Just be surrendered and willing; I will do the rest. Nothing else matters. My glory, My glory in you, is transformed from your shame when you release it to Me. Trust Me in this.

July 30

Do not conform any longer to the pattern of this world, but be transformed by the renewing of your mind. Romans 12:2

It's what's on the inside that matters to Me. Listen not to the voice of the world nor be caught up in its ways and priorities. What tickles the world's fancy is but rubbish to Me. The dailyness of the world would slide you like greased lightning into its mold, but that mold is not of My design. And when you fit yourself into it, there is something that is dear to Me that you lose. Measure not your worth using the world's yardsticks, for those measurements will fall far short when I stand face to face before My creation. Beauty, wealth, renown - they all spell success in worldly terms. But that success is not what I am after for you, My Child. What I hope for you, the world scoffs at. What I call wisdom, the world calls foolishness. Remember, I confound the likes of this world with My upside down agenda where the first is last, and the last is first. Such is the mold for which you were created. And remember, I see into your inmost parts where the world never ventures. It is there that I examine the intentions of your heart and mold you into My image, bit by bit.

July 31

Be alert and of sober mind. Your enemy the devil prowls around like a roaring lion looking for someone to devour. Resist him, standing firm in the faith, because you know that the family of believers throughout the world is undergoing the same kind of sufferings. And the God of all grace, who called you to his eternal glory in Christ, after you have suffered a little while, will

himself restore you and make you strong, firm and steadfast. To him be the power for ever and ever. Amen. 1 Peter 5:8-11

Your enemy is sold out to his Master; he thinks not of his own safety; he thinks not of the consequences of his actions; half deranged from eons of untruths and cruelty, your enemy stalks you without mercy. I know this sounds harsh, Dear One, but as a parent lays out the truth to a teen regarding the ultimate dangerous realities of driving a car, so I lay out the truths of the ultimate dangerous realities of having an eternal enemy who hates you simply because I love you. Both parent and I, your loving heavenly parent, speak thusly with the hope that the truths we share will not be brushed off like a stray piece of lint, but that they will be wisely heard and prudently examined and with vigilance digested. Your enemy prowls and seeks and listens; should not you do as much? With ill intent he ceaselessly awaits opportunity to strike at you, at your loved-ones, at any ideology that places Me at its center. To live in ignorance of his maneuverings only makes you an inattentive victim. Your enemy hates you and hates anything that has the odor of freedom; your personal freedom is abhorrent to Satan. Child, have you not noticed that the moment you look to Me to rescue you from a besetting sin that there is some remarkable availability to that very sin? Do not be naïve, little One; this IS the hand of your enemy offering you a bribe with one hand and with the other an unconscious message that slickly intimates: *'See, this temptation is impossible to avoid, and even if you avoid it this time, look how quickly another opportunity avails itself; you might as well not resist; might as well enjoy what you can. Because, as you can see, your "God" offers you nothing but difficulty and suffering.'* If you, Child, are not privy to the machinations of your enemy, you will succumb, grabbing for the immediate relief of sin as you take another step toward consequences I know your soul hates. Find Me in some quiet time; come to Me in the morning, and sit at My feet, and learn of Me. I will school you in wisdom and teach your hands to war. The pleasures of this world are fleeting, and they come with a price tag that you cannot afford; My pleasures are eternal, and I have paid the price for you to own them. With humility and transparency come to Me; your enemy prowls, but he makes not one motion that is undetected by Me; he breathes not one word of temptation that I do not hear; he offers you not one counterfeit pleasure that My pleasures do not trump. Look about you, Child; be vigilant; be wise; be prepared; be informed about your assailant, and be intimately acquainted with your Rescuer.

August 1

I have told you these things, so that in me you may have peace. In this world you will have trouble. But take heart! I have overcome the world. John 16:33
Yours is a life full of great sadness. From one end of the earth to the other the great master of torment stomps his feet, breathes his lies, and causes anguish in the hearts of all My created. Think not that you will somehow be exempt from his tortures because you love Me, because you are Mine, because I love you. There are no exemptions. This side of heaven there are no passes to escape the effects of the world's tormenter. His evil intents color the whole world; his voice of influence goes underground and appears in the most unlikely of places and peoples. Great sadness, although not your lot in life, will touch both your life and your heart. Tragedy, loss, corruption, pain, poverty of hand and spirit … all these My people too will encounter. There is no immunity, no escape. But know this too, Child, I have indeed overcome the world. Hope lies within the reach of your heart. Healing lies, if not right now, at least within your sight across the border of your time and place in this world. I am the Victorious One. Trust in Me; believe in Me; be made righteous in Me, and whatever the tormenter can throw your way will last but a moment, while My peace and victory will last for all eternity. Know that your great sadnesses will be replaced by even greater joys, for in My Kingdom all will be made right and the rough places will be made smooth.

Count on it, Child; believe it; wait for it. Take heart and wait for **Me**!

August 2

Keep your eyes on Jesus .... Hebrews 12:2 (MSG)

Turn toward Me. In your haste, do not too quickly pass Me by. In your pain and in your hurt and anger do not refuse to look Me in the eye. Your downfall is when you avert your gaze and your heart from Mine, for then I cannot reach you, and then all you can see are your surroundings and the relentless cacophony of your senses. But when you look at Me, meet My gaze, focus on Me, and hear the low whisperings of My heart for you, then you are protected from all else that assails you. Focused on Me you cannot be waylaid by anything else that this world dishes out. So orient your mind, your heart, your spirit, your gaze, your longings, yea even your pain, toward Me. I will not desert you. I will never turn away from you, never leave you alone with the harried racing of your heart and mind. Turn toward Me; see and feel My love for you; know My protective gaze; rest secure in My safe embrace.

August 3

And the peace of God, which transcends all understanding, will guard your hearts and your minds in Christ Jesus. Philippians 4:7

There is no real peace that isn't My peace - peace from the source of all Living Waters. In like manner, there is no real hope that isn't My hope - hope born of My promises and My faithfulness. The world will drive you crazy if you let it; focus on the things that aren't right, on the pain, on the incompleteness, and you will lose your focus on the only thing that can both save you and sustain you: Me! It is into exactly such a world that I came, My beloved One, bringing hope, bringing peace. I have not taken you out of the world, not yet, but I have infused your world with My bright light of love to bring you restoration and promises that give you glimpses of what is to come when all things are made right. As you dwell in this sad and painful world, dwell with Me, My loved One, for it is only in such dwelling that you will not lose your mind to the ravages of the brokenness around you and within you.

August 4

I have put my words in your mouth and covered you with the shadow of my hand - I who set the heavens in place, who laid the foundations of the earth, and who say to Zion, "You are my people." Isaiah 51:16
Be My echo. Be a voice that relays My cry as I thunder from the mountains, that heralds the waterfall of My love, that proclaims My words. Do not be afraid to open your mouth and let Me pour forth. Engraved on My palm, I have also infused Myself into you, into your very life's breath, your words, and even your thoughts. Give way, Child. Bow before Me. Release yourself. Surrender is not just a giving up, but a giving into - a removing of walls and fences and limits and fear that allows Me ever closer until I encompass you with Me. And then you will be Mine: Mine to use and Mine to rejoice in. Step back from yourself and let Me take up residence in your throne room. Perch at My feet, and let Me be the King of your heart. Bow your spirit breath and give way. Make My voice, make My heart, yours.

August 5

O Lord my God, I take refuge in You; save and deliver me from all who pursue me, or they will tear me like a lion and rip me to pieces with no one to rescue me.... My shield is God Most High, who saves the upright in heart. Psalm 7:1-2,10
Child of My heart, know that the battle is Mine. Even with your strength or speed or intrepidness, regardless of hearts that may hammer when you approach, you only have what I have given you. Do you think shepherd boy David defeated Goliath because of his skill or bravery? Do you think such

defeat would have occurred were he not My anointed? It is **My** strength that conquers, **My** speed that wins the race to the battlefield where enemies are overthrown, **My** intrepidness that calls out the pretender in the enemy and causes him to slink away. It is fear of Me that causes swords and shields to drop to the ground as the demons turn tail and flee. It is I who gave David the smooth stones for his slingshot and I who gave aim and strength to their path. The battle is Mine. I do not shirk, so ride on with Me. Take your place in what will be the victory line. Watch and see; give Me yourself, for like David I will use you.

August 6

As I was with Moses, so I will be with you; I will never leave you nor forsake you. Joshua 1:5
Though the way is hard and the road is long, I will never leave you nor forsake you. Though you can find neither the will nor the ability to lean in close to Me, I will never pull back from you. There is no contest here, My beloved One; I **will win**! Indeed, I have already won. The enemy will have his day, but that day is quickly drawing to an end. His sun is setting while My Son's reign is still rising in the east. You will have trials and troubles, but I beg you to remember that I have overcome the world. I will not leave you alone to face your disappointments and disasters. Even when your fleshly heart has played a role in crafting your own pain, I will not leave you alone to the consequences of a broken heart. Your pain I will take onto My already pierced body; your grief I will assuage with the light and life of My resurrection. Do not let discouragement have its way nor allow sadness a full measure in your life. Rejoice in Me always; I say it again: rejoice! Through your tears, through your pain, through your hardship, through plenty as well as deprivation, rejoice in Me. Where praises dwell, the enemy flees. Where hope paints a bright picture over darkness, Satan's hands are tied. Do not despair, for there is a future for you that you cannot yet see but that I have ordained and even now usher into existence. What you think is the end is only the beginning. What you

presume to be too hard and too painful is but the last minutes of the dark night before dawn breaks through into a New Day.

August 7

When I call you, it is neither to folly nor misfortune, for My calling on your life is to its truest form of worth and purpose. None will remain uncalled, though some will choose to not hear My call, while many others will hear and ignore it in either subtle or obvious ways. You were created by Me, and in that truth lies its twin: you were created **for** Me. My pride in you, My pleasure in you, My purpose for you should be what drive your days and your life. Yet far too often your passions rule the day, passions that are too frequently usurped by this world's fleshly king, too often poisoned by greed or selfishness or even fear and self-hatred. It is My calling, if you would call it that, to love you, and yours to respond to that love. If I take you to places and use you in ways that you had never imagined, what is that to you? Following Me is, after all, your only path to safety and comfort. If I challenge you to be and do things that seem far beyond yourself and your abilities, how excited you should be, for it is in precisely that too-hard-for-me place that My strength will overcome your impossibilities.

May God himself, the God of peace, sanctify you through and through. May your whole spirit, soul and body be kept blameless at the coming of our Lord Jesus Christ. The one who calls you is faithful and he will do it. 1 Thessalonians 5:23-24

August 8

As for me, I will always have hope; I will praise you more and more. Psalm 71:14

Child, thank Me for all the broken places, for all the places where relationship lies crumbled in dust, for all the places where disappointment and pain have brought everything to a dry, broken, barren place. Thank Me in those places, for your praise and thanksgiving I mix with the dust of your disappointments and the crumbled rock of your despair of broken things, and with it I build a new foundation for you. Sacrifice to Me praise in the hard; sacrifice to Me praise in the broken; sacrifice to Me praise in the dust, and I will mix and make a foundation of hope for your life and for the lives of those whom you love.

August 9

They will come with weeping; they will pray as I bring them back. I will lead them beside streams of water on a level path where they will not stumble, because I am Israel's father, and Ephraim is my firstborn son. Jeremiah 31:9

Feel My breath blow across your face and drift its way deep into your spirit. You are Mine, Child, surrendered, obedient, and beautiful in My sight. I ask nothing more from you than that. No fancy words. No perfect insight. No profound truths. Those are Mine to give if I choose. You have done all; now stand. Be still. I quiet your heart and calm your spirit. You are Mine, Dear One. I have drawn you close and you have come. I have asked for your new pieces, your hard pieces, and your painful pieces; you have brought them to Me and laid them at My feet. That is all that I ask. Now watch Me show up and use you. Watch My transformation, My restoration, and My training. It's Mine, Child, all Mine. Let it go. Just be My chosen, poured out vessel. Just be Mine.

August 10

"Am I not a God near at hand" - God's Decree – "and not a God far off? Can anyone hide out in a corner where I can't see him?" God's Decree. "Am I not present everywhere, whether seen or unseen?" Jeremiah 23:23-24 (MSG)

Let your walls tumble down, your great walls as well as your lesser walls. For I am the famous router of defenses, the God of the impregnable as well as the vulnerable. It is I who felled

Jericho's walls in order to make My people victorious. In like manner, it is I who will demolish **your** walls that you might be overtaken by My love for you. The defenses you have built against Me and My life for you will do you no good. You cower behind your ramparts when in fact your safety comes only as you move past your walls and into My presence. Do not hide from Me, My beloved Child. Your past, your painful circumstances, your fear of the future lead you to somehow protect yourself and hide away. But lo, I implore you to come out from your hiding places and find the real truth of My great love for you. My hands will tear down the walls that remain, the ones that bind you to your fears and your misgivings, for I would have you learn to know Me as friend, not foe - as intimate one, not stranger.

August 11

Wake up, North Wind, get moving, South Wind! Breathe on my garden, fill the air with spice fragrance. Oh, let my lover enter his garden! Yes, let him eat the fine, ripe fruits. Song of Songs 4:16 (MSG)
I'm not looking for good girls; I'm looking for **My** girls. I'm looking for the untamed. I'm looking for My Lionesses willing to move and run with the Wild wind of My Holy Spirit. Stop trying to be good girls, pressing and shoving your "self" into a girdle of restrained "you," thinking tamed is more acceptable. I have given you the personality that you have for a reason and a purpose. I challenge you today to be the woman I created you to be, to reject the mold never meant for you. Become who **I** desire you to be; become My lionesses because that's what this world needs: not good girls … His girls.

August 12

He had compassion on them, because they were harassed and helpless, like sheep without a shepherd. Matthew 9:36

It is I who shepherds your soul. It is I, the great El Shaddai, God Almighty, who shepherds your soul. It is I, Jesus the Christ, the Emmanuel who became God with you, who shepherds your soul. It is I, the Holy Spirit, the Great Comforter, who shepherds your soul. Your heart, your mind, your emotions, your will are Mine, if you let Me have them, to carry around the way a shepherd carries his sheep. I leave the 99, to go find **you**, to uncover your very soul, your needs, your feelings, your hurts, your woes, the things that debilitate you, the things that hold you and chain you and make you captive to the enemy of your heart. It is I who would shepherd your soul. I cry out to you, My Child, *'Come! Come today; come now. Come to My altar; come to My communion table. Come to My love; come to My grace. Come to My shepherding heart; come!'* And if you can't readily come, allow Me to take the crook of My staff and move you, draw you close, and pull you away from the dangerous places where you walk. It is I who shepherds your soul: God Almighty, Jesus Emmanuel with you, the Great Holy Spirit. And It is I who calls to **you** today - I, the Shepherd of **your** soul.

August 13

The Lord had said to Abram, "Go from your country, your people and your father's household to the land I will show you." Genesis 12:1

"That was then; this is now." If you don't let go of the "*that was then,"* you can never enjoy the "*this is now."* Every morning you awake to a new *this is now*. Every day you awake to forgiveness, for condemnation was then, and grace is now. For you who live with daily pain, today might be the day that, *that was then, and this is now!* You that don't have a job … expect … because today you may find that, *that was then, this is now!* I am a God who lives in the *this is now*. In your daily sin, in your daily struggles, you can always know and say, *'That was then and this is now!'* Child, don't focus on the *that was then*, whether that is a former job, a former place of worship, a former place of pain. Wake up this morning and embrace the *this is now!* because **that** is where you'll find Me.

August 14

Keep me from deceitful ways; be gracious to me through your law. I have chosen the way of truth; I have set my heart on your laws. I hold fast to your statutes, O Lord; do not let me be put to shame. I run in the path of your commands, for you have set my heart free.
Psalm 119:29-32

Restraint. It is what I call you to and what I intend for you in the fleshly, fallen areas of life. It is what will protect you - from yourself and from the enemy of your heart. Restraint: stopping to think and seeking Me before acting. Subduing your impulses with the promises and the protection that come from My Word. Restraint: looking to the power of My Holy Spirit to moderate your extremes as well as your addictions. Yet this kind of restraint is antithetical to the clawing, craving, mad carousel of this world. Faster, harder, more furiously is the cry that fuels this land's machinations. Only My Spirit can give you a different power, a different perspective. Only through Me can you find restraint; only by listening hard for My voice will you even hear My truths; only by My strength can you hold fast to My ways.

August 15

God has said, "Never will I leave you; never will I forsake you." Hebrews 13:5

Remember the words in the movie *Field of Dreams?* "If you build it they will come." I am like that My dear Child, for I have built this Abba daddy place of rest and comfort, and I beg you to come! If you listen, I will speak. If you turn toward Me, I will be there. If you look, you will see Me. There is no other that you can count on for any of that - not all the time. Friends will fail you. Time will constrain both their lives and yours, and they will not always be there; they will not always listen; they will not always look and see you when you fall or when you rejoice. Family will move to distant places, and their caring and attention will be siphoned between the here and the there in ways that often seem insufficient. Even with the most well-intentioned for-better-or-for-worse marriages, thoughts and feelings will slip between the cracks of daily living. Love between people with flesh and bones will never be enough. Rejoice, My beloved Child, that it will never be so with Me. I will **always** be with you. I will **never** leave or forsake you. My strong arms will forever hold you. You will always find Me in My Word and in My words spoken quietly to the depths of your heart. There is nothing about Me that is not quite enough. Never will I be too far away. Never will I be too busy. Never will I turn My back in frustration, or disgust, or fatigue. Will you take Me at My word? Will you believe My promises? Will you come? Will you stay?

August 16

[A]fter Pharaoh released the people, God didn't lead them by the road through the land of the Philistines, which was the shortest route .... God led the people on the wilderness road, looping around to the Red Sea. Exodus 13:17-18 (MSG)

You Child, who stands there hopeless, who can hardly find a voice to praise Me or the heart to trust Me, you Child, listen! For I tell you today that you cannot go where you need to go nor can you be who need to be without walking through where you are right now. It is not without My hand that you walk; it is not without My sight and My providence. I see you Child; I planted you there. I will bring you forth; I will bring you out. Do not lose hope, for in order for you to be who I call you to be, in order for you to do what I call you do, and in order for you to go where I call you to go, you must pass through where you are right now. Jobless, relationship-less, full of disease, full of despair, hopeless, a life full of tragedy ... whatever it is Child, I see you. I see **you**, and I give you My word right now, there is no place where you can be where I cannot see. There is no place where you can be that I am not. I have brought you there; I will bring you forth. Forty years I walked with My children in the wilderness and I brought them out. Think not that I will not walk with you, for a day, for a night, for a month, for a year, however long it takes for Me to bring you where you need to be and make of you what I need you to be. Rejoice in Me, Child, for that is My word, and that is My promise to you today. Lift your voice; bow your knee; surrender to where I have you **now** that I might teach you and guide you and bring you forth.

August 17

I call heaven and earth as witnesses today against you, that I have set before you life and death, blessing and cursing; therefore choose life, that both you and your descendants may live; that you may love the Lord your God, that you may obey His voice, and that you may cling to Him, for He is your life and the length of your days. Deuteronomy 30:19-20 (NKJV)
Life, Child; I speak life to you. My words pour out the evidence of My sweet love for you. Do not neglect to listen and receive those daily reminders. Your life is hidden in Me, and so you will be established: planted victorious on My Holy Hill, strolling like a triumphant king surveying all that he rules. The life I give you is the one that calls you to give away your very self, to surrender claim to the goods of the present life, and exchange them for the spiritual pleasures of life eternal in Me. It is only in such sacrifice that joy is found, where living waters wash away the stench of death, where the created all bow down to worship the Creator. Choose today which you will follow, which ways will hold your heart captive and claim all the allegiances of your days: life or death. Choose the life that I speak to you. Choose Me.

August 18

He is like a tree planted by streams of water, which yields its fruit in season and whose leaf does not wither. Psalm 1:3
I give you peace in the place of turmoil and restoration where there was heartache. In the middle of a whole forest of life and feelings, I preserve for you a single tree to claim as your

own. Tend it carefully. Water it. Prune it. Sit under its shelter. Do not be alarmed when it loses its leaves, for like you its seasons come and go and growth will return again. Although it lies dormant, sap still lives in the coldest of winters waiting for the time that the winter thaw will enable it to run again. Turmoil and heartache will come, but always I will transform such winters into the springtimes of growth and the summertime harvests of peace and restoration.

August 19

"The virgin will conceive and give birth to a son, and they will call him Immanuel" (which means "God with us"). Matthew 1:23

The parallels of your life are hard to navigate; you live in a realm of doctor appointments and deadlines, difficult people and dinner plans, all the while trying to live life in the Spirit. I know, Child, that these two worlds sometimes feel as if they will **never** find a melding point, never merge into a place that feels like they are walking in unison. This is the plight of Eden lost; man and woman used to walk a life of Spirit fullness in the midst of their days, enjoying and feeling My purpose and My pleasure in each moment of their lives. When Eve and Adam chose their own path, separate from My will, they lost their moment-by-moment awareness of Me. Added upon them were the increased trials of just getting by in life, every task suddenly drenched in difficulty and sweat; every need, once just an automatic reaching out and having, became an exercise in frustration. When Eve and Adam's heads hit their resting place at night, no longer did their bodies just melt into relaxed oblivion, full of rest and wellness. Now, their bodies ached and revolted against the hardness of the ground, and the hardness of the day's labors. Sleep, even sleep, once peaceful became clouded in unrest; the darkness became a hiding place of midnight terrors. This was mankind's lot after the rebellion, and it broke My heart to see such suffering in My beloved creation. In salvation, you realign yourself to a place of pre-rebellion presence of God. You have a right to awareness of Me, of My "Self" restored to your day. This physical world may be influenced by the enemy of your peace; your bodies will still moan for release from pain; your labors will still require almost every bit of your strength. But Child now … NOW you may have My moment-by-moment presence for all your tasks, for all your struggles, for all your minutes of work and play … there I AM. Practice My Presence; reach for Me in your imagining. I sit with you in traffic; I stand in line with you; I sit with you as you talk to your spouse, your child, your boss, your doctor. You are alone … NEVER; it is only in your unawareness of Me that your soul cries '… *alone!*' '… *alone!*'

August 20

My sheep listen to My voice; I know them, and they follow me. John 10:27
It is I: I who have called you forth and I who will accompany you. Doubt that not, even as fleshly fears and difficult circumstances assail you. My purposes stand far beyond the evil connivings of this world's temporary ruler. What I have called forth in you I will enable; what I have breathed into life, I will bring to fruition. I am stronger than flesh and blood, mightier than the world's most powerful, and My ways and My will prevail. Tremble not My little grasshopper, for you go in My name and in My strength. I cover you with My cloak and lead you safely through the paths of your enemies. Lift up your gaze; in confidence, trust that I will keep you. Go forth in the power of My presence, and know that I will do My good things through you.

August 21

Jesus said, "Come off by yourselves; let's take a break and get a little rest." For there was constant coming and going. Mark 6:31 (MSG)
Quiet, Child. Enter My stillness. There you will find My voice and My presence. There you will find safety and rest. Come away for awhile and sojourn with Me. Let Me gather you close to Myself and hide you under the shadow of My

wings. You are Mine, Child, in ways that you do not yet know. Your willing obedience has positioned you for My movement. You stand at the brink, power in your steps because they are My steps and truth in your words because they are My words. Hold fast to My strong right arm, for it is your vanguard. I go before you, sweeping My enemies out of your way, preparing the path for your feet to tread, waking those who sleep, calling forth the ones who will walk beside you and the ones whose lives you will touch. Rest now. I am ready and you are Mine; that is all that is needed.

August 22

Oh, give thanks to the Lord, for He is good! For His mercy endures forever. Let the redeemed of the Lord say so, Whom He has redeemed from the hand of the enemy. Psalm 107:1-2 (NKJV)

Shout! ... so My creation can hear it. Whisper ... so My people can know Me. My Message rides on the clouds. Far above the ways of the world, it does My bidding and travels forth encompassing the globe, stretching forth its hand, reaching out to the people, My people. How odd then, you think, that I rely on you too, for you understand that I could speak like a bullhorn with a volume that rises above the crowds and all the noises of the world. But My voice is often absent as I move across creation stealthily on the clouds, the winds, and the waves; My love and power are visible for all to see but silent. For sometimes I choose to let My people be My voice, My messengers. Then I will call you forth, and you will speak with your mouth, and My words of hope and deep affection will pour forth, or My gentle, quiet words of comfort and encouragement. Those who do not yet know Me will need My various voices to pursue them and capture their soul, so do not think yourself either unworthy or unnecessary, for you are My voice. Shout then! And whisper.

August 23

Do not be anxious about anything, but in everything, by prayer and petition, with thanksgiving, present your requests to God. And the peace of God, which transcends all understanding, will guard your hearts and your minds in Christ Jesus. Philippians 4:6-7

My little Child, you've called out. You've called out, and I have heard. In some situations I have healed or brought change instantaneously. And in others, you are still waiting. But I ask you, have you bowed your knees in praise to Me? Have your lifted your heart in thanksgiving to Me? Have you recognized and acknowledged who I have been for you? Who is your Healer? Who is your Provider? Who is the One that begins to enter into situations? And if you have not seen something instantaneously happen that you have asked for, are you waiting for Me? Are you **waiting**, with your eyes lifted up, and your voice full of praise, that I might enter and begin My redemption, My healing, My gifting? Or have you blocked Me because you have let the voices of the world and the gray clouds of circumstance dim your sight of Me? Fasten your eyes upon Me, O Child. What you have asked for I have heard. And though it may come in a package that looks different than what you expect or even what you hope, I will come. I have come. I am here. I have heard. I am answering. And for those concerns that I have not answered in a snap, I will answer, in My time and in My way. Praise Me. Praise Me! For it is your praise that opens up the doors of the heavenlies. It is your thankfulness that allows Me to be God in your life. Do not block Me with your worry and do not block My Spirit with your fear and your despair. For I have come; I am coming; I **will** come!

August 24

**He ... said to the man, "Stretch out your hand."
Mark 3:5**

Stretch out your hand, Child, for this gesture will serve many purposes. Your outstretched hand will allow Me to clasp it in

My own, to send a message of cherishing love like a siren call to your heart. Your stretched out hand, Dear One, is also a gesture of surrender, of reaching out, of acknowledging My presence and My purposes for you. Stretch out your hand little grown One, and in it find that I have filled it with My bounty, My gifts of wisdom, and My skills and talents that I have bequeathed to you to sow into My creation and to bless My creatures. Do not hold yourself so tightly unto yourself that you cannot pour yourself out. Do not withdraw thinking that alone will be easier or more satisfying. All that I ask of you is a stretching, a reaching, an offering. So stretch out your hand My Dear One, and see what I can do; see how I can use such simple willingness.

August 25

And that means killing off everything connected with that way of death: sexual promiscuity, impurity, lust, doing whatever you feel like whenever you feel like it, and grabbing whatever attracts your fancy. That's a life shaped by things and feelings instead of by God. Colossians 3:5 (MSG)

Hunger and thirst after Me, dear Child! Draw close, that I might draw close to you. My indwelling presence is the weapon that allows nothing to be formed against you that can prosper. It is in your hunger and in your thirst that you can be satisfied. I can only fill you as completely as you allow yourself to be emptied. Fast from your idols and make room for Me! Abstain from all that ordinarily fills you that you might become hungry for Me and seek Me out to fill you. The good things in life are only good; they are not the best, not the rarest, not Me. Seek Me; seek Me first. Like the deer panting in thirst, pant after Me. Let Me fill you with the Living Bread: Myself. Let Me feed you with the Word of Life. Let Me drown you in My Living Water. Empty yourself of yourself that I might fill you to overflowing with Me.

August 26

I counsel you to buy from me gold refined in the fire, so you can become rich; and white clothes to wear, so you can cover your shameful nakedness; and salve to put on your eyes, so you can see. Revelation 3:18

You are slow to hear, Child, and slower to obey. My voice cries out in your wildernesses, but you do not hear. My counsel and My instruction try to tame your recalcitrant heart, but you do not respond. Like the Laodicean church needed My salve for their blind eyes, you need My ointments for your deaf ears. Allow Me to train you, to tune your listening to My pitch, and to teach you My language and My ways.

August 27

He reached down from on high and took hold of me; he drew me out of deep waters. He rescued me from my powerful enemy, from my foes, who were too strong for me. They confronted me in the day of my disaster, but the Lord was my support. He brought me out into a spacious place; he rescued me because he delighted in me. 2 Samuel 22:17-20

I know, Child, that your heart sits in darkness; your spirit is like a coal car parked in some dark labyrinth, deep in the bowels of shame and depression and despair. A dismal, choking, stinking place that you feel right at home in, the circumstances of your life telling you from such an early age that this place is where you belong. The weight of your daily payload makes the trip to the surface seem impossible. Your solution is to not even struggle to the open air but to stay where you are, taking what little rest you can, what little comfort you can from the cold, harsh, lonely place you call home. Even the thought of being in the fresh air, the bright sunlight, the place of people and life and laughter and conflict is so rattling to your equilibrium as to send you deeper still. I understand this Child; I know, as well as you yourself know, the reasons for this place for you. But, Child, this is not where I want you to reside; it is time for your rescue. I alone know the way to where you are. Look up; see Me in your dark place. I have found My way to you, and I will stay here with you. Like a diver vulnerable to the "bends" if he ascends too quickly to the surface, so you are as well … ascending too quickly will make you unfit for surface dwelling ultimately driving you back below. So, for now, for today, just know I am with you. In time I will ask you to look at the circumstances that brought you here, and I will empower you to see My truth in those circumstances, perhaps truth you've not considered before. But for today, and tomorrow, and perhaps for some time I just ask you to be okay with Me being here with you. This is the beginning of your rescue. I am okay with the process; I am okay that it takes time. Rest in Me, cave-dweller, I have come to your rescue, and in time, you WILL know it.

August 28
Come near to God and he will come near to you.
James 4:8

O tortured soul of Mine, long have I called to you to come close and remain beside Me. But even longer have you brushed Me aside, day after day, season after season. Even as you have known Me, even as you have claimed Me as Savior and Lord, even then have you forgotten to allow Me to penetrate the deep recesses of your heart. It is not that you do not love Me; rather your indifferences to My presence keep you from allowing Me to love you in the way that I might. Those tears that you shed? You need not shed them alone, nor feel yourself uncared for as you shed them. It is your heart that I am after. As often as it beats in a minute, nay, even more frequently than that, that is how often I reach out to you. Yet, how infrequently you are aware of My approach. How infrequently you expect Me to show up. Today, My Child, know My great love for you. It is a once in a lifetime love that will meet you at every turn and will show up in every moment of your life if you let it. It is a love that will wipe every tear you shed, bind every wound that occurs, calm every fear that arises, accompany you in every joyous song you sing, and walk beside you through every dark place. Today, know Me and My great persistent love for you in all your moments. Learn to expect Me. Practice finding Me.

August 29

You have made known to me the paths of life; you will fill me with joy in your presence. Acts 2:28

I dwell wherever there is praise; it lures Me; it calls to Me but not as one that needs to be coaxed, for it is My great desire to be drawn into your presence. As a parent when your child calls, do you not enter your child's presence? Your praise calls to Me; it cries out to Me, *'Come near; come close; I cannot bear my burden; I cannot figure out my next move; I do not know what to say, what to do, where to turn.'* When you come to Me in praise, lifting up in words or song or even in silence your love and trust of Me, I hear each tone of pain, each tendril of burden, each and every unspoken angst. You do not have to verbalize everything that binds your heart to the basement of despair, for I know full well each strained cord. Praise is your secret arsenal; it is a bequeathed gift of your salvation; it penetrates every circumstance, shatters each barrier erected by man or the enemy of your soul; it obliterates defenses that you do not even know exist and opens the doors that you did not even know were locked against you. My Child, I am not an egoist; I ask you not to praise Me because I am self-seeking; it is because I know the power it unleashes in your life, in your spirit, in your circumstances for GOOD that I implore you to respond to My plea. Let your praise come from the stillness of your soul, realizing that in your own strength ... you can do nothing, and without My intervention all could be lost. Can you with your own power, change the mind of a child gone wayward who hears you no longer? Can you plant new seeds of hope in yourself in regards to a dead marriage, a seemingly hopeless addiction? Can you create the circumstances in the life of a loved one that will cause their weakness and pain to meet My "all sufficient"? Can you wield the knife of the Great Physician and cause a healing where all is despair? You well know the answer to all these inquiries, Child, and I tell you, your praise is what injects Me into your hopeless, into your "given ups," and into your "no way outs." JESUS IS MY NAME, AND I AM THAT I AM!

August 30

I will lead you. If you set forth on paths of your own making and deciding, you run the risk that they are not **My** paths for you. Take the time to seek Me, to ask, and wait and listen to My replies. It is not the doing itself that brings Me glory; I am honored when you do My will not when you just "do." In some cases, nothing is better than something, for if something is not branded and initiated by Me, it can do more harm than good. So slow down; await **My** words and **My** timing. Seek My face; hear My heart, for you and for all of Mine.

My dear brothers, take note of this: Everyone should be quick to listen .... James 1:19

August 31

Jesus said, "... See what I've given you? Safe passage as you walk on snakes and scorpions, and protection from every assault of the Enemy. No one can put a hand on you. All the same, the great triumph is not in your authority over evil, but in God's authority over you and presence with you." Luke 10:18-20 (MSG)

Wrest power from the Enemy, your enemy. You are not putty in his hands, unless you choose to be. Satan is a prowling lion, but you serve the Lion of Judah, the King of all kings and Lord of all lords. My power rules and reigns within you, but if you do not use it you are but a fancy piece of cutting-edge equipment sitting on a showroom floor. The power that works within you is there for a reason - to excise the demons that dwell within you and within this world, to make Me visible to those around you, to show forth My light. I have given you tools for this worldly fight that you might not be subdued and overtaken. Take My Word into the battle. Clothe yourself with both My peace and My righteousness. Know that it is I who fights for you and with you. Through Me you have the power to make the strongman impotent. No longer stand there quivering in your boots as the enemy stares you down with arrogance. Lay aside both your fears and your failures, and put on My mantle. It is a mantle of power and strength. I give you armor that will not rust, a voice that will never run out of words, and a sword that will never grow dull with use. With them I call you to take back that which the enemy has stolen and to prevent him from stealing more.

September 1

Create in me a clean heart, O God, and renew a right, persevering, and steadfast spirit within me. Psalm 51:10 (AMP)

I will create in you a clean heart. I will renew a right spirit within you. For I know how much My world needs cleanliness and purity and virtue and how that must start with each of My children. I will do it, but you must ask … and you must bow. It is easier to feel clean and pure and righteous when you are safe within the walls of My sanctuary, My holy temple. But, Child, I send you out into the world, and there you must be clean and righteous in Me. Call upon Me today; bow your knee and surrender your heart. Let the Holy Spirit look inside at what you hide from even those closest to you and show you the places where you need your heart cleaned and your spirit renewed. Do not hide from Me, My Beloved. I am indeed your Bridegroom; you are My bride, and I want you pure and white and holy and righteous for your reunion with Me. The world needs you too, so speak My words back to Me, Child, right now in your heart. Say to Me, *'Create in me, O Lord, a clean heart, and renew a right spirit within me.'* And I will do it; watch and see.

September 2

Therefore he is able to save completely those who come to God through him, because he always lives to intercede for them. Hebrews 7:25

Pray with confidence, My Child, for your prayers are nothing else but words of interchange with your great and powerful God. Do not be afraid to talk with Me, for like a mother, a father, a best friend, I revel in those times of conversation that we share. Do not shrink back; do not hide either your heart or your needs. It is with love that I embrace you and meet your needs. It is with joy that I lay a banquet of good pleasures before you. I am neither stingy nor unkind; you can count on Me for every good thing. Come fellowship with Me; bare your soul; cry your tears. It is only in such interchange that you will feel My love rise to overtake you, and you will know that the Great God is also your greatest friend and most powerful ally.

September 3

**[Y]ou have known the holy Scriptures, which are able to make you wise for salvation through faith in Christ Jesus. All Scripture is God-breathed and is useful for teaching, rebuking, correcting and training in righteousness, so that the man of God may be thoroughly equipped for every good work.
2 Timothy 3:15-17**

From My place of victory and of power, I call out to you, My Child. Pick up My Word, for it a light unto your path and a lamp for your eyes. It is the power of Me risen. Pick up My Word and dust it off from wherever you have left it. Bring it forth from the recesses of your mind. Speak it, for it is My voice that speaks through you when you speak My Word. Be not timid, Child, for yes, I am indeed worthy, for I have won, I have conquered, and the foe is vanquished. My Word is your sword. It is the power I have given you to slice through darkness, to cut through lies, to bind the mouth of the enemy who would assail you and bring you down. You forget too often to use it. In it is **My** power; in it is **My** truth. Stop speaking your own truth and looking for your own power. I have given you that which has conquered death, indeed what brought Me forth from the grave! It is in your hand; it is in your mouth. Be afraid no longer, My Child; you have all the tools and all the words you will ever need to speak to bring victory forth through Me and through your life, for My glory. Speak, Child; pick up My Word and use it.

September 4

In your majesty ride forth victoriously in behalf of truth, humility and justice; let your right hand achieve awesome deeds. Psalm 45:4

I thunder in, riding on My steed. This is what I have promised at the end of this season of time as you know it: Victory! My creation reclaimed! Wrongs made right! Hurts healed! Tears dried! And all will see Me as I am and bow before Me; all will see and know Truth and submit to it. Nonetheless, Child, you do not yet sufficiently believe that I ride beside you **now** on that same great white steed of authority and majesty. My time has not yet fully come because I in My mercy have made it so, but yet power and victory are Mine. **All** is Mine. You do not travel alone and you need not travel in fear. I am your constant companion; My banner of love is over you, and My eyes always have you in My sight. My kingdom and My power stretch forth on your behalf. Do not see yourself alone, a nomad wanderer in a desert wilderness, starving and thirsty. You have My Bread of Life; you live by My Streams of Living Water. You are not alone. My power indwells in you; My majesty walks by your side. My truth is always spoken into your heart, and your victory is sure. Take heart. Take heed.

September 5

If you were to ask Me what I would say to you today, you would hear My voice of calm tell you that I love you, Child, and for this love of you I have died. I would say that I hold you in close embrace and walk beside you in all your steps, no matter how far from Me they seem to take you. I feed you at My table, counsel you with both words of encouragement and correction, direct your paths. I would tell you, if you would listen, of My exploits in others' lives that changed the course of their future, led them to safety, healed them, and that I promise to do the same for you. I would speak to you of things to come, show you visions of your own heart for Me and what you will accomplish for My Kingdom, through My power and My grace. I would clasp your hand tightly in Mine and remind you that you never walk alone. I would show you the array of heavenly armies of angels who fight for you, who guard you, and the Spirit who will keep you in perfect peace if you only allow Me access to your heart. I would speak of the Great Day that is coming swiftly when pain and disease and sorrow and suffering will be vanquished forever. I would remind you that the end of history draws nigh, and the good guys win a permanent victory. I would speak to you of all this and more, Child, if you would only draw near and listen.

The Lord is my shepherd, I shall not be in want. He makes me lie down in green pastures, he leads me beside quiet waters, he restores my soul. He guides me in paths of righteousness for his name's sake. Even though I walk through the valley of the shadow of death, I will fear no evil, for you are with me; your rod and your staff, they comfort me. You prepare a table before me in the presence of my enemies. You anoint my head with oil; my cup overflows. Surely goodness and love will follow me all the days of my life, and I will dwell in the house of the Lord forever. Psalm 23

September 6

Do not love the world or anything in the world. If anyone loves the world, the love of the Father is not in him. For everything in the world - the cravings of sinful man, the lust of his eyes and the boasting of what he has

and does - comes not from the Father but from the world. The world and its desires pass away, but the man who does the will of God lives forever.
1 John 2:15-17

Not your will be done but Mine. It is the only path to true fulfillment and real happiness. A surrendered soul leaves room for Me to fill the empty places, to come alongside you with My strength and power, as well as My love. There are too many times when you cannot hear Me because you have closed yourself off from Me, afraid of what you might hear Me say or ask of you. That trade is a poor one, for while you think you avoid hard things that I might demand and you would somehow hate, what you really miss out on is My peace, My fulfillment, and the powerful feelings of My pleasure in you. I am a good God, Child, the One who wants only the best for you. The One who lays out a banquet for you not the table scraps that you feed on with little satisfaction or joy. Trust My heart for you; its commands will lead you beside still waters; your obediences will restore your soul. I have not come to bludgeon you or torture you; I have come to set you free from the false self that you so foolishly cling to so that who I created you to be can be revealed and rebuilt. Come off the trash heap that your fleshly spirit calls home; surrender your thoughts and your days to Me, and your spirit will soar in ways you cannot yet imagine, for My will is to fulfill you and make you whole.

September 7

For this God is our God for ever and ever; he will be our guide even to the end. Psalm 48:14

The wild horses of anxiety are pulling your arms from your sockets, and your hands are bloodied from trying to hold the reins. Child, your strength is no match for these relentless stallions. I AM the only One with strength enough to bridle these wild horses. Where there is no rescue, I AM your Rescuer. Where there is no redemption, I AM your Redeemer. Where there is no hope, I AM El Roi, the Strong One who sees. Where there is darkness, I AM the Light in that darkness. Where there is turmoil and nothing to hold onto, I AM the faithful Prince of Peace. Quit trying to manage the reins; you cannot ... **you cannot.** Release the reins of this team to Me, and I, with My sinewy arms, and strong back, I will pull those reins taut. Lean into Me, Child. Rest. Sit in the chariot where you belong and relinquish the control to Me.

September 8

Praise the Lord, O my soul; all my inmost being, praise his holy name. Praise the Lord, O my soul, and forget not all his benefits - who forgives all your sins and heals all your diseases, who redeems your life from the pit and crowns you with love and compassion.
Psalm 103:1-4
I do not bludgeon you with have-tos, ought-tos, or shoulds; instead, I offer you My heart. It is up to you which voice you hear, but if you listen I will reassure you which voice is Mine. The God who would sacrifice His Son for you is a God of mercy and love, not a God intent on squeezing life's juices out of His created. I am such a God: full of great compassion and endless grace, holding My love for you of much more importance than your service for Me.

September 9

As a father has compassion on his children, so the Lord has compassion on those who fear him; for he knows how we are formed, he remembers that we are dust.
Psalm 103:13-14
From heaven I have seen, and from heaven I have come down. There is not a breath of pain or a heartbeat of suffering that I do not notice. Every tear, every joyless blink of an eye, there too am I, for My eyes have not turned My gaze from the face of suffering. Child, you must allow Me to be God, to be Lord of this your trouble too. You must trust My love, My very nature, that I am indeed the God I claim to be, the Savior who has called and who will complete what He

has begun. Look to the heavens; see the broad expanse of My I AMness. In what seems to go on forever, find a glimpse of My eternity. It is only there that peace can be found, only in the boundlessness of My grace. My mercy is not curtailed; when you see it not, it is because you know it not. You see but a vague shadow of its substance, a fleeting glimpse of its true form. Yet you must trust that like I am, it is there. I call you not to understand but to trust. Make your stance firm. Trust, for I will deliver.

September 10

The Spirit and the bride say, "Come!" And let him who hears say, "Come!" Whoever is thirsty, let him come; and whoever wishes, let him take the free gift of the water of life. Revelation 22:17

Coming into My presence is not an elaborate thing. I require neither large amounts of time nor particulars of dress or circumstance. It is just you that I seek, My beloved Child, not the outward trappings of dress up clothes nor a dressed up heart. Come as you are; My presence always awaits. There is no perfect place, nor perfect time. Take some minutes captive from the things that capture your time and attentions, and steal away long enough for the measured beat of My heart of love for you to sift through the barren and the dark places of your life and your time. If you wait for your hours to become empty, you will never find My presence. Know this My much-loved One: I am in the midst of all the messy and preoccupied of your days and moments. If you stay away until you are presentable, you will never come. Yet, I wait for you in all your sin, all your confusions, all your misgivings. None of that alarms Me nor causes Me to withdraw. There is only one way you can break My heart: by not coming at all.

September 11

I love those who love me, and those who seek me find me. Proverbs 8:17

Time to come find Me, Child. Time to quit your wondering,

your worrying, your woe counting, and focus your heart's gaze upon Me. There is power in that focus because there is power in Me. There is nothing quite like clearing your mind's ramblings and setting yourself consciously and determinedly in My presence. Each morning when you wake, your mind will go somewhere. It is yours to choose, Child. Will you let it follow its natural inclination to start listing the day's doings: your appointments, the tasks from simple to complex that you must accomplish, and all the pain that walks with you there? Or will you open up your heart, your mind, your soul, your spirit to thoughts of Me? Will you let your awareness of Me bring forth praises that will clear your day's pathways and embolden your steps with My power? Will you set your gaze toward the face of the One who loves you best and always, rather than be distracted by the ones who know you not at all? Will you give power to the hurts and fears in your life by focusing on them first? Or will you ground your day in Me, in My ways, in My love for you, and in My protection? It is your choice, Child. Choose carefully; choose consciously, for look, the day has come and something will hold your attention. Something will capture your heart. Oh how I hope it will be Me!

September 12

Let this mind be in you, which was also in Christ Jesus: Who, being in the form of God, thought it not robbery to be equal with God: But made himself of no reputation, and took upon him the form of a servant, and was made in the likeness of men. Philippians 2:5-7 (KJV)

Yes Child, My mercies truly are new every morning; with generous ladle I pour out thick scrolls of kindness and grace, deserved or not, requested or ignored; in the night watches and in every new day, I pour. This is My standard, and I ask you, Child, to follow My lead. Those in your daily life need **you** to pour out measures of mercy upon them. This world writhes in injustices, hunger, and want; it wilts alone in a crowd that ignores or torments. Those in your own home, in your own influence sigh in heartache and loneliness, needing

your mercy to help them rejoin the land of the living. It is not easy; in fact, Child, without Me this undertaking is impossible. Refuse not My daily mercies toward you; do not forgo the nourishment of My presence, the acknowledgement of My mercies in your life. For without them you become brittle and dry, useless in the ladling out of kindness and grace, forgiveness and compassion to those who so need it. Become needy to help the needy; acknowledge your own thirst of fresh mercy so that you might pour mercy on others; reflect on your sins that you might be compassionate to those trapped in its sway. From My perspective, Child, **all** are equal just as from the great height of a jet, the depths of the Grand Canyon and the heights of the Himalayas are equal. You measure yourself against the depth and height of humanity, feeling superior to one and subjacent to another; this should not be. I bent My knee in mankind's presence; I chose this posture out of My great love. Choose as I chose.

September 13

Train me, God, to walk straight; then I'll follow your true path. Put me together, one heart and mind; then, undivided, I'll worship in joyful fear. From the bottom of my heart I thank you, dear Lord; I've never kept secret what you're up to. You've always been great towards me - what love! You snatched me from the brink of disaster! ... Make a show of how much you love me so the bullies who hate me will stand there slack-jawed, As you, God, gently and powerfully put me back on my feet. Psalm 86:11-13,17 (MSG)

When you stand still, stop your anxious ways, and breathe deeply of My Spirit breath, then I can meet you in your need. It is when you rush pell-mell into action, any action at all, that you lose sight of My peaceful ways. I am a warrior for you, not just any kind of warrior but a warrior with strategy and finesse, and such I also call you to be. Settle not for the vain imaginations of your own conflicted mind. Bid your restless thoughts cease, and turn to Me. There you will find

Me waiting. All I need is your attention; the rest I can take care of without your help. I wait not for your answers, your thoughts, your solutions; I wait for you.

September 14

But cling to the Lord your God .... Joshua 23:8 (AMP)
Cling to nothing but Me. What you hold onto will determine your course, so make sure that you cling tightly only to Me. The world teaches you to find safety and confidence in all that you stockpile: possessions, position, money, even relationships that you collect like chips that can be cashed in during a future hour of need. But I say, cling to Me! Store up all your treasures in My Kingdom, for only there will anything last, and only there is there anything of power. What you grab onto that is of this fleshly world only preoccupies your mind and fills your hands so that you cannot reach out to Me. The truth is, this world is fleeting and what seems both necessary and tantalizing right now will soon pass away, be transformed, and with new eyes you will know the truths of eternal importance. Clinging to the fruits of this age will not keep you from My grace and salvation, but it will make your way in this world harder. How ironic! What you think will guard you and give you ease, you will finally see was really just mist on the ocean, a mirage in the desert. All those things that seem so necessary now will be revealed for what they are: the fleeting dreams of a blind man. I have promised you everything; come close, and cling to Me now. I will lead you into the eternity where joy beyond imagining will live in your heart forever.

September 15

And while he lingered, the men laid hold upon his hand, and upon the hand of his wife, and upon the hand of his two daughters; the Lord being merciful unto him: and they brought him forth, and set him without the city. And it came to pass, when they had brought them forth abroad, that he said, Escape for thy life; look not behind

thee, neither stay thou in all the plain; escape to the mountain, lest thou be consumed. Genesis 19:16-17 (KJV)

Come to Me, Child. I know you have made choices to dive head first into sin; still I say ... come. This dark cavern of sin is not to be your dwelling place. Come to Me, for I desire to bring you out into the light. Turn and look upon My face; see that I look not upon you with frowning eyes, and stern face, pointing My finger at your sin. But see that I look upon you with compassion, grace, and mercy for I know the weakness of your human form. I know you've lingered in sin; I know you've said things, done things that your own heart knows are wrong. I condemn you not; I ask you instead to turn, take My hand, and come out of the cavern. Focus your eyes upon My heart. I condemn you not. Worship Me, for I will bring peace to your soul, and I will launder your sins.

September 16

This is what the Lord says to you: "Do not be afraid or discouraged because of this vast army. For the battle is not yours, but God's." 2 Chronicles 20:15

The fight is not yours. Although it seems to lie solely with your eyesight, your purview, and the reach of your feeble hands, the fight is not yours. Be mindful of the circumstances and attentive to the war that rages, but do not be deceived into thinking that the outcome relies on you. It is neither your wisdom nor your eyesight, neither your strength nor your goodness, not your compassion nor your endurance. The outcome relies on none of these, and nothing of you can turn the tide either toward victory or defeat. For I saw this battle of love long, long before it was waged against you. I saw troops gathered, forces mustered; I heard the warriors' screams and the victims' cries. I saw the blood that would run, the hurt that would come, the tears that would be shed. In all the dark and desolate days and nights that have been housed in the millenniums, I saw every battle and knew each of them before even one came to be. And so I rode forth, for

I knew the battle was Mine and Mine alone to fight and win. It is My love that has conquered, for it is only First Love, Eternal Love, Complete Love that wins this battle. Nothing human is strong enough, while nothing only of heaven is human enough to alone claim the victory of fleshly hearts. God made into man, Eternal made corporate, Holy became incarnate, and your Creator became your Bride as well as your Savior. This battle I have already fought. This battle I have already won. The fight was Mine, and I happily stretched out My arms and sacrificed My Holy that I might win. Victory comes with the break of day. Keep watch through the darkest of the night hours. The fight is Mine; the victor's crown is already upon My brow, and you will live to see the day!

September 17

Be joyful in hope, patient in affliction, faithful in prayer. Romans 12:12
Calm your restless thoughts and be still. I am here to speak to you, to infuse your heart with My presence and My love, but you cannot hear unless you still the calliope that is your life and your heart. Be still and know that I am God. It is I who dwells within you, mighty to save. It is I, Jehovah Jireh, who is your Provider, I and no other. Put no other gods before Me. Be careful that you do not allow the god of hurry, the god of circumstance, or the god of the clutter of your life to overtake Me and depose Me from My rightful throne. I am Lord of your life; I am the Alpha and Omega, your beginning as well as your end. I draw near. Will you hear Me? Will you see Me? Will you bow before Me? Will you worship at My feet?

September 18

The eternal God is your refuge, and underneath are the everlasting arms. Deuteronomy 33:27
Find the joy of surrender, the bliss of letting go and falling into the arms of the One who loves you best. I have not

come into your life for harm but for good. That which appears detrimental and feels cruel will yet be processed through My heart of love and caring for you. Evil intentions will be transformed; death that attempts to end all tomorrows will be nullified. I have overcome the world, and in that overcoming I willingly bring you with Me. All your days will be wrapped either in Me or in defeat; only you can choose your fate. Let go; fall back; surrender; your obedience of thanksgiving and praise breaks the handcuffs that bind you and the fears that defeat you. If you will let Me have My way with you, you will find that My bridegroom heart only wants the best for you. I sift what seems random and choose the finest just like a lover would do when shopping for a present for his beloved. If you trust Me in this, you will find your tight-fisted grip on your precarious days give way to the soaring eagle's flight. Ride My Spirit wind currents instead of struggling and resisting. What you hold onto so tightly will only crumble before you when the day dawns. Surrender is your only safety.

September 19

For though we live in the world, we do not wage war as the world does. The weapons we fight with are not the weapons of the world. On the contrary, they have divine power to demolish strongholds. We demolish arguments and every pretension that sets itself up against the knowledge of God, and we take captive every thought to make it obedient to Christ. 2 Corinthians 10:3-5

The enemy will never give up; his voice will never still. Always he will seek to convince you of your unworthiness and your insufficiency. Like a mosquito buzzing in your ear, you will hear his relentless taunting: '*Not enough. Not enough. Never enough. What you do and who you are are not enough.*' So Child, do not be alarmed by that voice. Learn to expect its coming and its persistence. Know it for what it is, but do not claim it for what it isn't. It is not My truth for your soul. My truth comes with power and with grace. It comes with both My tutoring and My love. My truth and the words of My

Spirit's voice to you leave you not condemned but empowered. Pray for discernment and be attentive to the gift that I long to give you that will enable you to distinguish My truth from the enemy's falsehoods. Crafty, deceitful liar he is; loving Abba Father I am, My riches and grace poured out on your behalf.

September 20

I know what I'm doing. I have it all planned out - plans to take care of you, not abandon you, plans to give you the future you hope for. Jeremiah 29:11 (MSG)

Do you trust Me? Do you trust Me with your tender heart, your heart broken by the things of this world that bleed sin and loss and wrong? Do you trust My truth that a thousand days are but a day in My sight will unravel all that seems hopeless and cruel to your heart in this flesh-soaked world? Do you trust that I see and care about your tired heart, your broken heart, your hungry, disappointed heart? Do you trust My goodness? Do you trust My love? Will you look into the eyes of the love that hung on the cross, broken and bleeding for you? Can you see My goodness, My love, in even that? Can you believe that this pain, this injustice, this new piece of impossible for your life can become part of My perfect plan for you? That fleshly horror can be made into healing balm by My hand? Do you know that I too cry and bleed over all the hurt and all the sorrow and all the injustices? Do you trust that I have not given up working in the world, that I have not deserted you, not abdicated My throne, not closed My door, not gone out of the God business? Do you trust My heart for you? It beats love through the days, the years, the eons. It plans your prosperity with eternity in mind, not just tomorrow. It is willing to allow discomfort knowing that your lack will drive you closer to Me. It sees this earth and your days on it as only temporary, as preparation for your eternal reunion with Me on a new earth no longer sin-scarred and blood-soaked where My perfect love and your halting, pain-filled surrender has made you perfect too. Can you trust that I work even this thing, this whatever thing, this **all**

things, together for your good - because of My love for you?
Do you trust Me, Child?
**He knows us far better than we know ourselves, knows
our pregnant condition, and keeps us present before
God. That's why we can be so sure that every detail in
our lives of love for God is worked into something good.
Romans 8:27-28 (MSG)**

September 21

**Whom have I in heaven but you? And earth has nothing
I desire besides you. My flesh and my heart may fail, but
God is the strength of my heart and my portion forever.
Psalm 73:25-26**

From far away I have called your name, spurring you to come
near, ever nearer. I have called out to you again and again,
*'Hear Me son; hear Me daughter; It is I, the Lord your God calling out
to you.'* Through the storm I have called; in the night watches,
I have whispered My love, My purposes for you. In the
lonely days, the stressful hours, the uncertain circumstances
… I call through them all. Not one of My children escapes
My attention. On a wintery day, when ice has fallen in the
form of freezing raindrops, look at nature; each
"insignificant" branch, each tiny tendril of nature is covered
with a cloak of shining, sparkling ice. So it is with you, Child;
you are the masterpiece of My creation. In choosing to create
you, I have chosen also to inhabit you, to abide with you, to
pursue you, to comfort you, to keep you, and to encourage
you. To what degree you "own" these truths about Me in
regards to you is within your own determining. You, even in
your redeemed standing, can live your life practically void of
acknowledging My "choosings" in regards to you, walking in
and out of life's circumstances feeling alone, abandoned,
uncomforted, and unknown. Or, My One, you can fling open
your arms and your heart to My presence and begin to feel
and know My "choosings" in regard to you, feeling My care
and friendship and guidance in all that life brings to you,
growing in grace and knowledge. The knowledge of My
unrestrained commitment to you transcends human

understanding and bridges the gap between the seen and the unseen, adding depth, fullness, and wholeness to your life. The choice seems clear to Me, My Dear One; choose Me; choose to hear My wooing call; choose life ... true life, abundant life.

September 22

Summing it all up, friends, I'd say you'll do best by filling your minds and meditating on things true, noble, reputable, authentic, compelling, gracious - the best, not the worst; the beautiful, not the ugly; things to praise, not things to curse. Philippians 4:8 (MSG)
Think on these things, Child. Hear My sweet voice, My Holy Spirit voice reminding you to think on **these** things. You are My child and I am your King. The world, **My** world, but nonetheless the fallen world would have you think on so many other things that take your mind far from thoughts of My Words, your memory far from places where you have known My faithfulness, and your Spirit far from My Spirit. So think on these things, Child: My love for you, My sacrifice for you, My always and forever holding of you. There is nothing that is outside of My hand that happens to you or will ever happen to you. There is nothing in which you will not be able to find My grace and My truth, even the hardest of situations, if you hold yourself close to Me and think on **these** things. So I call you, Child, today: think on these things. As you commune with Me think on these things. As you praise and worship Me, as you read My Word, and as you go through your day, think on these things.

September 23

From the ends of the earth I call to you, I call as my heart grows faint; lead me to the rock that is higher than I. Psalm 61:2
You have lost your way, My beloved One. Your strength is gone; your hope that was thin to begin with has been washed away by the constant rainfall of life's complexities. There is

nothing tender, nor anything of strength nor certainty left to convince your heart that all will be well. You are left alone with the hard, the bruised, and the tattered of your world, and the rains have not stopped just because you have lost your umbrella. The sand shifts in the deluge and suddenly what once seemed like rock solid ground in the midst of your life and circumstances has turned into sinking sand. Oh where is your confidence, My Child? Where is the voice that you used to hear that sang of love and faith and joy that would come in the morning? Where is the light that smote its piercing blade into the darkness? Where am I? Peer around the corners of your despair O little, lost One. Raise your eyes and fear not the intimacy of Mine when you seek Me. Cry out to Me in the wilderness that has swallowed you whole, for wisdom can only be found in Me, and only through Me can courage be regained. Seek My Holy Spirit who will lead you back to My High Rock. Cling to the promises that you once knew like you knew the contours of your own hand. There and only there will you find rest for your soul and hope for your grieving heart. Though trials rise up against you like mountains on your path and though your energies wane and your heart grows faint, I will be found by you if you seek Me with your whole heart. Your rescue will come, for even now your Savior draws near.

September 24

I sought the Lord, and he answered me .... Psalm 34:4
Nothing is wasted. Hear Me again, Child: nothing is wasted. You've lived so long in this world's economy that you can hardly imagine the truth of that. Ask Me to open the eyes of your heart that you might see, in **My** Kingdom economy, nothing is wasted. Every trip to My altar, every knee bowed down, every single tear that you have shed, none of it is wasted. Your biggest sin that you're so ashamed of and that haunts you, even that; nothing is wasted. The sorrow that dwells deep in your heart and all that you grieve over: finances, losses, hopelessness, relationships, sickness; nothing, Child, is wasted. There is no garbage dump in My

Kingdom. There is no place where hopes are lost, and fears conquer everything, and things rot, for nothing perishes in My Kingdom. Today, even now, even when you don't yet know it in your head or with your eyes, know with your heart that I transform, that I remake, that I use, that I hone your sword, build your heart, and make of you what I would have you be with all the circumstances that swell around you, and all the things that feel too hard to bear. Child, none of that is wasted. Claim My promise that all things will work together for your good. Believe My heart for you and let Me give you the eyes of **My** heart that you might see that **whatever** it is, nothing is wasted.

The Lord appeared to us in the past, saying: "I have loved you with an everlasting love; I have drawn you with loving-kindness." Jeremiah 31:3

September 25

Listen to me, O Jacob, Israel, whom I have called: I am he; I am the first and I am the last. Isaiah 48:12

I AM. Such simple words … and yet, so complex, so mysterious to your fleshly heart. I created you for simplicity, for life in the easier place that knows Me with certainty and trust. My hope for you has always been that you would know the I AM even more thoroughly than you know your own heartbeat, your own face. I AM, God Almighty, risen Savior. What more need you know? What more do you need to hold onto? I AM, and because of that, you are … you. Welcome to My world, Child; welcome to My love. Your only peace and hope are found in traveling this road of truth: I. AM. Believe it. Know it. Live in it. Walk this road.

September 26

The Spirit of the Lord is on me, because he has anointed me to proclaim good news to the poor. He has sent me to proclaim freedom for the prisoners and recovery of sight for the blind, to set the oppressed free. Luke 4:18

Take your stand for freedom, for **your** freedom. Long have you been shackled to the past, shackled to habit, shackled to unhealthy ways and unhealthy words. This place of confinement, of imprisonment has been home to you; your memory of anything else is vague at best. From your earliest memories you have been bound, bound by circumstance, bound by expectations, bound by habits, bound by willfulness. Like a tired swimmer with sodden, heavy garments, you tread and sink and struggle and grab a gulp of air …. This is the life of the forever incarcerated, captive not perhaps by bars and cement, but by obsession and weakness, addiction and routine, and mostly by fear. I speak to you, prisoner of self: *'Break free';* loose the clamps on your lips, and give voice to your heart's cry for freedom. Shake off the constraints of past lying voices and past rejections, and speak with a **new voice**, **new words** that express MY LOVE and MY ACCEPTANCE of you. I embrace your whole self, the good, the bad, and the ugly. Hide none of it from Me, for none of it is a surprise to Me; none of it is shocking to Me. Imagine Me in your most secret, most hidden, camouflaged, boarded-up place, and experience My light and wind and freedom. For when you **"see"** Me there in that place, not with furrowed brow and pointing finger with a *'tsk-tsk'* on My lips, but with open hand and open face and open heart, not even Satan himself can stop the tide of freedom that will overcome **any** internment of heart and mind. Sing My praises; voice your gratitude; open your eyes to My goodness, and stubbornly grab hold of freedom's coat tails resolving to never again be held by your enemy's sway nor by your own voice of self-loathing.

September 27

By day the Lord went ahead of them in a pillar of cloud to guide them on their way and by night in a pillar of fire to give them light, so that they could travel by day or night. Exodus 13:21

I've been waiting for you out here in the dark. My Fire is burning, and you are not alone. It is Satan who would try to convince you of your lostness, your failure, your deserved solitude, and God's desertion. Shame is his game, not Mine. I play by different rules - where all can win if they choose to, where none of the rounds need to be played in the dark because I bring My light there too, and where there are always do-overs available for the asking. So do not cower where darkness lingers. Take the veil from your troubled heart and eyes, and see Me waiting for you with longing. Remember the Israelites and My provision for their nighttime wilderness wanderings. Such provision is for you as well, Child. Lift your gaze now and find Me, a beacon in the darkest of places, a search beam when all seems lost.

September 28

Let us throw off everything that hinders and the sin that so easily entangles. And let us run with perseverance the race marked out for us, fixing our eyes on Jesus, the pioneer and perfecter of faith. Hebrew 12:1-2
Seek Me while I may be found, and do not harden your heart when I call to you. On bended knee see My love for you. Like Abraham with his much loved son Isaac, it is from such a position that you see My provision for you. If Abraham had not been on his knees when he was ready to sacrifice his only son in obedience, would he have even seen the ram that I provided caught in the thicket before him? What I ask of you will not always be easy, but it will always be marked by both My goodness and My love. Do not shirk from My calling. Neither turn away. You have started on this good path; you have faithfully pursued what I have for you. If you stop now because you fear what I might ask of you, your loss will be great. How sad to quit when the best is yet to come because you can't see your victory around the next corner. Strengthen your feeble knees, and straighten your back. Seek My peace; pursue Me. Knock down every hindrance; crush all the idols that would waylay your focus. I call for your attention today, for tomorrow may be too late. Both the promise and the prize beckon you toward the finish line of your faith. Answer My call; pursue Me.

September 29

You are the light of the world. A city on a hill cannot be hidden. Neither do people light a lamp and put it under a bowl. Instead they put it on its stand, and it gives light to everyone in the house. In the same way, let your light shine before men, that they may see your good deeds and praise your Father in heaven. Matthew 5:14-16
AWAKE! Dawn has come. The night is over. Shake off your lethargy. Be done with your sleepiness. The world awaits; today it needs your wakeful energy that is born in Me. Light your candle from My Light, and live all your hours in that light. So many dwell sunk in the mire of hopelessness where darkness and fear reign. I call you to come forth, for the world needs you. ARISE! Sing the songs that are My melodies. Plant the hope that grows from My promises. Dip your feet in My Living Water, and make all your steps leave footprints of My love. The world needs the Me that is in you far, far more than you think. AWAKE! ARISE!

September 30

Jesus said unto them, Verily, verily, I say unto you, Before Abraham was, I am. John 8:58 (KJV)
Close your eyes and speak a word of gratitude to the One who is big enough to be small enough to know your every minute. I AM is My name, and before there was light and life, I AM. The complexity of this age changes not the truth of I AM; technology and tyranny change not My rule and reign. This world thinks I AM of times old and obsolete, that I AM simple and out of touch with the speed and pressures of today's world. From before the beginning of all things, I knew what this time would hold; I AM the author of all things; from the thousands of creatures man has not even laid his finite eyes on, to every breakthrough in every science that man heralds and claims as his own. I AM not an historical figure of the past; I live TODAY. See Me not as just a man confined by time and space; before there was anything ... I AM; today ... I AM; in every tomorrow ... I

AM; in the last minute of the last day ... I AM; in the unknown forever ... I AM. Man, look on your life from My perspective, a breath, a vapor ... there ... then gone. Consider the thought, created One, that you might not know all there is to know, for what has man done that I have not ordained? You think you are smart; you think you are wise; I tell you ... become as a child that you might find wisdom.

October 1

O Child, you've locked your heart against Me. You opened it to receive My love, My great, saving grace, but yet now the door of your heart stands firmly closed. Realize this, Dear One; I have poured much into you that much might flow from you. I have graced you with My gifts, given you words to speak and talents to use, not to edify **you**, but to empower you to be My voice and My hands for this time, in this place. Your heart's door has handles only on **your** side of the door. Your pride, your shame, and your lethargy all too often keep you from opening that door to My riches. Be done with all that would keep you from Me, with all that would cause you to lock your heart's door against Me. Draw back the deadbolt; unhinge the latch; bid Me enter. Take My gifts, My **good** gifts, and spread them forth, and you will find yourself refilled and refueled over and over again.
Let us not become weary in doing good. Galatians 6:9

October 2

Surrender yourself to the Lord, and wait patiently for him. Do not be preoccupied with an evildoer who succeeds in his way when he carries out his schemes. Psalm 37:7 (GW)
Surrender. Not often is the key to a joyous life able to be expressed in a single word. You hear it so often you don't even recognize its value. Like the people in My own town could not see The Glory walking among them day by day, this word rolls off the tongue and is quickly forgotten. Child, the key to **every** lock in your life is forged in this word.

Dwell with Me for a moment and think what this word may bring forth in your life, in your spirit, in your relations. Think for a time what might happen in your heart if you surrendered to Me your expectations of your spouse, your child, your boss, your friend, your church. Your expectations of others hold both you and them hostage in a vise-like grip of changelessness. Until you completely surrender to Me your expectations, no-thing can happen to change the circumstances of your relationships. Until you surrender, it is YOUR will striving to MAKE change happen. This comes from impatience and your faithless thoughts that lie, *'Jesus does not care to help Me; He is not capable of changing my circumstances.'* You know that My timing is not your timing, and your unwillingness to surrender shows only your restlessness for My hand to move. You, like a stubborn toddler, want what you want, when you want it. Wave your white flag, Child; bend your knee; relinquish your desire for attention or revenge or justification, and in My time and My way you will see My will accomplished. Your stubborn grip on expectations of others usually means your expectations of your "self" are harsh and restrictive and void of My grace and mercy .... Surrender this too Child, for it holds you in a straightjacket of judgment and intolerance toward yourself and toward your others.

October 3

A white-tailed deer drinks from the creek; I want to drink God, deep draughts of God. Psalm 42:1 (MSG)

Do not neglect meeting with Me. Do not think that I am so far away, so ethereal, so other worldly, so godly that I have no real use for the likes of you. *'Come find Me!'* I cry, for My heart is lonely for you. I am God who created man in My own image. I could have made you more like a ... mosquito or a ... worm. But no, I made you like ... **Me**! Don't you know what that means? You long for friendship, for connection, for fellowship with others, because that is what **I** desire. I did not create heaven and earth so that I would have a big space where I could stand apart from My creation. I created that entire expanse and all the things in it for the crown of My creation: you! I am lonely for you, yet you stare far off mindless of My call to you, heeding not My outstretched hand or My heart that are ever turned toward you. Rise early and meet with Me. Find Me in the minutes of your day, and talk to Me. Unburden your heart when the path gets steep and hope feels lost. In the nighttime hours, feel Me close to your side desiring the intimacy that only you can choose to allow. I always wait. Whether you too cherish time with Me, rebuff My overtures, or are just ignorant of My attentions toward you, I always hunger for your return. Your wild forays into fleshly pursuits do not cause Me to love you less. O Dear One, do not neglect meeting with Me! Here I am: nearby, and around the corner too. Raise your eyes, and you will meet My gaze. Your choice; always and forever your choice: will you treat Me like a stranger, or will you too enter the circle of the love I have for you and love Me back?

October 4

Glory in his holy name; let the hearts of those who seek the Lord rejoice. Look to the Lord and his strength; seek his face always. 1 Chronicles 16:10-11
Truth teller you are, **My** truth teller. You speak of Me and offer My light to others, but what of yourself? How often do you neglect the precepts of My ways that you are so quick to point out to others? Awake your soul, My Child; heed the truths that you know and so freely share. Sit under the fountain of My love and be refreshed. I call you to help tend My sheep, but you too are one of those sheep. Allow Me close that I might tend you as well. Think not that what your mind holds is sufficient for your heart needs, for you have need of Me. Never lose sight of your own inadequacies, for it is only with those eyes that you will see your need of Me. Come as you are, Child: thirsty, ill-clothed, tired. Feed on Me. Rest in Me. Let Me give you My garments of grace and of peace.

OCTOBER

October 5

No eye has seen, no ear has heard, no mind has conceived what God has prepared for those who love him. 1 Corinthians 2:9

I will have My way with you. Peek your head out of whatever hole you hide in, whatever pit you are stuck in; cry out however faintly and there I will be, claiming you and transforming you. When your captivities feel old, and you feel tired, know that there is no **too old**, there is no **too long** in My Kingdom vocabulary. Days and years that march by in what feels to you like an odd kind of endless forever are just a moment in My timekeeping. For I have My eye on the prize, and I will have My way in your life. A bowed knee, a surrendered heartbeat, a painful relinquishment of just one of your many idols ... even just one small sign that you will give up a piece of your flesh and give in to Me, and there I will be taking advantage of even one small crack and pouring forth My presence and My power. I mean to overtake you; I intend to subdue you. How else can I show My passion for you or My intention to win the war over your heart? This world may have its way in some of your days, and the woe it brings may seem endless, but take heart: I will have **My** way in your life, and I will bring both hope and a victory that will last forever. My promises will have the final word as grief gives way to joy and lack turns into the ease and prosperity that will mark your life in My new world. I **will** have My way, and My Day **will** come!

October 6

He was so hungry he would have eaten the corncobs in the pig slop, but no one would give him any. "That brought him to his senses. He said, 'All those farmhands working for my father sit down to three meals a day, and here I am starving to death.'"
Luke 15:16-17 (MSG)

You act as one on a deserted island, stranded, unprepared, without the tools or the company that would make this place easier. Such is life on this earth sometimes; you find yourself in these places of great need or even greater aloneness. It is mankind's bent in these times to yell and scream, to run back and forth looking for help, looking for companionship, looking for **anything** that will make this place of hardness … easier. Oh, lost One, how I wish in these times you would call out for My help, for My tools, for My company. I said I would give wisdom if it is sought … without measure even, and My provision has been also promised to you; who knows what you need better than I? My presence also is your trusted and faithful companion, yet Child, you act as if I AM the one stranded on a desert island with no means to get off, much less to find you. You beat your head bloody striving for people that do you no good and for goods that only highlight the emptiness of your spirit. In your panic you thrash about, inviting danger and misuse and chaos into your life. Can you … WILL you "**STOP**," Child? Will you give up your thin gruel for My rich presence, give up bad company for the company of My Spirit, give up busyness for peace of soul? I cannot make you do this My Beloved; I can only invite you to do so; I can only whisper in your ear, *'There is another way, a different path, a peaceful glen.'* You are responsible for deciding if you are in love with Me or in love with the drama. I can offer you excitement as you have never known, but to grasp one you must release the other.

October 7

For the Son of Man came to seek and to save what was lost. Luke 19:10

You. You there. Yes, I mean YOU! I love you; I see you; I know you. Aware of it or not, it is truth for your life. There is nothing about you that goes unnoticed. And there is nothing about you that is unclaimed by My hand of Lordship and love. Stumble not in shame; hide not in disbelief. It is you whom I love! What you cannot fathom is true. It matters not, from My perspective, how long it takes you to come to Me. Your pain and suffering, the trials along the way, the upward path, the rocks and thorns that you encounter, I am mindful of it all. I come to you in those barren, hard places. I visit My Spirit of peace and comfort upon your brow in those most difficult of times. It is not just others that I am aware of, that I watch over, that I lead through the valleys that are full of shadow and fear - it is you! YOU!

October 8

By him all things were created: things in heaven and on earth, visible and invisible, whether thrones or powers or rulers or authorities; all things were created by him and for him. He is before all things, and in him all things hold together. Colossians 1:16-17

Stop talking **about** Me and talk **to** Me. It is not enough that you dissect your thoughts and feelings with exuberance and precession. Instead you need to bring that which fills your head and your heart straight to Me, emptying yourself before My throne, pausing to feel My presence and hear My words of comfort and counsel. Consider yourself the baker taking the ingredients that I give you and making them into something of both value and beauty. But always remember the baker is not the Creator. You put things together, mix, and form them, but I must create and enable all those pieces. Flour, sugar, yeast are Mine; you only use them. Put your head together with Mine, and do not try to do anything on your own.

October 9

Come near to God and he will come near to you. Wash your hands, you sinners, and purify your hearts, you double-minded. James 4:8

I am the One who works My will and My ways within you. It is in your surrender that you find who you are, who I have created and called you to be. Your task, your role, is to submit, to lay down mind and heart and soul and spirit. Mine is to pick up what you surrender and to craft and use it. Your own work is but broken flesh. The seed you sow without Me is doomed to fail, to grow with choking weeds wrapped around it. Come forth, lay your offering before Me, and become rich in the finest of fare that I can extend to you. Know that only when you give up what you hold so tightly can I loose the storehouse vaults on your behalf. Only when you lay yourself before Me can I pick you up and use you.

October 10

But you, O God, are both tender and kind, not easily angered, immense in love, and you never, never quit. Psalm 86:15 (MSG)

Potent is My love for you. More potent than anything this world holds if you will only breathe in its powerful fragrance, and embrace the depth and breadth of its power. Love has become such an ordinary word. Both misused and overused, it substitutes for something that is altogether too lukewarm to even resemble what My feelings are toward you. Do not be tricked by this well-used verbiage. I don't love you the way you love your favorite drink *('I love milk!')* or the newest, brightest fashion (*'I just love that outfit!'*). Rather, I love you with grandeur like the majesty of the fire blaze of a setting sun. I love you with fervor, like the ferociousness of a lion's roar. I love you with completeness, from here on earth to the infinity of space that lies beyond your sight. I do not love either politely or with moderation; I love you to the depth of Myself, to the limits of My blood poured out in sacrifice for you. I love you from before the beginning of time until the endless end of the eternity that you cannot even contemplate. I love you. I **love** you. I LOVE YOU!

October 11

Thus says the Lord: "The people who survived the sword Found grace in the wilderness - Israel, when I went to give him rest." The Lord has appeared of old to me, saying: "Yes, I have loved you with an everlasting love; Therefore with lovingkindness I have drawn you." Jeremiah 31:2-3 (NKJV)

I just walked through your spirit, left it ripe and ready with the footprints of My love for you. Do you feel Me close? Draw near, for I have something of importance to teach you. Grace you see, dear Child, is not always easy grace, nor is it really ever cheap. My grace in your life cost a stiff, fleshing-ripping price. And you Dear One will also have to work to claim its power in your life. Gift it is to you; yet this hard, blood-burnished love is not always easy to spot. The Accuser spoils the true picture, warps it into a Funny House view that isn't at all amusing. My Grace doesn't mean easy or pain free; it doesn't come with a guarantee that nothing will hurt you because I love you. I don't work that way; I never intended that somehow you would think that I do. Sly serpent, the stealer of satisfaction and soul riches, would turn you against Me, teach you to say that love never allows pain and good never allows hurt or catastrophe. But that is not so, just his slow, steady, torturous lie to sway you from My safe bosom. All is grace, Child, even when it hurts, for all is claimed by Me and refashioned for the eternity that you cannot yet see. Grace and peace are your gifts from Me in full measure. Grasp them, and hold them close.

October 12

God, pick up the pieces. Put me back together again. You are my praise! Jeremiah 17:14 (MSG)
Surrender Child. Give it up. Make room; make way. When it gets messy is precisely when I enter in and am able to pick up the pieces and weave them together. Child, sometimes your good intentions get in your own way, and also get in the way of Me doing and being what I need to. Neat. Done. Finished. That may be what your flesh longs for, but those are not My ways. All of My creation lives and breathes unfinished, messy, and undone right now. Other than Satan getting the victory, that is how it must be for the present. There is no other way. It is in such ambiguity that I am found. It is in the very places of messy life that I best do My work. Look for Me there. Do not desire what is not yet meant to be. Yearn for what will come only in eternity, but

do not allow such yearning to be a stumbling block for your present.

October 13

Peace I leave with you; my peace I give you. I do not give to you as the world gives. Do not let your hearts be troubled and do not be afraid. John 14:27

The stranglehold of shame, fear, and confusion that wraps around your heart is not of Me. My way is a path of heart peace, of contentment, of daylight. Darkness is the tool of the enemy. If he can bring confusion and a loss of direction then half of his battle is already won. What you are not sure of, he will manhandle in order to point it, and you, in his direction. What you are ashamed of, he will use to taunt you, to reduce you to a sniveling criminal who locks herself up in a prison of the enemy's making. What you are afraid of, either lack or loss, will swiftly become glib words on the liar's tongue telling you that your God is neither fair nor loving and that He withholds what is your due and deprives you of His best. Hear all this for what it truly is, My Child: the inner workings of the malevolent one. I hold your life in the palm of My great and glorious hand, and I have only loving intentions toward you. Let your imperfections drive you to Me not to shame. Let your discontent urge you to seek both My face and My love for you. Let your fear lure you to shelter under the cover of My wings. And there peace and contentment will guard your heart and still the clamor of the lies of the enemy of your soul.

October 14

"For my thoughts are not your thoughts, neither are your ways my ways," declares the Lord. "As the heavens are higher than the earth, so are my ways higher than your ways and my thoughts than your thoughts." Isaiah 55:8-9

Be mindful.
Be mindful of My ways, My beloved One, for they are far

from the ways of the world. They speak unconditional love, unreasonable acceptance, unmerited favor, unfathomable blessing. If you do not focus on Me, if you get caught up in the world and how it works, unthinkingly you will attribute worldly ways to Me. You will miss My love, My care, and My gifts, for they are bestowed in a different way than the world hands out good things. And you will misunderstand difficulty and hardship, for unlike the world, My eternal love will always cushion the blows that the world hammers upon you so freely. Mine is a hand that stretches from here into eternity, Mine a love that surpasses the boundaries of your understanding. Take your eyes off Me and My heart, and you will be lost in the hard of the here and the now, missing the blessings, missing the joys, missing your future. Be mindful of My ways, My beloved One....

Be mindful.

Be mindful of My gaze upon you, for you are never unnoticed and never left alone. Take care that you do not let your heart translate My attention into condemnation. I do not look at you with eyes of impatience or frustration; like a parent with his baby, I do not punish you for falling when you are learning to walk. You will always be learning to walk this side of heaven, My beloved One; you will always be subject to sin, to mistakes, to mishearing, to fatigue. It is My gaze, if you can only see it and feel it, which will give you the strength to get up again, to try again, to hope again. It is My gaze and My love-stuck eyes that will convince you that repentance is enough and remind you that I already bore your punishment for all eternity. Be mindful of My gaze upon you, My beloved One....

Be mindful.

October 15

When my heart whispered, "Seek God," my whole being replied, "I'm seeking him!" Don't hide from me now! Psalm 27:8-9 (MSG)

What is the posture of your heart, Child? Must I **always** bang on its door to gain entry? Might you sometimes be the one who comes calling on Me instead? You take for granted My hunger for you, knowing that I call you My Beloved, My Bride. But I too wish to be desired, to be sought after, to be pursued. Does that surprise you My Child? It shouldn't. After all, you are made in **My** image, not the world's. Your heart is patterned after Mine. Your longing, your heart full of hungers, is designed to cause you to reach for Me, even as I reach for you. It is in this place of seeking that you can learn to see Me and know Me best. It is here that you can abandon yourself to Creator rather than be captured by created. Here in the seeking is where you will find and be found.

October 16

Then he said to me, "Prophesy to the breath; prophesy, son of man, and say to it, 'This is what the Sovereign Lord says: Come, breath, from the four winds and breathe into these slain, that they may live.'" So I prophesied as he commanded me, and breath entered them; they came to life and stood up on their feet - a vast army. Ezekiel 37:9-10

Truly I tell you, this IS a lost generation, weaned on chaos, broken by abandonment; they live like hell because they truly have no hope. I tell you ... they **can** be reached, and I charge you My people to reach them. But to do so will require you to abandon the traditional and embrace the Pneumatic. It's about positioning yourself to hear and to flow with My Spirit Wind; the darkness is so deep that this is the only thing that can penetrate. Know My Spirit moving and working through you; hear My still, small voice in the midst of your daily, and act upon its instruction. Open your heart to the Holy Spirit, for there **is** hope for this generation, and it lies in your hands; it lies in your heart, and it lies in opening your mind to the fresh wind I am poised to breathe upon you.

October 17

I've told you all this so that trusting me, you will be unshakable and assured, deeply at peace. In this godless world you will continue to experience difficulties. But take heart! I've conquered the world. John 16:33 (MSG)
When the world gives you a stomachache, I am your Pepto-Bismol. When anxiety intrudes and grows like a weed in your heart intent on overtaking all that flowers and produces, I am your Tranquility. When loneliness intrudes and covers your feelings with loss and lack, I am your Forever Friend. When wisdom eludes you and you don't know where to turn, I am your Counselor and the Director of your steps. There is much in life that will assail you, and rocks will be on your path to slow you down, but I will never leave nor forsake you. There is nothing that you can encounter that will either surprise or perplex Me, so take heart. I have covered **all** the bases and seen the end from the beginning, and I will stay close and see you through it all.

October 18

Give thanks to the Lord, for he is good; his love endures forever. Let Israel say: "His love endures forever." Let the house of Aaron say: "His love endures forever." Let those who fear the Lord say: "His love endures forever." In my anguish I cried to the Lord, and he answered by setting me free. Psalm 118:1-5
I stretch forth My hand and send healing and redemption into the world. It is for this that you must continually wait. Go forth in your own strength and wisdom, and you will find only failure and frustration. I am your Source, the backbone to your life and the heartbeat of your spirit. It is in your reliance on Me and your listening to Me that you find your way in your world. Keep your focus on My truth; set your gaze upon Me and upon My ways. Be not alarmed by either the floods that rise or the dark and lonely nights, for I am right by your side through it all. Wait for Me. Listen for Me.

October 19

Even though you have sung My praises and rehearsed My promises and remembered My great love for you, do you still feel like there's a hole in your heart that could sink you? A sadness that is almost too much to bear? A grief and a waiting that if you're honest make you doubt My love for you, make you wonder if I'm indifferent? Dear One, **My Dear One**, let Me retell the story of Mary and Martha when they came weeping and said, '*If you had been here, Lord, our brother would not have died.*' So I ask you, Child, do you have the same question for Me today? If I had been there something would have happened - or not happened? If I had been there, surely this circumstance would have changed? It is not lack of faith, Child, as much as it is your real truth. I see you and I feel you; I know your pain, and I see your tears and your anxiety. I see your lack of strength and the endurance that's almost ready to give out. And as I did with Mary and Martha, I weep with you. I weep with you today, for it is not yet time for you to understand, but someday you will. Until then, My son, My daughter, let Me hold you as you weep. See Me weeping with you as I draw you close, and know that in My strength, and in My power, I pitch a tent over your tears.

You've kept track of my every toss and turn through the sleepless nights, Each tear entered in your ledger, each ache written in your book. Psalm 56:8 (MSG)

October 20

When Moses came down from Mount Sinai with the two tablets of the covenant law in his hands, he was not aware that his face was radiant because he had spoken with the Lord. Exodus 34:29

You are indeed lost, Child, not because I have left you, but because you have left Me. Willfully, you choose other things over Me. Your morning rush is just that, a rush: no time to hear, no time to dwell, no time to prepare. Child, do you know what your day holds? Do you know what your next minute may involve? Do not let the daily-ness of life fool you into thinking that this day will bring no change. I threaten you not, Child; I am not shaking My fist promising calamity in the midst of your peace. But, I do admonish you; I do remind you that life, as always, does not come with any written guarantees. Your soul **needs** My presence; I **know** I am with you, Child; I do not need time with you to convince **Myself** that I am in your midst, fully present in your every moment. But YOU, My Child, do need time with Me to convince your own soul that I am with you in every moment of your day, that I KNOW what this day holds and that I have prepared a space for your soul to breathe in that knowledge. I urge you to plan Me into your morning; create some space for time with your Father; I will give you what you don't even know you need. When you walk out the door without Me, it's like walking out the door without your tools, your computer, your shoes, your very clothing. Naked and vulnerable, you enter your day without even a small sense of My attendance. Come Child, for some minutes; still yourself; put a Psalm under your belt; give Me a chance to pour into you what you need for this day; like warm sun on cooled skin, feel My presence melt over you …. Now, you are ready.

October 21

Yet I am always with you; you hold me by my right hand. Psalm 73:23

Think not that I stand in some far off dominion and watch your little goings on with indifference. No Child, I am not a watcher but a doer. Do you not know by now that it was My love for you that took Me down into your world to live and breath and dwell amongst the likes of you? Heaven could not contain Me because heaven would not be enough for Me without you. I came then and have sent My Holy Spirit after Me that you might never, ever be alone. Though the present world holds both terror and tragedy, you need never face it alone, for I am there with you. In your darkest hour I will always come to you, covering you with My presence, pitching

My tent of strength and power over your poor weak and fearful shivering form. In your moments of unbearable grief, when you can find no speck of sanity and only confusion swirls in your brain, I will be there to weep with you. It was never My intent that My holiness preclude My mercy. Is that not the very message of God made flesh in the form of a baby? Of perfect God dying for imperfect man? Of resurrection victory forever? I have come down; I am here now both around you and within you, and I will continue to walk with you in the midst of all that ails you and all that concerns you, weeping with you as you go.

October 22

But I will trust in you. Psalm 55:23 (NKJV)

Even when your day dawns darkly, I call you to trust Me to be your Light. When your resources seem to contradict the truth that I own the cattle on a thousand hills and never allow My children to beg for bread, still I tell you to trust Me to be your Provider. When all seems lost, trust Me to be your Finder. In the midst of the storm of ill health, trust Me to be your Healer, both for this world and the next. When your faithful steps take you to the edge of a cliff with no apparent safe way forward, trust Me to be the Wings that will hold you up and the Director of each of your steps. When confusion reigns in relationship and all hope seems lost, trust Me to be the Wisdom and the Counsel that will set you straight and repair that which has been broken. When the earth and all of its ways say '*No way*,' trust Me to be your Yes-sayer, your Way-maker. When all your optimism has fled, trust Me to be your eternal Hope. To everything that would distract you from My love, My light, and My peace, let Me be the "but" that will change the trajectory of your story. Trust in Me, for your sake, and for My Glory!

October 23

Don't panic. I'm with you. There's no need to fear for I'm your God. I'll give you strength. I'll help you. I'll

hold you steady, keep a firm grip on you. Isaiah 41:10 (MSG)

Look at Me, Child. Do not avert your gaze. You have nothing to fear, nothing to dread from Me. There is nothing that you can do, or neglect to do, that will make Me turn My back or withdraw My hand. Those are **your** feelings, the effect of the snake's betrayal of My truth for you in the Garden, the twisting of reality to suit his purposes. Let the fact that you have once again missed the mark lure you back to Me, not drive you from Me. I wait for you, eager to kill the fatted calf and feast and dance. Do not stay outside, hidden and reluctant. Come forth. No longer wonder if there is such a thing as too sinful or a place that is too far away from your repentance. My grace, My love, is sufficient. Taste and see My goodness. Dally no longer in the wilderness, for I await you. Come!

October 24

You hem me in - behind and before; you have laid your hand upon me.... [Y]our right hand will hold me fast. Psalm 139:5,10

Ours must be a mutual holding. It avails you not for Me to hold you up if you do not cling to Me. Check your posture, Child. Like a youngster in the midst of a tantrum while held in his parent's arms, you often arch your back, clench your teeth, and wail for release. How then is there safety for your heart when your very spirit demands its release from My embrace of you? I have always left the choice up to My created ones: to be held or not to be held. You will find peace for your soul when you lean in and cling to Me, when you wrap your arms around My neck the way a toddler does while dozing off against her father's neck. It is then that I can clasp you steadily and securely. It is then that you will learn of safety. My right hand will hold you fast when you hold onto Me.

I hold on to you for dear life, and you hold me steady as a post. Psalm 63:8 (MSG)

October 25

God, the one and only - I'll wait as long as he says. Everything I need comes from him, so why not?
Psalm 62:1 (MSG)

You come to Me empty. The Pretender would have you believe that your soul made full and your heart made content comes from who you are and what you do and how much you accumulate. The truth is, Child, it is I who bless and I who orchestrate your life into a peaceful symphony. Look around you. Name all that lures you that is not of Me. Name even those things that you strive for with vigor that is not My vigor and with longing that comes from your flesh and not your spirit. I counsel you in the way to go, but you must listen. I lead you on the paths designed for your feet, but you must follow. I set the pace, cause even the regularity of your breathing, but you must believe. The wait for My good things will be easier if you trust My unflagging heart of love for you. The voices of the Pretender will grow fainter if you draw near and listen to My voice and My counsel. Wait. Hope. Trust. Believe. I am the Dependable, Bountiful One.

October 26

As obedient children, let yourselves be pulled into a way of life shaped by God's life, a life energetic and blazing with holiness. God said, "I am holy; you be holy."
1 Peter 1:15-16 (MSG)

What do you know of My holy, earth-child? Sin-caught One, trapped in the lies and the nets of your enemies' plans for you, makes sure that you know My holy! It is My love that rescues and redeems you, but it is My holy that sets the standard that makes you know that you need Me. Oh how comfortable you are in your sins sometimes - those things that have become so much a part of you that you barely recognize them as transgressions. Come into My presence, and open your eyes to My holiness. Do life in the face of that holiness, not that fear might be your guide, but that My Spirit might kindle a sense of who I am and what I breathed

into you as I formed and made you. I will teach you of holy.
I will unsheathe My claws and roar My Aslan roar. I will
instruct you in My ways and show you the other side of My
kind and generous nature. Then you will understand that
love and holiness are not in contradiction. Together they
complete My character. Together they call to you to walk the
walk of faith in My image. Open your heart to My truth, to
this truth, and prepare to stretch to receive and be challenged
by My Holy!

October 27

**We thank you, God, we thank you - your Name is our
favorite word; your mighty works are all we talk about.
Psalm 75:1 (MSG)**
It is not just into My courts that I bid you come with
thanksgiving. A beating heart, pounding with gratitude, will
serve you well in all your days. Even if you feel there are no
big things to thank Me for, count all the small favors and
protections, all the seemingly minor gifts, and talk about
them! You claim to be Mine, but when was the last time you
were heard declaring My praises about the bounties of your
life, crying out to all who will listen that I your God am the
Great God, the Mighty God, the Amazing One? When does
My Name flow from your lips like water from a turned on
faucet? Have you nothing to thank Me for that you remain
silent? Have you other gods that you turn your attention to
instead? What **are** your favorite words after all? To whom or
what do you turn your attentions? If your thanks and
attentions flow most often to a person or to fame or wealth
or career or sport or leisure … well, Child, it is not too late to
recognize the idolatries of your heart and repent. Make **Me**
your most talked about. Respond with grateful heart to all
that I am and all that I do. Line up both your pleasures and
your miracles, and think carefully about who is responsible
for them all. Is it not I? Let your tongue, then, be loosed to
speak of Me and My good deeds.

October 28

For you created my inmost being; you knit me together in my mother's womb. I praise you because I am fearfully and wonderfully made; your works are wonderful, I know that full well. Psalm 139:13-14

Hear Me, Child? Hear Me? No, you cannot, for the hounds of hell gather in your quiet, baying and howling and snarling at the very point you come to still yourself. Your memory is short, My little One; remember not that last time you came to find Me in the stillness? These carnivores of your soul awaited you then as well, did they not? Tell Me, Mine, why do you not question their right to invade your sanctum? You hear their incessant barks, see their salivating fangs, and almost immediately you bend to their will. They howl to convince you that they are the voice of My conviction sent to chastise you as soon as you take a moment to lean in to hear My voice. Know you so little of Me that you think thusly? Sadly, you listen to their angry, condemning howls as they insist that you look at all your weakness, that you examine all the reasons your Lord would not choose to look upon you with mercy. Like a mongrel dog, digging up a long forgotten shank, they dig until they find a sin you tried to bury, waggling it in your face until you cast your eyes down and roll onto your back in surrender to the memory. This is not what I desire for you, Dear One; I wish for you to seek Me, not so I can condemn, but that I might gather you to Myself and pour mercy upon you. Pick up sword and shield and stand in the position I have ordained for you, and when the hounds of hell come barking, snapping, and howling for fresh meat, I command that you slap them with the flat of your sword until you still their riotous clamor. THAT is what I desire for you, Child; then when you quiet yourself before Me, quiet it will be … and you may hear My tender voice of love and affection for you. I created you; I conceived you …. What loving parent would want their child to be daily attacked by angry dogs? Wisdom, Child, wisdom … hear her call.

October 29

But thanks be to God, who always leads us as captives in Christ's triumphal procession and uses us to spread the aroma of the knowledge of him everywhere.
2 Corinthians 2:14

My Child, your life speaks a language many are longing to hear. This world is full of posers, people with false faces and false words and false lives, where untruths are the norm and drama has replaced respect. I have called you beyond the trite; your authentic life will speak to those weary and fed-up with the trivial and paltry that is common to this age. You won't be heard by everyone; many are still infatuated with the theater. But, there are those, longing for real, and I send **you** to them, to live authentic life with language infused with grace and truth. Trust Me, and walk, and I will reveal those waiting.

October 30

Every desirable and beneficial gift comes out of heaven. The gifts are rivers of light cascading down from the Father of Light. James 1:17 (MSG)

Don't confuse the gift with the Giver. Good things are not the Best Thing; I and only I hold that role. Let what I give you, what I so freely bestow upon you with the hand of an eager lover, lure you to Me. Let the face of your blessings be the mirror for your Blesser. In the gift of Me as Creator I release all the creative impulses and visions that make your eyes dance with joy. In the gift of Me as Friend and Abba Daddy, I bestow relational intimacy, the heartbeat of a soul toward another, the possible magnetic attraction of a spirit created in My own image. The gift of Me as Counselor releases all wisdom and knowledge that lures your mind toward puzzle solving and invention, toward healing and harmony, for I have made you too creator in your own right. But remember to focus on Me, the Giver, not on My good gifts to you.

October 31

Wait for the Lord; be strong and take heart and wait for the Lord. Psalm 27:14

Do not get too far ahead of yourself. Danger lurks there, both in demon imaginings and dreams that get tortured by your thoughts of impossibility. It is I who created your mind and I who must sometimes rein it in for you. I endowed you with a creative spirit; who else but Creator God could make you such a dreamer? Yet it is I who also must be the boundary line for all your thoughts. Do not get ahead of Me either, for in that unknown place fear lurks, waiting to jump out at you and scare you to death quite literally, for death of the heart is the worst death of all. And there also failure is bred, for if your plan is not from Me, nor of Me, it will not come to pass, at least not in the way that you might hope. You are an ox who needs My yoke; a workhorse who needs My blinders and My bridle and reins. I say all this not to discourage you but rather to help you color within the lines of My design for your life. The frustration of unanswered prayer and discouragement from unfulfilled desires in your life too often come because you have run far out ahead, not bothering to consult, not stopping to wait. Like a toddler by the side of a busy road, there is danger there in your missteps, and peril, much peril for your fragile heart. Do not step forth without consulting Me; do not move forward if I have not called you. But once I have, step out knowing that even if you experience what feels like failure, I am with you and My hand of blessing and calling have not and will not desert you. Do not be afraid to follow Me. Know that fear has been swallowed up in the victory that is eternal, the hope that never ends, the pot of gold at the end of the rainbow that is shadowed by My cross.

November 1

Trust God from the bottom of your heart; don't try to figure out everything on your own. Listen for God's

voice in everything you do, everywhere you go; he's the one who will keep you on track. Proverbs 3:5-6 (MSG)

Lift up your head. Set your gaze toward the heavens, your steps toward My kingdom ways, and your heart toward home. Why spend your days despondent when you know the Lord of the universe and His love for you? Why ponder quitting, stepping back, giving up when you are on the winning team? Victory is likely not immediate, and until then pain and trouble still hang around. But victory is promised: thorough, forever victory. I **will** have My way in this world, and the next one will be nothing but Mine. You may court disaster, but whatever overtakes you will not be permanent. Do not let your heart slide out of My grasp. Do not avert your gaze from the truth. Do not let My name, My words of power, or My truths disappear from your mouth. O you little One of bowed head and broken heart, fear assails you when you look away from Me. Fix your gaze upon Me, and your heartsteps as well as your footsteps will be firm, always leading you toward the grace and the glory of My Kingdom. You, Child, lift up your head!

When these things begin to take place, stand up and lift up your heads, because your redemption is drawing near. Luke 21:28

November 2

The Lord is my shepherd, I lack nothing. He makes me lie down in green pastures, he leads me beside quiet waters, he refreshes my soul. He guides me along the right paths for his name's sake. Even though I walk through the darkest valley, I will fear no evil, for you are with me; your rod and your staff, they comfort me. Psalm 23:1-4

If you lack peace, ask of Me, for I am your God who does not withhold from you. My hand and My heart are forever open to you. As you look to the future the long path may seem dark; the noise and chaos of this world are increasing in volume and frequency. But, I have created a garden of peace for you, and I bid you come. Here you may dwell in peace regardless of what happens around you. Cast your eyes toward Me, for I hold your peace; I hold your future, and I hold the futures of those whom you love in My hand. Do not be discouraged, for no matter who or what claims to hold dominion, I AM **still** God; I AM **still** King of the angel armies, and I hold all of time in My sovereign hand. Rest in these truths.

November 3

When the storm has swept by, the wicked are gone, but the righteous stand firm forever. Proverbs 10:25
I want you to look at your hands; if you could see what I see in the Spirit, you would see your fingers bloody, your nails torn from grasping and scraping against dirt and rock, desperately trying to hold on. I want you to look at your feet, Child, and see that you stand on the Solid Rock; as you flail desperately for a handhold, you're mindlessly unaware that your feet are planted firmly on the Rock that **never** gives way. Many of you face situations that you know will be with you for some time. Things take time to be righted it's true, but know that in this waiting time, My Presence never leaves you. Moment by moment, there is a choice to be made; walk in the Garden with Me and feel the Solid Rock beneath your feet, or continue to grasp and claw at the cliff frantic to hold on. Child, look at your feet and realize on Whom you stand.

November 4

Don't look for shortcuts to God. The market is flooded with surefire, easygoing formulas for a successful life that can be practiced in your spare time. Don't fall for that stuff, even though crowds of people do. The way to life - to God! - is vigorous and requires total attention. Matthew 7:13-14 (MSG)
Do you not know? I come to gather My own from the four corners of the earth. My love rides forth and I appear, ready to rule and to reign in all hearts open to Me. I do not barge in where I am uninvited, but to those who welcome Me, My

coming is swift and My overtaking total. Feel My pleasure in your openness and My joy in consummating what I have ordained. What I have begun, I will complete. This is what you were designed for: this closeness that takes your flesh and joins it with My Spirit. The melding of created with Creator. The depths of you that call out to the Deep that before your formation was carved canyon-like within you. Until you come home to this, recognize it, and allow it to write its purpose across the book that is your life, you will wander.

November 5

Steep your life in God-reality, God-initiative, God-provisions. Don't worry about missing out. You'll find all your everyday human concerns will be met. Give your entire attention to what God is doing right now, and don't get worked up about what may or may not happen tomorrow. God will help you deal with whatever hard things come up when the time comes. Matthew 6:33-34 (MSG)

Cherish what you have. Today is gift enough; don't rush through it. Tomorrow will take care of itself, whether it comes with ease or pain, joy or grief, if you plow the soil of today. Today is what I have given you. Tomorrow is never promised, and the truth is I am the only One who can both know it and manage it. You waste your todays if you spend them hoping for or worrying about your tomorrows. Seize the day in My name - **My** day, **this** day. Walk headlong into it, cloaked in My image, bearing My name. And the rest? Leave it in My hands where it belongs, where it is safe, and where I can take care of it.

November 6

Drench the plowed fields, soak the dirt clods With rainfall as harrow and rake bring her to blossom and fruit. Psalm 65:10 (MSG)

My Child, I want to speak of the bitter root. The hearts of even My children lie wounded and abandoned, lost in forlorn desperation and despair. There are causes for this bitter root in your life, and I condemn you not; I scold you not, and I admonish you not to scold yourself. But angry, resentful One, there are choices to be made. Choose to nurture it not, but instead dig around this bitter root exposing it to the air, again and again and again; deny it sustenance, and the root will begin to shrivel, and I will then break it and destroy the fruit it has born in your life. Look! I plant a new seed of grace in your life, bringing forth a new root from which new life will spring. Test Me and see if I will not do as I say!

November 7

Saturate. Let Me cover you like the soft finger fall of an early morning mist.

Saturate. Lower yourself deep into My love like a diver slides his body smoothly into the waiting waters.

Saturate. Take My word and compass it round about you as you read and meditate. If you read with the cry *'Come, Holy Spirit'* on your lips I will indeed be present and instruct your very spirit in My ways and My purposes.

Saturate. This walk of a sold out believer is not for the dainty who would skirt the messy and the deep. It is for the all-in who purposefully surrender their all, over and over again.

Saturate. The world calls you to surround yourself with your own needs and wants, to see life from the very limited perspective of your own eyes. I call you to see with **My** eyes, and then to pour yourself out into the needs of My fallen, broken created ones.

Saturate yourself with My love that your sodden soul might saturate My love starved ones who surround you.

Saturate.

Live full lives, full in the fullness of God. God can do anything, you know - far more than you could ever imagine or guess or request in your wildest dreams! He does it not by pushing us around but by working within

**us, his Spirit deeply and gently within us.
Ephesians 3:19-20 (MSG)**

November 8

**I will remember the deeds of the Lord; yes, I will
remember your miracles of long ago. I will meditate on
all your works and consider all your mighty deeds.
Psalm 77:11-12**

Remember. Remember when I bought your life with the
sacrifice of My own. Remember the times when although you
felt alone in your world you later discovered just how close I
was to you, hovering nearby, carrying you when your
strength was gone, leading you when you'd lost your way.
Remember the many stories of My faithfulness that you have
heard your friends and fellow sojourners tell, for your life
needs to build its foundation deep into the bedrock of My
constancy and love. Remember the truths I have told you
about your enemy: although neither corporal nor visible in a
fleshly sense that you are aware of, he never averts his gaze
from you and never stops trying to bring you down. You are
hated and you are a target. Remember whose will prevails,
whose way will finally and forever win, whose story holds the
ultimate and final happy ending. Remember My love, for it
never forgets you and never lets you go. Remember.

November 9

**They only cared about pleasing themselves in that
desert, provoked God with their insistent demands. He
gave them exactly what they asked for - but along with it
they got an empty heart. Psalm 106:14-15 (MSG)**

Too long you have bartered for independence, too long
argued with defiance for the release of My claim on your life.
What you haven't yet said in words, you have said with the
intents of your actions and your avoidance of any intimacy
with Me. O Child, you want My salvation and My rescue and
you beg for My miraculous interventions, but then you
continue independently on the path seeking only comfort.

Do you not know that with My rescue comes My claim on you? I save you and I make you Mine. My plans and My purposes are all that will ultimately satisfy your heart greedy for comfort. But you cannot see that; indeed, you refuse to see that, and you run willfully hither and thither, gathering up food that will not satisfy and pleasure that will only lead to unholy addictions. Your heart is empty only because it seeks not what it truly longs for, what it was created for: Me. An intimate journey and a close walk with your Creator are what you were made for, but you shy away from those and seek gods who will not demand much and comforts that only momentarily assuage your desires. You leave Me with no other choice than to give you over to what you seek and what you demand. When finally you recognize their insufficiency, your empty heart and your empty hands will lead you back to Me.

November 10

"For even if the mountains walk away and the hills fall to pieces, My love won't walk away from you, my covenant commitment of peace won't fall apart." The God who has compassion on you says so. Isaiah 54:10 (MSG)

O My pilgrim, you who walk with bowed head and broken heart through the valleys of grief and fear and worry and pain. O My pilgrim, you who keep your head down to watch the road for the rocks that will trip you and the holes that you might fall into and the dips and the hills of your paths. See **Me**, pilgrim! See Me as I lift My hand, the one that was pierced and shed blood for you. See Me as I tuck My finger under your chin and lift until your eyes meet Mine and see My love and My compassion for you. Watch Me as I take your hand on that path through your own valley, My pilgrim. My compassion is so great for you. You know not the tears that I shed on your behalf. You know not the prayers that the Holy Spirit raises to the Father's ears on your behalf. You only see what brings you down, what causes you panic, what makes you cry in the night, and even what you hide behind the veil of your good looks and your "good person" today. But, Child, My compassion is great. And what you cannot see that I can is the end to those valleys. The time when I will take My rightful place, and all that is evil, and all that is death, and all that is pain, and all that is worry, and all the curses that were brought forth by your forefather's fall in the Garden ... when all of those things are banished. So, lift your head. Look at Me. Let Me continue to hold your hand and guide you in those valleys. I will begin to give you a vision of what is at the end of that road. Rest in Me, Child, for I do not want any of My pilgrims to walk with bowed heads and broken hearts, seeing only what the enemy would have them see. I would have you look forward into the paradise that awaits you, the new creation that I will give you, the joy, the love, the glory, the victory, and the broad shouts of *'Hallelujah!'* that you will join in. For I love you, My pilgrim; I love you with a deep love. Feel that love today.

November 11

For surely it is not angels he helps, but Abraham's descendants. For this reason he had to be made like them, fully human in every way, in order that he might become a merciful and faithful high priest in service to God, and that he might make atonement for the sins of the people. Because he himself suffered when he was tempted, he is able to help those who are being tempted. Hebrews 2:16-18

The tyranny of soul and spirit is a testament to your earthy roots: born into sin, created from created, from created, from created; generations creating a legacy of dysfunction. Mankind is broken, wounded, transgressed, and abandoned. From the president of the United States to the addict, to the second grade teacher at the local elementary school, there is none on this afflicted planet that do not suffer from dysfunction birthed and nurtured generations ago. Each generation reveals a new strain morphed and adapted to this era's stubborn ailments. You walk in the wounding of your father's father's father, or your mother's mother's mother ....

It is not a punishment; it is just life in a broken world. In this lineage of broken, I come and splice Myself with your broken genetics. My holy, My sacrificial grafting to your lost and broken bloodline is THE hope for you and for your offspring. This connecting, this melding of earthly and divine was planned before your ancestors ever took breath, before their sins led them to habit and habit led to addiction and murder and incest and a host of other catastrophes that have wound their way through the ages. These sins have been diluted by some generations, amplified by others; the good, the bad and the ugly all joining in a whirlpool of intents and circumstance to form ... you. No one escapes this human routine, the pastor, the thief, the prostitute, and the Sunday school teacher ... no one. Can you, Child, grasp this knowledge? Can you see My divine intention in the person that some would tell you was just "spit out" by a random genetic pool? I Am; I Am that I AM. I Myself orchestrated the you that looks back at you from the mirror's reflection, through all the generations of purposed circumstance; do you see My intent, or do you view the reflection with a sense of valueless contempt? The choice is yours to make, and the consequences of that choice are yours to live out. Every son of Adam and every daughter of Eve have reason to give up and fail and leave wreckage in their wake; conversely, every son of Adam and every daughter of Eve have every reason to lift up their heads and rejoice at the intervention of Holy God with unholy man ... restoring grace and bringing mercy back to family.

November 12

He [the Devil] was a killer from the very start. He couldn't stand the truth because there wasn't a shred of truth in him. When the Liar speaks, he makes it up out of his lying nature and fills the world with lies. John 8:44 (MSG)
Deluded by the forces of darkness are saints and sinners alike. Swept into the pale by promises that seem attractive, men and women fall for the dark trickster over and over

again. Evil is not a person; injustice and recklessness with human life do not bear names. Don't confuse the person with the force that holds sway. Evil is just that, evil. It lives in the dark, breeds in the dark, brooding about how to trick the ones God created. Fallen angel turned malignant and malicious enough to seek each My created ones. None are immune to his ways; his forked tongue that drips with poison while pretending to care slithers its way into each human's small world of need. Be careful who you accuse of being loveless, for you too are lacking in both virtue and restraint. Add to that this truth, and take care that you are not deluded as well, for fear and worry are also such delusions.

November 13

Good friend, take to heart what I'm telling you; collect my counsels and guard them with your life. Tune your ears to the world of Wisdom; set your heart on a life of Understanding. That's right - if you make Insight your priority, and won't take no for an answer, Searching for it like a prospector panning for gold, like an adventurer on a treasure hunt, Believe me, before you know it Fear-of-God will be yours; you'll have come upon the Knowledge of God. Proverbs 2:1-5 (MSG)

My glory swirls around you and fills the space wherein you dwell. You will see it with your heart's eyes if you will only be attentive. You choose, My Child, what you tune into. Like trying to find a station on the radio, your ears are continually in seek mode. You scan and pause at what strikes your fancy. All too often it is fleshly entanglements, or even worse, Satan's endless games and posturings, that catch your attention. And My glory slips past your senses, somehow surprisingly unremarkable to your unsanctified ears. Surrender your thinking, your hearing, and your seeing to Me. Ask to distinguish My glory. Seek My face. Pursue My heart. For therein lies both your joy and your safety.

November 14

Still, when God saw the trouble they were in and heard their cries for help, He remembered his Covenant with them, and, immense with love, took them by the hand. Psalm 106:44-45 (MSG)

Trouble follows you wherever you go; such is the way of this world. Sadly, you try to bear it on your own much too often, trying to take it in hand and master it with your mind and your will. How frustrating it is to discover that you cannot conquer trouble on your own. It is I alone, the Great God Almighty, who has both power and strength to bend trouble and turn it to My will and My glory. Cry out to Me, and I will answer; cry out to Me, and I will not leave you alone, overwhelmed, helpless or frightened. It is My great pleasure to bring My love to bear in your life. Like a mother who swoops in at her youngster's first cries, I too come racing to your aid. O troubled One, give up your attachment to independence; give up your sense that your failings make you ineligible for My Fatherly graces. I hold mercy in My hand; such mercy has no bounds for it is attached to My great love for you and My commitment to save you at all costs. Such is the story of My Son's sacrifice, death, and resurrection. I have vowed to save you if only you will allow yourself to be saved. I have covenanted to love you; unworthy, unholy, unable, still you are Mine, and still I will take you by the hand and rescue you.

November 15

Quiet down before God, be prayerful before him. Psalm 37:7 (MSG)

Be still, O restless One, be still. It is in the quiet that you will find Me and in that same quiet I find you. Your strength comes in the silence, not in the noise. Too many voices compete for your attention in your busyness. Too many cries are heard. Anguish surrounds you; need overwhelms; the call to action stirs your blood, and yet you do not know what to do or where to go. It is in your stillness that you will know your way. Come before Me; wait; listen. In the striving are only confusion and despair. My peace will come to you as you still yourself. I will anoint you with strength for today and set you on the path that I would have you, My warrior, take. Otherwise your churning mind will result only in agitated feet, dashing this way and that to no avail, like an arrow set forth from an uncocked bow only to fall to the ground spent and useless. I will give My warrior directions, purpose, and strength in the stillness. I will trade your restless confusion for My certain knowledge and send you forth. You will fly with confidence and accuracy straight to the target I have for you. Be still. Be quiet. Let Me position your feet, your mind, your arm pulled back in readiness.

November 16

Do you think anyone is going to be able to drive a wedge between us and Christ's love for us? There is no way! Not trouble, not hard times, not hatred, not hunger, not homelessness, not bullying threats, not backstabbing, not even the worst sins listed in Scripture .... I'm absolutely convinced that nothing - nothing living or dead, angelic or demonic, today or tomorrow, high or low, thinkable or unthinkable - absolutely nothing can get between us and God's love because of the way that Jesus our Master has embraced us. Romans 8:35,38-39 (MSG)

Hear My heart for you, Child: it is you whom I love. Just the way you are - both because of and despite all that you are - it is you whom I love. Today. Tomorrow. Always. Only love can change you. Only My passion for you can move you. Only through Me and My love can you rest and find sanctuary. But bottom line, whatever you do, whatever you don't do, I love you. I will never leave nor forsake you. I will always walk beside you. I will always dwell within you. I will always speak to you, embrace you, save you from both this world and yourself.

November 17

She obeys no one, she accepts no correction. She does not trust in the Lord, she does not draw near to her God. Zephaniah 3:2

This morning I came to find you, and I couldn't. Oh, you were there, and yes, I could see you. But your heart was closed against Me, and you could neither see Me nor feel My presence. How sad it made Me, Dear One, to be so close and yet so far from one whom I love. What is it that keeps you from Me? That keeps your gaze fixed on all others than the One who loves you best? Is it your sin? I have remedy for that; come quickly without fear or shame and know that I will meet your repentance and your sorrow without condemnation. I will wipe the slate clean; I will remember your failings no more. Is it your own low self-esteem? Have you lost faith in Me because you have lost all faith in yourself? Child, have you not yet caught even a glimpse of the ways I already use you when you release yourself and let Me flow through you? I am not appalled by you; why then are you? You are a gem, buried deeply still perhaps, but nonetheless wonderfully made, exquisite in your uniqueness, hand crafted by your Creator. Stop calling '*Useless*,' '*Hopeless*,' '*Failure*' what I have called '*My beloved One*.' It is time for healing, Dear One, time for your eyes to be opened and your anxious, reluctant heart to be healed. It is your disbelief that keeps you from Me, your incredulity that I could love and call a hopeless one such as you to hope. Truth is, you are perfect in Me: picked up, restored, renewed, and used. It is safe, Dear One, to meet My gaze when I come looking, safe to walk with Me, safe to let Me melt both your shame and disbelief into willingness.

November 18

Dear child, I want your full attention; please do what I show you. Proverbs 23:26 (MSG)

It is in drawing close to Me that you are known and that I can reveal Myself. Yet you stay in the shadows, often watching instead of participating, mindful of Me but alarmed by what you think I might ask of you. You, Child, are My Beloved. In Me and Me alone is the strength for your days, the directions for your journey, and the hope for your darknesses and confusions. Strip off the scales of fear that leave you unwilling to come close. Allow Me to open the eyes of your heart that you might really see Me, know Me, and know My love for you. Safety is in My coming near and your true understanding of My love for you. The distance that you think keeps you from whatever I might ask of you is but a fog that clouds the sunrise of your soul. Draw close; I am waiting, longing, hoping. It is **with** Me that you will find both peace and protection. It is **in** Me that you will find your true self.

November 19

Do you think this is the kind of fast day I'm after: a day to show off humility? To put on a pious long face and parade around solemnly in black? Do you call that fasting, a fast day that I, God, would like? This is the kind of fast day I'm after: to break the chains of injustice, get rid of exploitation in the workplace, free the oppressed, cancel debts. What I'm interested in seeing you do is: sharing your food with the hungry, inviting the homeless poor into your homes, putting clothes on the shivering ill-clad, being available to your own families. Isaiah 58:5-7 (MSG)

The fast I require, the kind I delight in, is one with willing sacrifice, one that costs you something. One that offers something of value and lays it at My throne and does not snatch it back with greedy hands. It is your heart that I am after, My Child, for it is that heart that directs both your thoughts and your actions. Your spirit is full of Me, but sometimes you recognize it not, focusing only on My gifts or the outward trappings of both your pleasures and your pains. Look to Me, Child; fall on your face and worship all that I am that you need not be, all that I have given that you need not find for yourself, all that I will make of you that you could never craft on your own. The fast that is Mine is a humbling of heart, a sacrificing of your flesh, an offering of your best and of what you hold most dear.

November 20

Immediately Jesus reached out his hand and caught him. "You of little faith," he said, "why did you doubt?" Matthew 14:31

Do you trust Me? Not just with your mind, knowing that theoretically I am trustworthy? Do you trust Me with your heart? If I ask you to do something that stretches far beyond your capability to manage, does your heart know, does your heart really believe, that I will show up, that I will show My face, that I will provide all the missing pieces, all that is needful? Or does your heart remain risk adverse, sure in a theoretical sense that I will enable what I call you to, but unwilling to step out onto the water, pretty sure that when all is said and done, that you will sink and will make a fool of both Me and yourself. Trust Me - all or nothing. No safeguards that are not of Me. No promises except the ones I make. Trust **Me**. If you don't, you lose nothing, but you also gain nothing. If you do, your boundaries will never be the same and your vision no longer constrained by only what you can see with your physical eyes. Take My Spirit wings and fly, for I have said you can. Try Me and see if it isn't so; try Me and see if I don't show up.

November 21

And surely I am with you always, to the very end of the age. Matthew 28:20

My dearly beloved Child, there are things in this world for you to worry about, things for you to cry about, things for you to be anxious about. Do you think I don't know that? Hear My call today, Child; let Me be in the midst of those things. Invite Me into them. It should come as no surprise to you, for I told you that in this world you will have troubles, but I have overcome the world, and I will walk with you every step of your way through the world. Set down Satan's lie that it's your job to handle this alone, that it is you who cries alone in the dark watches of the night, that it is you alone who takes control of your life with your worry and your anxiety and your cares. That is the lie of the enemy and to believe it is to destroy peace. I have promised you My peace; I have also promised My overcoming, but Child you have to let Me walk with you. No longer walk alone. Know that I am the One who slays giants. Know that I am the One who notices each of your tears and collects them in a bottle. Know that I am the One who promises peace and either stops the storm or walks through the storm with you to keep you safe. No longer walk alone, Child; invite Me in to walk with you.

November 22

No one can serve two masters. Either you will hate the one and love the other, or will be devoted to the one and despise the other. Matthew 6:24

Glory. Esteem. Laud. Honor. If that is what you strive for, it will always force you to make a choice. Is it My glory that compels you? Or do you seek glory for yourself? That choice dictates a large portion of the trajectory of your life. There can be only one master on the throne of your life. Will it be you? Or Me? Will you seek that which brings glory to My name, or will you strive for fame and fortune on your own? Know this; My Word has proclaimed it and it is so: no man can have two masters. You will hate one and love the other, for there is great competition for your heart. Either lean into Me, or lean into yourself. Your Spirit can no more go in two directions simultaneously than your body can. Forsake all for My sake. Turn from everything that does not have My stamp on it. Surrender your selfishness, and you will find in Me more than you ever dreamed of, more than you ever hoped for, fathom upon fathom of more than you could possibly craft for yourself on your own. Live to glorify Me, and I will satisfy the desires of your heart.

November 23

As a result, it has become clear throughout the whole palace guard and to everyone else that I am in chains for Christ. Philippians 1:13

Weak and wounded One, bending under the weight of your own thoughts, I have come to free you from the shackles that bind you to these old, broken thought pillars. For your entire life you have been bound to them; when you strive to move, you find your wrists are bound; when you work to put your head in a different place, the shackle around your brain holds you fast; when you stretch your leg to stride away, again you are held fast. Who can save you from such a fate? Time and again it has been proven to you that you are no match for these old thought patterns; bound to them you move along familiar paths, trenches really, dug by your own shuffling movements over decades of use. Left to yourself surely you would never gather enough strength to pull yourself out from these ruts and move along different paths. Truly, I could give you eons more, and this would still hold true. If you doubt, look at the course of mankind over his centuries; deep ruts cut across cultures and governments, kings and paupers; again and again mankind takes the broken paths the generation before him took, and so it will continue until the end. I am the ONLY hindrance to the broken path. I AM the only hindrance to the broken path. It is only through My sacrifice that I now may have access to the wounded paths of thought that torture and torment and create havoc and chaos in your mind and bring bruising to your life and relationships. Pray for your mind's renewal; seek to give Me praise for what I have done, what I am doing, and what I will continue to do, for that praise fills in the trenches; that praise makes the locks shake that hold you to old thought pillars. Come, Child, and know Me better; let My loving gaze melt your stiffened heart. Feel the ladles of mercy and grace flow over you like oil down Aaron's beard. I stand ready, I stand able, and I stand willing to show you new paths of thought that will lead you to new places you've only dared to dream even exist. I come as Locksmith; I come as Warrior-God; I come as Companion and Helper; let us travel to new places.

November 24

Jesus once again addressed them: "I am the world's Light. No one who follows me stumbles around in the darkness. I provide plenty of light to live in." John 8:12 (MSG)

Stretch toward the light. Follow its rays, for I **am** the light. My light dwells deep within your heart since you are Mine now, and My children can never be taken from Me. My ways often defy what you can see, even what you can discern. So know this: even in the darkness My light dwells, for there is no darkness in Me, and I am in you and you in Me. Day gives way to night, and sunshine gives way to rain clouds, but nothing and no one drives Me from you. Know, then, even when it is pitch black, My light still reigns. I gave Myself for you that I might be victor and you might dwell in light eternal through Me. So it is that you must open your spiritual eyes along the way that you might see the light of hope and peace and truth, even when the darkness of trouble and pain and fear cloud your way. So, stretch toward the light. Follow My rays. If you open your eyes, you will find My sprinkles of light in the darkest of places and My Spirit will lead you through.

November 25

Whether you turn to the right or to the left, your ears will hear a voice behind you, saying, "This is the way; walk in it." Isaiah 30:21

I am the Gyroscope of your soul; whatever brings you low today, know that I will right you to your true north. Whatever hits you hard, knocks you down, brings you to your knees, know that **I** am your Gyroscope. My love, My mercy, My grace will always right you to your true north. Fear not, for whatever this world hits you with, whatever comes down your path, although you may feel like your face is in the dust, do not fear because I am your True North, and I will bring you up. I am the Gyroscope of your soul.

November 26

Yours, O Lord, is the greatness and the power and the glory and the majesty and the splendor, for everything in heaven and earth is yours. Yours, O Lord, is the kingdom; you are exalted as head over all.
1 Chronicles 29:11

Majesty. Worship My majesty. As you live and breathe, breathe your worship of Me. Step by step, day by day, enter into My presence with joy. It is your choice and your choice alone, My Child, whether you live with Me or without Me. Your choice is made every day, every hour, even every moment, and the consequences of your choice have ramifications far beyond what you imagine. When you tackle your world and your needs without praise of Me and without the close touch of My Spirit, there will be pain and worry in your aloneness. Think not that money or recognition or a comfortable job or a faithful family can fill the need that you have for Me. Your preoccupation with all of those things, although good in and of themselves, costs you pieces of your life that you so desperately try to hold on to and control. It is only as I meet you in your praise of Me and your surrender to My holiness that I can come close. Only then that I can meet you and join My breath with yours, pouring both the comfort and the wisdom of My Holy Spirit into your life. Come worship Me, Child. Draw near, and I will meet you here.

November 27

The body we're talking about is Christ's body of chosen people. Each of us finds our meaning and function as a part of his body. But as a chopped-off finger or cut-off toe we wouldn't amount to much, would we?
Romans 12:5 (MSG)

I have called you forth, sung songs over the depths of your soul, and whispered truth into your life. It is My heartbeat that fashions the rhythm of your life's flow and of your very breath. You stand not as a solitary figure, alone and self-made, but as a tree in the forest of My creation, an upright, strong tower that is part of a hedge of protection. You are not to stand alone, but rather to position yourself in community: a forest dweller, not a solitary scrub in a desert oasis. Your coming forth allows strength to grow, places you as a beacon, allows Me to position you in usefulness and Kingdom building, and enables you to be both protector and protected.

November 28

Don't let this throw you. You trust God, don't you? Trust me. John 14:1 (MSG)

Let not your heart be troubled. Through Me find rest for your soul. Trust in Me and I will bring the days that I have planned for you to pass. You do not need to know the end of your situations in order to find peace in the midst of them. The challenge of My love for you is to wholly embrace all of your days and nights because you know that I hold them, as I hold you, in the palm of My hand. There is nothing about you that is outside My grasp or beyond My knowing. Both My will and My ways hold you fast. Step out of the dark caves that close you in and tie you down with fear and uncertainty and live within the vast high ceilinged vaults of spacious possibility and promise - My places of opportunity for you. Believe in Me!

November 29

Let me give you a new command: Love one another. In the same way I loved you, you love one another. John 13:34 (MSG)

My love is not an easy love. Not a simple, rah-rah pat you on the back kind of love. Unflagging love is never simple precisely because My created ones aren't simple. My love must work and shine through all the hard parts of life on this planet. It must shine into all the dark corners and musty areas that have grown stale for lack of it. My love is not for just the cleaned up and spit polished people. It is for those broken ones living in complicated war zones and for the addicts shooting up in the midst of their disreputable lives. It is for the children whose lives are lived out and dragged through the garbage dumps of the endless slums of poverty. My love finds a home in the complicated facets of life, in the ragged and the worn, in the tear-stained and the despairing. Since such love is really best suited for those who are meek because they are disreputable and those whose shame has driven their hope far afield, do not be too quick to beg Me to rescue you from the hard places. It is in precisely those hard places that My love lives, and if you would endeavor to be My love and bring My love, it is to those hard places that you too must go.

November 30

And he said, Go forth, and stand upon the mount before the Lord. And, behold, the Lord passed by, and a great and strong wind rent the mountains, and brake in pieces the rocks before the Lord; but the Lord was not in the wind: and after the wind an earthquake; but the Lord was not in the earthquake: And after the earthquake a fire; but the Lord was not in the fire: and after the fire a still small voice. 1 Kings 19:11-12 (KJV)

Create some quiet space, Child; the world spins, and howls, and spits its panic, its urgency, its shell-shocked anxiety onto your path each and every day. There is no joy, no peace to be found in its company; your peace may only be found in the Prince of Peace. The world urges you to **"DO SOMETHING"**; they know not what, but the only way they know to handle the all-encompassing stress is movement: keep moving; keep talking; keep doing. This is not the path for My chosen ones; this is not the way of the Children of Shalom. Remove yourself from the calliope of noise, from the shrill shriek of hysteria that blasts its warning shots across your bow at an ever-increasing pace. Remember My servant Elijah. Child, his day too was wracked by fear and anxiety;

running for his very life, weary and abandoned (so he thought), he sought My face alone on the Mountain, Horeb, the Mountain of God. There was howling wind, but I was not found in the wind; there was a violent earthquake, but I was not found in the earthquake; there was consuming fire, but I was not found in the fire. Stunned into quietude, Elijah found Me not in the chaos, frightening for all its strength and wildness, but I revealed Myself in My own still, small voice. Remember, Child, true strength need not boast of its strength; true strength has such assured confidence that it need only whisper. Find for yourself, Child, a cleft in the rock and take your rest; let the fury and violence and heat pass by you, but own them not. Stay in the cleft and wait for My still, small voice; with it I will speak encouragement, wisdom, strength, and direction to your battered senses; I will bring My peace, My calm, My equilibrium back to your overwhelmed spirit. This will be your joy; this will be your peace; this will be your strength, and you shall walk as one quieted and satisfied at his mother's breast. Try Me, Child; see if My voice cannot bring peace to your storm.

December 1

Give thanks to the Lord, for he is good; his love endures forever. Psalm 107:1

A grateful heart ... a thankful spirit ... those draw Me close, and those allow you to feel Me close. Those teach you My ways more powerfully than many sermons can. It is in gratitude for what you **do** have that you will find My peace for what you don't. It is in your thanksgiving that you find the grace for living in the midst of the warfare of this world. You know enough of Me, dear Child, to trust that which you do not understand. Mine has been a heart of love for you from the very beginning. That heart has pursued you with endless fervor. It has tracked you in even the minefields that you have sown to keep Me at a distance. My love has poured over you even when you have retreated far from Me. When your confusion about Me and My ways has so baffled you that you lash out in anger and distance yourself in ways that you think will keep you safe, even then My love flows. Even then My compassion for you surrounds you in unlikely ways. It is your gratitude, your praise, your thankfulness, even in those times when you don't understand Me, **especially** in those times, that is your safety. Your submission to Me as faithful and holy and all-knowing God puts boundaries on the evil that tries to assail you. Your faith-filled praise for My love for you, which sometimes you cannot feel but which you nonetheless trust, is what banishes the storm clouds and opens the door to hope.

December 2

Oh! May the God of green hope fill you up with joy, fill you up with peace, so that your believing lives, filled with the life-giving energy of the Holy Spirit, will brim over with hope! Romans 15:13 (MSG)
Let you who are without hope hear this. I came to bring a hope that would never fail. My years on earth taught My people much about My mercy and grace and unexpected love for those unlikely ones who had been left behind or shunned by the powers that be. My death and resurrection sang the song again, *'I love you with a fierceness that will never abandon. I love you from your beginning to your end. I love you from before your birth through the eternity that will eventually come. I love you enough to die for all the mistakes you have made and for all the injustices that have been perpetrated against you. Nothing and no one can stop the assault of love, for My love WILL find a way.'* This is your victory call, Dear One. This is My promise to you. This is My hope given freely, passed on to you like a loving father passes on his inheritance to his beloved children. Gather it up and hold it close to you, for it is your shield and protector. It is a weightless burden, an unending joy, and it is yours if you will only embrace it.

December 3

And the Lord asked me, "What do you see, Amos?" "A plumb line," I replied. Then the Lord said, "Look, I am

**setting a plumb line among my people Israel; I will
spare them no longer." Amos 7:8**

I hold a plumb line in My hand - and I make it straight and
true across the fabric of your life. But it is your eyes that
must choose to recognize the truth of it. No longer can you
pretend integrity and faithfulness when the plumb line shows
you those places where your life has veered from the path
upon which you should walk. Build your house straight and
true. Let Me, the Son of the Architect, be the Builder who
brings vision to life, who squares the corners, who fashions
the foundation and lines it up with Me. Your life is like
earthen clay before it has dried in the sun and been hardened
in the oven. Keep it pliable. Build with your eye on the
plumb line and the One who holds it.

December 4

**Not only so, but we also rejoice in our
sufferings, because we know that suffering produces
perseverance; perseverance, character; and character,
hope. And hope does not disappoint us, because God
has poured out his love into our hearts by the Holy
Spirit, whom he has given us. Romans 5:3-5**

The difficult things of your life are but the means by which I
make you soft and pliable. What you don't understand and
what your mind rebels against are the tools by which I teach
you that you are smaller than I. I call you to faith, not
comprehension. I invite you to trust the truths that you
already know of Me: My compassion, My love, and My
goodness. In that trust you will find strength to endure what
seems too hard to bear and faith to believe even when the
clouds conceal the light of that belief in Me. Someday, but
not yet, you will know. Someday, but not yet, you will
understand. Someday, but not yet, you will see with perfect
vision from the vantage point of eternity. And then you will
know why things happened thusly, and why even bad things
were honed into good for you, and how both you and your
loved ones profited from what seemed like only hardship and
incessant suffering. In the meantime, no matter how long

that time lasts, I ask you to trust the God who loves you and to find safety in My arms, for only when your heart is close to Mine, will you endure and not be undone.

December 5

You, Lord, hear the desire of the afflicted; you encourage them, and you listen to their cry ....
Psalm 10:17

Indeed My Child, I have come. In this Advent season it's easy to forget that many about you face hard and painful places; there is someone on your street this week that's starting chemo; there is someone in your neighborhood that has lost someone this year, and they don't know how they're going to face this Christmas. Child, go for Me; be My kind word; be My listening ear. But, even if you don't know them or of their trouble, they are still there, and they're hurting this week, and they'll be hurting next week, so pray for your neighbors. Your prayers, dropping like raindrops from your lips, will bring a measure of peace to their hurting souls, and I will send someone else in your stead for they need a visit from Me this season. So don't forget them because you're busy; don't forget the hurting because you're having a good time. Go for Me! And even though there may not be a story to tell or a name to attach to that story on this earth, there will be stories in heaven, and you'll know, and you'll see, and you'll talk to the ones that I touched because of your obedience. Don't forget Me, and don't forget them in this Advent season.

December 6

Don't fool yourself into thinking that you are a listener when you are anything but, letting the Word go in one ear and out the other. Act on what you hear! James 1:22 (MSG)

Today! Today is your day. Today is your hour; today is your moment. Today! Today is when I call you to bow your knee, to surrender sin, to give up anxiety, to stand and believe.

Today is the day that I ask you to come out of your fear, that I offer you My bravery to do what I have called you to do, to speak what I have called you to speak, and to go the places that only you can go. Today, Child, today! You come to Me day after day, but sometimes you just won't hear. Listen, Child, for I call you today. I call you to be unafraid, not because you have no fear, but because I am your Brave One. I call you to go to the dark places because, Child, if you won't go to the places I call you to, there may be no one who goes. Child, I weep; I weep for the days that you leave My presence and you haven't heard My heart. You haven't heard My heart for **you**. You haven't heard My heart for the person you live with. And you haven't heard My heart for the people whose lives you will intersect. There is no such thing as chance; nothing happens without My plan, without My hand of grace and blessing. And there is nowhere that is too far, too difficult, too hard, too scary, or too without resources that I will not bring what you need for your day. So bow your knee today, Child. Bow your knee. Do not leave Me with tears in My eyes because you have not been obedient to hear what I call you to today. Today, Child. Today! Now! Please listen. It's your time.

December 7

But he said to me, "My grace is sufficient for you, for my power is made perfect in weakness." Therefore I will boast all the more gladly about my weaknesses, so that Christ's power may rest on me. 2 Corinthians 12:9

It is in your quiet places, in your still, in your lonely that I meet you. It is when you are undone, used up, and unprepared that I show My face. It is when you have not ... strength, hope, understanding ... it is then that I bring what **I** have. It is when you are not, that I can be. When you are empty that I can fill. When you are wordless that I can speak. It is in your poverty that I bring My wealth and in your impotence that I show My strength and power. What you lack, dear Child, is My opportunity. I can do far more in and for a child of Mine who is undone by her own insufficiency than for one who is propelled by his own prowess and wisdom. It is only emptiness that I can fill and only need that even recognizes Me.

December 8

Treat my prayer as sweet incense rising; my raised hands are my evening prayers. Psalm 141:2 (MSG)

Take the days and the ways of your walking with Me and willingly offer them back to Me as a sacrifice. It is not enough for the health of your own soul to offer yourself to Me as a blank slate in the mornings. You must also relinquish all that the day has brought, and all that the enemy has brought with it, back into My hands at day's end. When your hours become past tense, it is then that I must hold them and hold you too. All that you have faithfully done and tried to do in My name, all of that, must be surrendered to Me. The accumulation of your days walked out in Me is Mine to keep, not yours. Both the pain and the pleasure of those days and those circumstances must remain in My hand. When you try to hold them tightly in your own grip, they only torment you, both with pleasure and with pain. Yesterday is Mine, Child, all your yesterdays, all your days and all your nights. Release them to Me.

December 9

In your stillness, in your quiet, in your poured out and opened up I come. I come. I often sneak up to you, but you hear Me not and sense Me not because you have bought into the lie of the world that it is in your thoughts and your movements and your actions that problems are solved and cares are lessened. Breathe in, Child; breathe Me in and exhale those lies. Breathe in My Spirit and exhale the belief that **you** must know, that **you** must conquer. It is I, Child, who finds room in your stillness. It is I, Child, who brings words when you are voiceless. It is I, Child, who ministers to the deepest and sorest and darkest of places. Do not think that I require you to first figure it out, to first come up with the solution, to first see the end. Nay, Child, that will only distract you; that will only be the hammer that beats on your heart and makes it sore. My Holy Spirit, My promised presence, My springing forth words and deeds and hope and peace, those are all Mine, Child, but how I long to gift them to you. As mothers and fathers gift to their children, so I long to give you My peace and My rest. So come to Me. Be still; be quiet. Open the ears of your heart that My Spirit might invade you.

The Friend, the Holy Spirit whom the Father will send at my request, will make everything plain to you. He will remind you of all the things I have told you. John 14:26 (MSG)

December 10

Keep your eyes on Jesus, who both began and finished this race we're in. Hebrews 12:2 (MSG)

Fix your eyes on Me, for I am the author and the perfecter of your faith. My Friend, My dearly beloved Child, listen to Me, for I have something to teach your spirit today. Where is your focus? My Word tells you to fix your eyes on **Me**, for there you will find My comfort, and there you will find My truth. Do you think I do not know all that you come with today? All that is heavy on your heart and a burden on your spirit? All the questions that you have, even the wondering, *'God, are you good?'* I hear all that, Child, for I see deep inside you. But today I ask you to focus on **Me**. Praise Me. PRAISE ME! You so often focus on all that ails you, all that concerns you, uncertain if I hear and know. Yet it is I, Child, who woke you this morning. And it is I, Child, who keeps you safe as you go about your day, who protects you from all the many things that could happen. I beg you, Child, to focus on Me that you might see the things that I keep you from in this world of sin and sorrow, the things that I protect you from, the many ways that I show My love and My blessing to you. Fix your eyes on **Me**, ON ME, that you might be captivated by the love that I show instead of led astray by the enemy's lies. I know your sorrows; I know your pain. I see your tears; I know your hesitations. There is nothing that is hidden from Me. But, Child, I am love, and, Child, I am good. Fix your eyes on Me.

December 11

The thief comes only to steal and kill and destroy; I have come that they may have life, and have it to the full. John 10:10

You have seen many of My miracles: people transformed, relationships healed, diseases cured. Today I come and speak to **you** - you who think you have not yet gotten your **own** miracle. You wonder why, and in the dark of the night the liar and the thief whispers words that bring you to tears and drive you to your knees in despair. I tell you now, Child, that I answer your prayer. **I answer your prayer.** The answer is not always what pleases you or what makes it easy, but I answer your prayer. Sometimes it's a '*Yes*'; sometimes it's a '*No*'; sometimes it's a '*Wait, Child, wait,*' but I answer your prayers. I give you healing, if not this side of eternity then in the next. I bring restoration to you, restoration of **all** things, even if such restoration does not come on your timetable. What the locusts have stolen from your life, I **will** restore. Take heed, Child; if you listen to the one who prowls and wants to bring you down, you will not hear or feel My love. But My love is there! My love is constant and My promises are true. Hold tight to My hand. Look into My eyes. I am your Lover who has sought and gone after you for all good things. Take hope. This is **My** truth for you!

December 12

I'm feeling terrible - I couldn't feel worse! Get me on my feet again. You promised, remember?... My sad life's dilapidated, a falling-down barn; build me up again by your Word. Barricade the road that goes Nowhere; grace me with your clear revelation. Psalm 119:25, 28-29 (MSG)

Child with a wounded heart, loved one of My designing, feel, Child, feel. Don't be afraid; don't yet search for control or understanding. Just surrender to the moments that are Mine. I am there, right beside you. My arm is slung over your shoulder, pouring My love out, standing My ground, protecting your heart. I see the end from the beginning, and the end is a good one: wholeness and purity with all of the loose cords cinched up and tightened. Take hope; the King of the universe has this firmly in His hand. Truly I **have** given you, I **am** giving you, and I **will** give you strength for the tasks ahead. Be unafraid. There is no minion of the enemy's army that can conquer you, not even Satan himself. I have sworn an oath that the blood of My victorious Lamb will cover you and protect you. There is nothing that His sword will not slay, His victory not surely win. March forth, eyes open with nothing hidden, into the light of His love. You are free; you will be even freer.

December 13

And then I'll marry you for good - forever! I'll marry you true and proper, in love and tenderness. Yes, I'll marry you and neither leave you nor let you go. You'll know me, God, for who I really am.   Hosea 2:19-20 (MSG)

Draw close to Me, My beloved Spouse. Today I do not call you child, although My Child you still are. Today I call you My Beloved, My covenant Partner. I have vowed My unending love; I have spoken My commitment. My token, so much more than a ring, is My life sacrificed for you. And you, Dear One, you also have proclaimed your love. You have made public declaration of our union. You have promised your heart. You have made known your covenant with Me. Such covenant will stand the test of time, for I will faithfully woo you. I will provide; I will protect; I will continue to give Myself to you. In My strength you will find your safety. In My provisions you will find all that you need for each of your days. There will never come a time that I will tire of you. I will never be tempted to replace you with another. I have become the bridegroom of your heart. I have taken you to our marriage bed and made you Mine. I have planted My seed within you - body, soul and mind.

Allow My love to overtake you and consume you. Allow our covenantal relationship to be the rebar that undergirds you. I will be the certainty upon which you build your life. No more wandering in the wilderness. No more unfaithful lovers. No more walking alone.

December 14

He heals the brokenhearted and binds up their wounds. Psalm 147:3

For you who are broken: I have come; I am here. For you who are broken - your mind is broken, or your heart is broken, or your body is broken - I have come! I am here! For you who are hungry - your spirit is hungry, or your body is hungry, or your soul cries out with a hunger that is not filled by this world - I am here; I have come. I will take your wounded broken places, and I will heal them. I will Spirit-glue them back together so you are stronger and more whole than you have ever been. For I am here, and I have come ... for you! Bring Me your brokenness; bring Me your hunger; bring Me your woundedness. Bring Me that of your loved ones as well, for I am here; I have come.

December 15

Keep me safe, my God, for in you I take refuge. Psalm 16:1

From everlasting to everlasting, man has called upon My name, and from everlasting to everlasting, I have been faithful to answer his call. I change not; My attributes and assignments have not changed; I am The God concerned with the affairs of mankind from forever behind to forever forward. Mark not My seeming silence as disinterest or impotence, for I AM God of the angel armies, and all things move or don't move under the length and breath of My sovereign will. Any advance of darkness is always still within the bounds of My omnipotence and My watchful gaze, and I will always answer with righteous might. Through the generations man has used his will for evil, ignoring the seeds planted in himself by Yahweh, and instead coveting the seeds of disharmony and discord placed there by the enemy of man. Man's heart loves itself and feeds itself what appeals to his selfish eye and hungry heart, grasping and clawing at power and riches and anarchy, not even aware that his own soul will be raped and pillaged by the things he covets. For in man's foolishness he thinks he will not be devoured by the evil he lays his hand to, that his own heart, his own mind, his own soul will somehow not be affected by what is evil in My sight. Those that seek their own goals without the boundaries of mercy and honor and truth will eventually find themselves unable to turn the tide of the evil within themselves in the course they have set. Thinking only that their deeds will affect others and not themselves, they will continue forward until the day they look into the mirror and realize that they indeed have killed their own soul, and all the goals they had set out to obtain will be as dung because there is nothing left of goodness looking back at them from their reflection. This is the fate of evil, forever behind and forever forward; it blusters, then burgeons and eventually breaks under its own evil weight. In all the eons of evil intent, still, the lessons of that evil are never learned, and each new generation must eventually drink its own dredges. Good wins! **Child,... GOOD WINS!** The days may be dark, but be not dismayed; even those most deceived by the Evil One are beginning to feel the weight of their own evil. When foolish man says evil is good, it matters not because Jehovah God has always been and forever will be the standard maker, and the wrong done in the name of false gods will always double back and destroy the lives of its own warriors.

December 16

Take my yoke upon you and learn from me, for I am gentle and humble in heart, and you will find rest for your souls. Matthew 11:29
Be gentle with yourself today. Treat yourself with the kindness and the empathy that you display to others but too often do not feel that you yourself deserve. This world is

harsh ofttimes, and even the love of family and friends does not override the intentions of the enemy to keep your heart cut off from its only true source of comfort and strength: My love. Like on a cloudy day, your mind must choose: is the sun still there, just hidden? Or has it disappeared all together? You too, My loved One, must determine whether or not My heart for you is one of patience and protection or one of harsh and vengeful impatience and wrath. You feel that which you believe, so let My Word be your guide and allow it to mentor your feelings that you might finally be convinced that the clouds that you see may veil My truth for you but never change it. Be gentle, My beloved One. Your harshness toward yourself makes you neither more obedient nor more faithful, just more vulnerable. You cannot goad yourself into more Christlikeness by slapping your fallen, recalcitrant heart around. Only a full acceptance of My love for you can draw you to Me and make you more like Me. Be gentle, O heart of Mine, for gentle is My heart toward you.

December 17

As it turned out, it was the best thing that could have happened. Instead of trusting in our own strength or wits to get out of it, we were forced to trust God totally - not a bad idea since he's the God who raises the dead! And he did it, rescued us from certain doom. And he'll do it again, rescuing us as many times as we need rescuing. 2 Corinthians 1:9-10 (MSG)

Be still, My loved One. I have delivered, I am delivering, and I will yet deliver you. Your cry does not fall on deaf ears, and I am pleased to answer such a plea from your heart. There is no shame in admitting your need for Me. You were created with that need, and until you surrender to it, you can only be a fraction of who I intend for you to become. The despair that you feel in your own inability to control and fend for yourself is the door to the joy of My transforming provision. When you finally say, '*I cannot*,' you position yourself for what **I** can and will do. Relinquish your control; repent of your pride; refuse to set foot in the mire of self-loathing that the enemy evilly beckons you toward. All Mine you are - only Mine. Come to Me knowing that I reign over all that holds you captive. Rest safely, knowing that I will both set you free and redeem the ill intent of your enemy. Call out to Me that you might hear your own voice proclaiming your need and insufficiency as well as My power and love.

December 18

And we, who with unveiled faces all reflect the Lord's glory, are being transformed into his likeness with ever-increasing glory, which comes from the Lord, who is the Spirit. 2 Corinthians 3:18

Cease your striving, My Child. It is not by your might nor by your power that anything good is accomplished in and through your life. Rather, your life's hope lies in My Spirit. Therein is your deliverance. Take My breath, and allow Me to make it your breath. Take My thoughts and let the Holy Spirit renew your mind with them. If My ways are higher than your ways and My thoughts higher than your thoughts, how can you gain holy ground except as I transform you? You cannot will good works; you cannot create your own heart change. Your only hope is in Me, in the help that I freely offer you. Open yourself before Me; allow Me to pour in. Let My Spirit overtake you. As you are consumed by My holy fire of love, so will you be transformed. As you surrender, My Spirit will reclaim and make of you a more holy offering. I will make your heart My home.

December 19

God, the Master, The Holy of Israel, has this solemn counsel: "Your salvation requires you to turn back to me and stop your silly efforts to save yourselves. Your strength will come from settling down in complete dependence on me - The very thing you've been unwilling to do." Isaiah 30:15 (MSG)

Come rest awhile. In quietness and trust is your strength. Your power lies in both your waiting for Me and your walk with Me. Lay down your burdens. Surrender the things that perplex you, the things that you do not know and cannot solve. It is My peace that you must seek and not your own. The difference rests in who you allow to sit on the throne of your life: yourself or Me. Walk with Me now and be no longer alone. Submit your ways to Me. Invite Me on your paths. Call Me close to you. Lean in. Let Me come beside you. All power is Mine, but the invitation is yours to answer. I will never force Myself on you, never demand an audience in your heart. Oh, but how hungry I am to be your constant companion, to walk and talk together in all the hours and days of your life. I love you Child, and I desire oneness with you. I long to weave My heart into yours, to make you My own. Come.

December 20

If you really know me, you will know my Father as well. From now on, you do know him and have seen him. John 14:7

Hear Me, Child; hear My Parent-heart for you; when you avoid Me, when you postpone Me, when you give heed to the shame in your heart and mind instead of giving heed to My grace and mercy, it hurts us both. I speak not to fill again your cup with more shame and more reason to avoid and postpone, but to help you redefine your interpretation of Me, of who I am and who I am not. Your decades of living in a guilt-driven mindset have limited our ability to have a relationship. Imagine, Child, if every time you walked up to your "best friend," you did so with trepidation and a sense of shame; you would not count this as a "best friend" relationship very long. Yet, this has been your mindset with Me for nearly your whole life. Each morning you wake not to the anticipation of meeting with your True Best Friend, but you come like a dog not sure of his standing with his master; your demeanor is one of unease, nervousness, uncertainty. Dear One, can you not see how this gouges My heart? I am not what you have made Me to be; can you see what you have done? You have carved out your own god, made him in your own faulty image, purposed him from your own limited wells of love, affection and patience. This idol you have fashioned is not I. I am Jehovah-God; My thoughts and ways are far above yours which means that My affection and patience come from My own limitless well of Living Water and not from broken cisterns that are stagnant and brackish. They are running, cold, clean, refreshing, life-giving waters full of affection for you, full of attraction to you, full of patient understanding of your self. I ask you, Child, to look at the god you've fashioned and reject his evil intentions for you; the very fact that you cower each morning, postponing your face-to-face time with him should be enough to prove to you that this false god is not I. Yes, repent of your sins; recognize your very limited abilities to change yourself, but Child, come to Me as you would come to a cherished friend knowing you will find affection, laughter, and acceptance in her presence. This is My will for My children: to know Me in full, joy-filled relationship. You will find all that you need in this acceptance, in this affection, in this stability, no longer as a cowering dog but cherished friend. Test Me; see if what I say is not true. Find Me as your True Best Friend; imagine Me waiting for you in joyful anticipation, and the power of this Savior-Friend bond will bring with it the changes you seek in yourself and the peace in God that you crave. Yes Child ... know Me, but know Me in My true nature and not the false nature you have imagined.

December 21

Immediately he received his sight and followed Jesus, praising God. When all the people saw it, they also praised God. Luke 18:43

And what of you? When you see My might, My miracles at work in your life and in the lives of those around you, what is your response? Do you even stop to acknowledge My hand of mercy? Do you know that it is I, holy God, faithful Father and Friend, who accomplishes all good things? Do you understand healing and hope and even patience in affliction to be gifts that I bestow on a heart that is open to Me? Do you treat Me with casualness instead, the inattentive complacency of a believer who has grown too accustomed to My appearing that you don't even notice it anymore? Or do you break forth in praise? Praise for your Savior who redeems and heals? Praise for His hand of love that reaches down into your own life and the lives of others who surround you? How sad that My people go about their lives unthankful, dismissive, unaware when every minute My hand is at work in some miraculous way, giving sight and healing and strength to those Who seek Me, to those who follow after Me with praises, to those who notice.

December 22

For with God nothing is ever impossible and no word from God shall be without power or impossible of fulfillment. Luke 1:37 (AMP)

There is **nothing** that I cannot do. The same God who caused the sun to rise this morning, who kept you from flying off the earth, who gives you a good night's sleep, who brings rain, and who brings all of your bounty … I am the same God who is at work today. And there is **nothing** that I cannot do. Think not, Child, that I am oblivious to your heart today, for I hear your questions as you come to Me. I hear your wonderings: *'If there's nothing that you cannot do, my God, why do you not spare me? Why do you not spare my friends? Why do you not take the world into your hands and bring justice now?'* I know, Child; I know your confusions and your hurts and even your fears, but again I say, *'There is* **nothing** *that I cannot do.'* You will see that truth someday, and all your confusions will be swept away. Oh, the stories I will tell you when you are in My Kingdom forever, on the New Earth! All the stories I will tell you about My faithfulness to you, all the things that I averted; all the things I did to keep you safe and to keep you Mine, you will understand one day. You will understand it **all,** and all your questions and all your tears will vanish in the face of My love for you that you finally, finally understand. Until then, know that My hand **is** at work; that My hand does stay principalities and powers; that My hand upholds you; that I cushion the blows; that I walk with you through the storms; that I wipe your tears and then collect them, for they like you are precious unto Me. So take heart with what you don't yet see and don't yet feel, for I **have** overcome, and I **am** overcoming, and I **will** overcome, and there is nothing, **nothing** that I cannot do.

December 23

Therefore, since we are receiving a kingdom that cannot be shaken, let us be thankful, and so worship God acceptably with reverence and awe, for our "God is a consuming fire." Hebrews 12:28-29

You have lost your awe of Me and with that some of your reverence. I live and move and have My being within you, and I am jealous of My relationship with you. It is true that I urge you to see Me as Abba, as the daddy heart to your very soul. Indeed I also come to you as lover, take you and make you Mine, insert Myself into the deep places of your very life, and make you one with Me. But you must never forget that I am the Almighty God, that I AM Who I AM, that I am Creator God, resplendent in both majesty and power, and that I deserve all honor and praise. I call you to intimacy, but awe must fill that intimacy. I call you to safety, but holy reverence must abide in that safe place that you find in Me.

December 24

Deliver me out of the mire, and let me not sink: let me be delivered from them that hate me, and out of the deep waters. Psalm 69:14 (KJV)

You're wrecked; you're wired; you're weary, and you're worn; as Great Physician I recognize the symptoms: overwhelming circumstances, unrealistic expectations, unmet physical needs, and almost constant self-chastisement. There is no real escape from the mountainous responsibilities and dramas of living in today's reality. Old prescriptions seem like putting a poultice on a cancerous lesion. Today's world, in your home, outside your home, locally, domestically, internationally, carry a wounding that folksy remedies don't seem to be able to meet. What does this mean, Child? Does it mean God has gone into hiding, afraid to come into the open and meekly share His impotent remedy for the ills of the world? LAUGH!... At times, My Child, this is what you think. Does God no longer possess the "cure" for the meth-addict, the porn-addict, the religious-addict, the broken-down, smashed-to-bits marriage? Is Yahweh somehow disconnected because the times have changed, and He is somehow unable to "get with the program"? As life comes barreling down on you with demands and problems you NEVER thought you'd have to face, what happens to your faith? Are the dramas that unfold in your life too embarrassing, too real, too complicated for the Simple Man that came to save the world? If I am not God of the REAL in your life, then I am not God AT ALL in your life. Stop trying to sugarcoat or hold truths back from Me ... sharing them with a friend who will "understand" and not with the God that formed all matter and gave you breath. I chide you not, but I give you truth so that you can see the folly of your own thought processes. I am REAL GOD acquainted with all grief, privy to all wounding of body, mind and spirit; I cringe not at the unsavory, the unpleasant, the humiliating ... not when it is truth. The days are upon us that demand a real relationship with a real up-to-date God, a God intimately familiar with all of man's ways and woes. A transition must be made in your heart; like the realization that your 26-year-old child is no longer a child and you begin to treat them as an adult, so you must now look at Me and treat Me as the God that I truly am. If you are honest with yourself, you will find that you have been God of your own life up to this point; and now, only now as you see the piles sinking and the decks crumbling and the walls cracking do you see that you must surrender control to the One and Only True God with each day's question being *'What, if anything, do you want me to do Lord, regarding (fill in the blank).'* This is the new way, Child; learn its lesson, and you may yet find the rest you seek.

December 25

Therefore, whatsoever ye have spoken in darkness shall be heard in the light; and that which ye have spoken in the ear in closets shall be proclaimed upon the housetops. Luke 12:3 (KJV)
I have not come to undo you; truly I have come to bind you up. The slings and arrows of all of man's days create bleeding, aching heart wounds, confusion, and void; I have come to fill that void; I have come to heal those wounds; I have come to banish that confusion with My light and life. To your prayer closet I come, Me ... My very presence, My very person; not to find fault, I come Child to release you from your prisoner stance. Hear now these words of freedom; let them permeate your mind and spirit; they have great power to overcome your long practiced restraining voices, forever holding you back, holding you down, forever speaking lies ... *'He cannot love me.' 'He does not care.' 'I am not enough.'* Child, I hear your whispered pain; now you hear My Whispered Call to your heart. Let My words of love, of mercy, of affection echo against your cavernous need, bouncing and rebounding across the years of your fractured and lonely life. I've come and you never again step alone; I've come and you never again stand alone; I've come and you never again reach out to find no one reaching back; I've come to speak; hear now My Whispered Call, and know wholeness.

December 26

He proved he's on my side; I've thrown my lot in with him. Now I'm jumping for joy, and shouting and singing my thanks to him. Psalm 28:7 (MSG)
When you seek Me, you will find Me: full of grace and truth, longing to bestow understanding on you. I do not leave you alone, mired in confusion, nor lost in a deep jungle of ignorance. I come to you in My Word; My Holy Spirit speaks truth to you and teaches you that which I would have you know. Invisible God draws near to you in holiness, but

also in great love for you. I have not set Myself apart from you in order to distance Myself from you. My apartness is in order to be Holy God who also makes you holy for My purposes. Press in closer, Child, ever closer. Allow My Holy Spirit access to the doors of your heart and your mind. I will reveal My ways and My paths; I will show you My very self. Come expectantly when you seek Me, for I honor and rejoice in the cry of a heart eager to find Me. As the dawn moves swiftly toward you every morning, so I also pick up the hem of My holy robe and run toward your seeking form. Cast your eyes toward Me; you will find Me more eager to be found by you than you ever imagined possible.

December 27

I pray that out of his glorious riches he may strengthen you with power through his Spirit in your inner being. Ephesians 3:16

I desire to strengthen you in your inner man. Take My Word and write it on your heart. Allow Me to bolster your weak knees and embolden your every step. It is not in your own might that you face your todays, but in Mine. Know that it is your inmost parts that I am most concerned about. Your outward trappings and the circumstances of your life will quickly be revealed for what they are and fall away in My presence. They are only wrapping paper made of thin tissue covering the gift of substance and importance that is you. Find Me and you will find My truths and My power to guide that core of you. Look to Me for direction. Seek My voice in the night; find Me in your mornings. Engrave My words and My ways onto each blank page that is your heart's life.

December 28

God's Spirit touches our spirits and confirms who we really are. We know who he is, and we know who we are: Father and children. Romans 8:16 (MSG)

I have put My name on you. You have no idea really how remarkable that is, for you quickly take for granted what you have become accustomed to. Adopted child as well as spouse, I have bequeathed you both your innocence and your identity. Though you were fallen and lost in your sin, I have made you new. I have written My righteousness and My laws in your heart and have given you My name, yea, My very identity. With My name comes your blessing. Hide not your marriage to Me, your very identity through Me. Rather proclaim to all who will listen what I have done for you: My provisions throughout your wilderness wanderings, the sacrifice of God-son on your behalf that you might always draw close, the mystery of My limitless love for you despite all your blemishes and all your failures. I have removed the taunt of your illegitimacy and given you the adopted name of the Most High King. Child of the Most High, you are Mine, and I invite you to step into that birthright.

December 29

Drink, yes, drink abundantly of love, O precious one [for now I know you are mine, irrevocably mine!] Song of Songs 5:1 (AMP)

You are Mine. Everything about you is Mine: breath and thoughts, words and deeds - all of who you are and who you will yet be. All that stems from your past days, both the good and the bad of it, is in My hand. There is nothing of you that I do not know, nothing that escapes My gaze. Whether that brings you great relief or strikes fear into your tender heart is really up to you. Believe the truths of My covenantal, changeless love for you that My word teaches, and you will embrace My watchful, all-knowing eye and find peace with Me.

December 30

Examine me, God, from head to foot, order your battery of tests. Make sure I'm fit inside and out So I never lose sight of your love, But keep in step with you, never missing a beat. Psalm 26:2-3 (MSG)

You need to stop looking at your heart as though it is your

own. In fact, it is My heart, bought with a price, a very high price. Protect it not, for I will protect it. Hide it not, for I cannot use a heart that is hidden. Treasure it as a gift from Me, but also relinquish your tight grasp upon it. Allow it to be broken, spilled, and poured out, for I will both heal it and replenish it. Hoard it not, for the more of it you give, the bigger it will be and the larger the pleasures that can fit inside it.

December 31

For unto us was the gospel preached, as well as unto them: but the word preached did not profit them, not being mixed with faith in them that heard it. For we which have believed do enter into rest, as he said, As I have sworn in my wrath, if they shall enter into my rest: although the works were finished from the foundation of the world. Hebrews 4:2-3 (KJV)

I am the initiator of intimacy, the creator of connectedness; it matters not what your story is in regards to this; I have come to author a new story in your life. Your history of "not safe," of "handle it, fix it on your own" is the past; I desire to forge a new template for your future. Those that should have, could have, but did not, did not out of their own broken histories; release them from blame, but then turn to Me as parent, as teacher, as guide, as advocate. It matters not if you are young or old; it is time to begin life, true life, life where your minutes and hours and days are known by you to be under My hand of administration. It's time to seek Me and to know Me and to release to My care those burdens, those worries that up to this day you have struggled to carry, to influence, to manage on your own. I am God over all, but if you feel that not in your own bosom, what good does that do for you Child? It is the main objective of man's heart to be known; known for what he is and is not, and to be loved, accepted, and cherished in spite of it. This is a state of being that very few enjoy without effort; broken hearts, wounded stories have infiltrated almost every single child of Mine on earth. But, with God, ALL things are possible. Begin life anew; I am the good parent; I am the intimate spouse; I am the best-friend of your heart who always has time and space and enthusiasm for you. But think not that this comes without effort; the enemy of your soul knows what peaceful gains await you when I am embraced thusly; therefore, know he uses all his wiles of circumstance and lies to convince you otherwise. To own the truth of My love, of My like, of My nearness, of My affection you must live life actively engaged with seeking My heart for you and owning the truths I speak of My children from My Holy Word while renouncing the lies that are relentlessly fired at your brain by the enemy who seeks to convince you that you are lost with no help and no hope. It is a fight; it is a war, and it is not easy, but you'll never, ever fight a more worthwhile cause.

ABOUT THE AUTHORS

There's nothing of any real importance left to say about Sue and Sandy, not really. Our stories, in short version, are found at the end of our first two devotionals, *God Whispers* and *Still... God Whispers.*

The important story in all of this is God's story, and that story is the same for all of us: His love redeems us; His love remakes us; His love uses us. He is a pursuing God who never gives up on His created ones.

This third book is a product of the patient, persistent, and compelling whispered call that the God of the universe showers on both of our lives. We are learning to step out of His way in order that His powerful love might speak through these words.

We pray that you would see and hear only Him as you meet him in these meditations. It is He who yearns to be heard; our pens are but a vehicle.

If you'd like to contact us, please feel free to email us at SandPiper1122@gmail.com.